All local lads

St Helens and Pilkington Recs RLFC

Alex Service and Denis Whittle

London League Publications Ltd

All local lads
St Helens and Pilkington Recs RLFC

Front cover photo: Pilkington Recs celebrate their 2007–08 North West Counties Premiership Cup Final success. Back cover photos: St Helens Recs with the Lancashire Cup in 1930; Recs blazer badge (Courtesy Billy Simmons); skipper Sid Wright holds the trophy as his mud-spattered team-mates celebrate the Lancashire Cup Final victory against Leigh Miners Welfare in December 1975 at Knowsley Road (Courtesy Ken Cross).

Title page: An early St Helens Recs trade card (Courtesy Curtis Johnstone)

A CIP catalogue record for this book is available from the British Library.

First published in Great Britain in November 2008 by:
London League Publications Ltd, P.O. Box 10441, London E14 8WR

ISBN: 978-1903659-43-4

Cover design by: Stephen McCarthy Graphic Design
46, Clarence Road, London N15 5BB

Layout: Peter Lush

Printed and bound by: Biddles Ltd
King's Lynn, Great Britain

This book is dedicated to the memory of William Taylor (1887)
and Jackie Pimblett (1971). Both lost their lives playing the game they loved.

"Their indomitable spirit, their unfaltering resolution, their unrivalled tenacity in hanging on and still on, when further struggling seems nothing but folly, to come out on top – or nearly on top in the end – in this, I say,
St Helens Recs stand alone"
Tom Reynolds ('Premier') 1928

President's Foreword

As your President (only the second in over 100 years!), I pay tribute to Alex Service and Denis Whittle for producing an excellent new history of the Recs, following on from Les Corns' sterling first effort in 1999.

When I think of Recs, my mind is full of happy memories and images:

- As a teenager, attending matches at the old City Road ground with my father Guy, the first President, in the old wooden stand.
- Billy and Johnny Greenall's mother clasping me (and my brothers and sister) to her bosom... "I luvs 'em Mr Guy, I luvs 'em."
- The excitement of the game with shouts (screams) from the stand by Mrs Greenall and Mr Guy..."Pass it out, Billy! Pass it out!"
- The magic sponge, carried dripping from the touch-line. A cure-all for every ill. What was in that water?
- And through the fog, often swirling round the ground, mixed in a memorable cocktail with household smoke, the Red, Amber and Black.

Those were the glory days, when the Recs were in the professional league, like gladiators fighting on behalf of us all. Battles by proxy. There were only two teams at City Road, with many of the lads taken into employment by Pilks because they were good players of the game. It is not known how much the company and / or Pilkington family subsidised the team, but it must have been a considerable sum.

The Recs club today is a fitting successor to those glory days. The glory of today is seen in a much wider involvement of many more people participating in the club as both officials and players and proud parents, attending every match and shouting (and screaming) encouragement to their offspring. Not two, but 12 teams of active players, some as young as seven! And at the top end, players who, from time to time, move into the professional game, as well as those who play for the amateur representative teams.

The story of the Recs is one which we can all be proud, whatever our connections.

David F. Pilkington CBE
Club President

Photo: David Pilkington (right) congratulates Ernie Forber on his international selection in 1961. (Courtesy Ernie Forber)

Chairman's Foreword

There have been various publications and articles over the years that have detailed the history of Pilkington Recs Rugby League Club and of course there is a great deal of folklore evidence of their memorable games.

It gives me great pleasure to be able to write this foreword to what is probably the most comprehensive piece of work to date on the story of the Recs. Alex Service and Denis Whittle have compiled this book after interviews with former and current players, past and present club officials and painstaking research through various archived material. They have captured the highs and lows and the anecdotes from people associated with this great club. The Recs have an enviable history in the amateur rugby league world, having been a professional outfit in a former life and having achieved notable playing records. These include memorable games against top professional sides with a great game against Wigan at Knowsley Road in 1979. Alex and Denis bring this together in a book that will appeal to all and which, no doubt, will evoke great memories of past times and leave us to expect a great future.

I commend the book to you and thank Alex and Denis for all the hard work and dedication in producing it and to the people who have contributed to it.

Ralph E. Rawsthorne
Club Chairman

Photo: Chairman Ralph Rawsthorne and Recs skipper Sam Rawsthorne with the North West Counties Premiership trophy in 2008.

Acknowledgements and thanks

The authors would like to acknowledge the following publications and articles:

Billy Greenall article first appeared in *Code 13* Issue 4 August 1987. Edited and published by Trevor Delaney
Small, Gordon: *The Lancashire Cup – a complete record 1879–80 to 2006–07* published by Soccer Data Publications on behalf of the Lancashire Football Association 2007
Wood, Niel: A History of Pilkington Recreation – Part One. *Code 13* Issue 2 December 1986
Wood, Niel: A History of Pilkington Recreation – Part Two. *Code 13* Issue 3 March 1987
Wood, Niel: A History of Pilkington Recreation – Part Three. *Code 13* Issue 4 August 1987
Corns, Les: *The Glorious Recs* 1999
The Cullet, the Pilkington Company magazine 1912 to 1945 and the *Pilkington News*
The *St Helens Star* newspaper (various articles)
Rugby Leaguer
St Helens Reporter

We also acknowledge the help of the following organisations and websites:
Since 1888 the searchable Premiership and Football League player database has been an invaluable reference source, especially www.allfootballers.com
The Museum of Association Football at Preston and archivist Peter Holme, without whose help we would have floundered indefinitely.
Pilkington Group Limited and Julie Woodward, external communications manager
Liverpool Football Club Museum
Commonwealth War Graves Commission website
North West Counties Rugby League website
Max Dunbar (RFU Museum, Twickenham)

This work could not have been completed without the help of the staff of the St Helens Local History and Archives Library. Special thanks to Vivien Hainsworth, senior heritage officer and her staff.

We are also indebted to the following people who, alas, are no longer with us:
The late Harold Gibbins, a former Recs season ticket holder, who provided some of the signed portraits in this book
The late Billy Greenall a true legend of rugby league and a Recs man through and through.
The late Jack Potter for his observations of both Northern Union and Association Football
The late Albert Pimblett, George 'Jumbo' Highcock and Horace Randolph – legends all.
The late George Morrison for his tireless work at City Road.
The late Bob Webster, whose rugby league archives were invaluable.

We are also indebted to the following individuals who helped to make this publication a reality:
Robert Gate – the doyen of rugby league historians, who provided much of the pre-Northern Union statistics in this book.
Billy Simmons – a genuine Recs great, whose archive has been utilised extensively during production of this book.
John Rees of the modern day Recs – a superb representative for the club.

Bill Bates; Mrs Britch; Ian Cartwright; Bobby Chisnall; John Clegg; Mike Critchley; Kenny Cross; Terry Cross; Mike Denning; John 'Todder' Dickinson; Billy Dillon; Eric Doig; John Ellaby; Harry Edgar; Andrew Fairhurst; Ernie Forber; Geoff Fletcher; Andy Foreman; John Forster (The Warhorse); Eric 'Big E' Frodsham; Eric 'Little E' Frodsham; Gareth Frodsham; Albert Garner; Josh Gaskell; Rob Gerrard (Ruskin Leisure); Ron Girvin; Brian Glover; Jeff Gormley; Mr and Mrs Hand; George and Sheila Highcock; The inimitable Bernard 'Archie' Hill; Mrs Irwin; Curtis Johnstone; Andrew Kilmurray; John Ledger; Hughie Leyland; Denis Litherland; Len Lowe; Dave Manning; John McCabe; Peter Metcalfe; Alan Molyneux; Gerry Moore; Paul Morris; Tommy Morris; Keith Nutter; Harry Ody; Brian Peers; Geoff 'Jethro' Phillips; Harry Pimblett; Bernard Platt; Jim Pyke; Wilf Roach; June Shorter (nee Greenall); Johnny Smith; Wilf Smith; Noel and Andy Swift; Eddie Tinsley; Kevin Wellens; Margaret Whittle (Rainford); Kevin Whittle; Niel Wood; Julie Woodward (external communications manager, Pilkington Group Ltd)

Thanks to Michael O'Hare for subediting, Steve McCarthy for designing the cover, the staff of Biddles for printing the book, Dave Farrar and Peter Lush of London League Publications Ltd for agreeing to publish it, and everyone who lent us photographs or other illustrations.

Special thanks to:

Club President Mr. David Pilkington
Ralph Rawsthorne – Chairman Pilkington Recs ARLFC

Introduction

The starting point for this publication came, rather ironically, before the 2006 Super League Grand Final at Old Trafford between St Helens and Hull. Talking with Recs legend Denis Litherland, he was delighted that his former professional team (Saints) had reached the Final, yet he was deeply troubled about the prospects for his beloved Pilkington Recs, who were faced with losing their famous old ground at City Road. What is it about this club that means so much to those associated with it? It has always been an ambition of ours to set about chronicling the full history of the Recreation club and here was our opportunity to find out. A case of *'It's now or never!'*

A host of great sportsmen appear in this book, particularly from rugby league, including those who wore the red amber and black in those famous local derbies with Saints; those who created unparalleled history for the club with a record number of four BARLA National Cup victories and the current Recs teams, who have brought home silverware at open age, under-18 and under-12 level. There are numerous characters chronicled, but the one thing that stands out above all is the Recs famous fighting spirit, formally recognised in print by the journalist Tom Reynolds after a real 'backs-to-the-wall' cup tie at Headingley in 1928.

Past players, such as prop-forward Kenny Cross, talk in such glowing terms of their time at City Road: "Two new knees and no regrets whatsoever" he says, with great pride. Indeed, the club engenders a fierce loyalty and remains very much a part of the local sporting scene in our rugby-mad town.

Although the Recs were still at their spiritual home at the end of the 2007-08 season, the next decade will certainly be one of change, one way or another. Yet with such devoted and dedicated people associated with it, the club must surely live on and continue to prosper. Although he was overjoyed when Saints defeated Hull in the 2006 Grand Final, the fact is that Denis Litherland would swap anything for the continued existence of his beloved Pilks Recs at City Road.

It has been a real pleasure to compile this history of such a great club. Our thanks to everyone who gave their time to the cause and we hope you enjoy what is one of the most enduring tales of any sporting club anywhere in Britain.

Long live the ***'Good Old Rekerashun.'***

Alex Service and Denis Whittle
St Helens, September 2008

Photo: Denis Litherland at the 2006 Super League Grand Final, complete with a Saints hat and Recs polo shirt.

Contents

Photographs and illustrations

Some of the photographs in this book are quite old, and therefore have not reproduced perfectly. We thought that readers would prefer to have them like this than not at all. Unless otherwise credited, photographs and illustrations are from private collections. No copyright has been intentionally breached; please contact London League Publications Ltd if you believe there has been a breach of copyright. All photographs and illustrations were provided by Alex Service, unless credited otherwise.

Left: Warrington captain Ben Jolley (right) shakes hands with Jack 'Tot' Wallace before the Challenge Cup tie against St Helens Recs in February 1926. The referee is the Reverend Frank Chambers of Dewsbury. Warrington won 17-12 after a magnificent game. The gate receipts were £1,260 – a then record for a cup tie at Wilderspool.
(Courtesy Eddie Fuller and Gary Slater)

Recs skipper Billy Greenall (right) shakes hands with popular singer Gracie Fields before a game against Rochdale in the mid-1930s. Victor Armbruster is on the left. (Courtesy the estate of June Shorter).

1. 1878 to 1897: A hotbed of rugbyism

There are two things that St Helens is renowned for throughout the world - rugby and glass and in terms of the sporting history of the town, the two are inexorably linked. St Helens Recreation, the works rugby team for the Pilkington Glass Company, appeared in 1878, some five years after the formation of their rivals, St Helens RFC – the Saints. Yet there is a common thread. The Saints were founded by William Douglas Herman, the head chemist at Pilkingtons and this is where the story begins.

The finest chemists in Europe at this time were considered to be German, although Pilkingtons settled for a young Englishman of Franco-German extraction from London who, at the age of 18, was already making a name for himself in the field of metallurgy. He took up the post of chemist at the firm's Crown Glass Works with a starting salary of £150 a year. 'Herman the German', as he became known, soon felt at home in St Helens. Yet he missed one aspect of his former life in the south. He was a capable sportsman who had played rugby in his school and college days. To his disappointment, there was a dearth of winter games in St Helens. On many a cold afternoon, the 'sporting chemist' could be seen kicking a rugby ball about with some of his newly found friends on a field near Boundary Road. These were professional gentlemen and budding entrepreneurs who were keen to try their hand at this new game which would fill a gap in their sporting calendar.

By 1872, the second season of the Rugby Union's existence, clubs had been successfully set up in Liverpool, Manchester and Wigan, and it was Herman's dearest wish to establish a rugby club in St Helens. He looked initially to his workmates but this, apparently came to nothing. Herman then called a meeting in a local hostelry for interested parties, from which the first St Helens team originated. Two or three years after Douglas Herman's sporting ambition had been realised he found, like a number of his team-mates, that he could no longer play regularly because of the demands of his career. By 1892, for example, he had become a key man in Pilkingtons' glass-making operations. He located and supervised the supply of sand, dealt with all kinds of chemical problems and introduced Pilkingtons into business activity on the continent, earning more than £1,000 a year by this time. Herman's 'Old Originals' were largely superseded by some younger lads, who became known as the Eccleston Rangers, later the St Helens Rangers, before dropping the 'Rangers' to become St Helens Rugby Club in 1885.

Worrall's Directory in 1876 describes St Helens as "the principal seat of glass manufacture in the United Kingdom...covering large areas and employing a large proportion of the population." Subsequent industrial growth meant that the town's population had expanded from 45,000 in 1868 to over 70,000 20 years later, by which time it had attained the status of County Borough. St Helens was a typical industrial town of tall crowding chimneys, with waste tips galore, seemingly enveloped by a permanent pall of smoke and chemical haze.

The Pilkington company was the major employer and benefactor in St Helens and as long ago as 1847 had taken the enlightened decision to form a works recreation club. Its aim was to provide sport and amusement for the workforce, which was to become a key issue in the years to come. The club was initially set up to provide the workforce with a cricket team, both for workers to play in and to watch and support. A bowls section was added a few years later, with rugby football making an appearance in 1878. The minutes of the Recreation club at that time state that: "Footballers are to be put on the same footing as cricketers and bowlers".

The first land used by the Recreation club for cricket was bounded by Peter Street, Westfield Street and the 'Bruk', near St Thomas's Church. The legacy of those times is the Cricketers' Arms in Peter Street, which was used for post-match refreshment. As a result of rapidly-expanding urban development, however, it was time to move on and a farmer's field was obtained just off Boundary Road, which became the regular headquarters for the cricket and rugby sections until the end of the century. This was virtually on the same piece of land where Herman and his friends had first played their *ad hoc* rugby games all those years before. The cricketers later moved to the firm's new sports ground at Ruskin Drive, which opened in 1901, while the rugby section moved up to a pitch adjacent to the Cowley Hill works at Windle City. The old ground in Boundary Road was donated to the Borough of St Helens, and was named Queen's Recreation Park as a lasting memorial to those times.

In the early days, however, the Boundary Road ground was the hub of the Recs' rugby activities. Match reports were rare then, although a report of the first practice match of the season, on 2 October 1880, can be found in the *St Helens Newspaper*: "The season was formally opened with the Recreation Club on Saturday 1st by a match on their ground, Boundary Road. Sides, 14 each, were chosen on the field by W.R. Thomson and J. Burrill, when a couple of hours' splendid practice followed. All played well up and the members who displayed themselves so well last season again came to the front in good style, especially Cunliffe, Valentine, Cook, W.E. Taylor, Reynolds, Atkinson, Clegg and Tickle. At first the teams seemed well-matched but before the conclusion of the game it was noticed that Burrill had the majority of the good players and accordingly won the victory. At the close, the result was Burrill 1 goal 3 tries and 2 touchdowns, to Thomson's 3 touchdowns." In those days goals were decisive in deciding the result.

Their first captain of the rugby section, Major William Thomson, had been one of the founder members of the first rugby club with Douglas Herman and was to become the manager of the plate works at Cowley Hill. Like Herman, who was listed as a vice-president of the Recs club, Thomson did not play for too many years, but remained as chairman of the rugby committee. However, it appears that it was no longer a game purely for gentlemen anymore. "Only those as are used to working hard every day can tackle it," remarked William 'Monsey' Parr, the Saints captain and later a key member of the Recreation team. "Even we working men have to keep ourselves in trim by boxing with the gloves and exercising with the dumb-bells, which we do every Tuesday and Thursday night during the season."

Alas Thomson was to meet an unfortunate end in August 1917, when his body was found in a pond at Windle Hall fields. A popular figure, he had not been able to work for some months after a serious operation, followed by a nervous breakdown. He held the rank of Honorary Major in the 5th South Lancashire Regiment and was chairman of Windle Bowling Club. His body was found by his daughter Henrietta after the alarm was raised by the maid at his home at Stone Leigh, Hard Lane. Although an ornamental Japanese dagger was found by the scene, there were no marks on the body to suggest it had been used. News of his suicide at the age of 64 shocked his wide circle of friends and work colleagues. During his tenure as chairman of the football committee, Major Thomson was to see the Recs become one of the most feared teams in the whole of Lancashire – a great achievement indeed.

In the early years of the Recreation club, games were arranged on an *ad hoc* basis against teams from the local area and derby games against the Saints were played by the 1882–83 season, at both Boundary Road and Saints' new ground at Denton's Green. The rugby section continued to grow, with the addition of an 'A' team and a third team, who played their games at City Road, followed much later by the first team themselves. The Recs, with their distinctive maroon jerseys and green collars, which were to change to red by the end of the decade, became one of the most powerful teams in Lancashire and beyond by the end of the decade. The formidable Recs pack even provided the town with its first England international, Jim Pyke, as well as several county representatives.

Throughout the club's history until 1939, the rivalry between the Recs and Saints was always apparent, although this rapidly diminished over the years following the changing status of the two teams. Perhaps it was at its most intense between the two World Wars, when both clubs were members of the Rugby Football League, but even in the 1880s it could be a major issue. When it was found out, for example, that Mr C. Anders was not just a member of the Recs committee but also a member of the St Helens Football Club, he was asked to resign forthwith, never to be seen at Boundary Road again.

After one particularly fierce derby encounter in November 1887, the Recs committee objected in no uncertain terms about "the unfair action" of the St Helens club secretary in his one-sided report of the game to the press. The Recs duly cancelled the return fixture on Good Friday only for the Saints to replace it with a lucrative clash against a Manchester XV at their Denton's Green ground.

The Recs football committee was aware of the need to maintain the interest of the public, who were watching the games in ever-increasing numbers. This interest could soon begin to wane with what were only friendly fixtures. As a result the club applied to and were accepted into the West Lancashire and Border Towns Rugby Union. This provided Recs with cup ties to give an extra impetus to the club, as did the increasing number of crack Yorkshire teams visiting Boundary Road by the late 1880s, such as Heckmondwike and Holbeck. Yet there was a price to pay for the advent of more competitive football into the Recs fixture list.

The more competitive nature of the cup ties could bring out more unsavoury aspects of the game. These were not always welcomed by the Recs committee and board of directors at Pilkingtons. Relations with the Widnes club were somewhat soured after a particularly rough 'A' team game at Boundary Road on 12 November 1887. William Taylor, the Recs threequarter, caught the ball close to his own line and punted it back downfield. Unfortunately, Taylor was the victim of a late challenge after he had put boot to ball, with disastrous consequences. The 27-year-old ledger clerk, of Croppers Hill, St Helens died on the night after the game from "severe concussion of the brain". At the inquest, a spectator witness, William Carlow, reported that although Taylor had fallen on his back after the initial challenge, he got up and rubbed the back of his head. He kept playing for about eight minutes before he collapsed and later became unconscious. The incident had seemed so trivial at the time that none of the players could be sure who had been the perpetrator.

Taylor's funeral took place at the town cemetery at Windleshaw Abbey, with the Recreation Club sending a "handsome cross" and £100 for Taylor's father. The inscription on his tombstone reads as follows:
"Merciful Jesus Give Rest to the Soul of William Edward Taylor
Youngest Son of Henry Helsby and Ann Taylor
Who was accidentally injured whilst playing football Nov. 12th 1887 and died Nov. 13th 1887 aged 27 years."

St Helens Recs 1887: Back: Bill Dean, Jim Dolan, Jim Pyke, Jim Hankinson, Jim Mousedale, Harry Gregson, Jack Ready. Seated: Albert 'Dummy' Tickle, Jimmy Pilkington, William Parr (capt), Albert Smith, Henry Greenall. Front: Henry Gerrard, Billy Matthews, Billy Lund, Alex McGeichan.

The incident seemed to have implications for the Recs club, with the Pilkington directors requesting the cessation of fixtures with Widnes. The minutes of the company's plate (Cowley Hill) board of 17 November 1887 explained that "as they are a notably rough club and Warrington and Runcorn won't play them, that we don't wish our men to play them again." The directors were always uneasy about competitive football and the ramifications were significant some years later when the club decided not to join the new competitive Northern Rugby Football Union in 1895. The issues of professionalism and 'broken time' – payments to compensate players who missed work to play in matches – were at the heart of the split at this time although the Recs were involved in payments to their players, or expenses for away games. Players were entitled to one shilling for first or second team matches and sixpence for the third team. These sums were quite substantial, given the wages of the time. It was not just the players who received some financial inducement from rugby. The Recs committee donated three guineas towards a testimonial for Mr Parry, the secretary of the West Lancashire Rugby Union – a good move in essence, because shortly afterwards, two Recs players, Jimmy Pyke and Jimmy Pilkington were nominated to play for West Lancashire.

The photograph above was taken on 6 November 1887 - the day after the Recs had defeated their deadly rivals Saints on their Boundary Road ground – today Queen's Recreation Ground – by 1 goal, 2 tries, to a single try. Their club colours were maroon jerseys, green collars and long white breeches. It is interesting to note that several members of the team would later have sons playing in the famous Northern Union Recs team between the Wars, namely Jim Dolan (hooker Oliver Dolan – 1928 Lions tourist), Jim Pyke (centre Jim Pyke Junior – later assistant secretary at City Road) and Henry Greenall (scrum-halves Johnny and Billy Greenall, who both captained the side; another son, Henry Junior, played on the wing for Saints). The team was beginning to establish a formidable reputation in Lancashire and beyond. There were characters in abundance in those far-off days and their loyalty and enthusiasm for their sport was beyond question.

Captain William 'Monsey' Parr was the leader on and off the field, a brilliant scrimmager, he would always be in the thick of the action. A tough and durable player, his orders would be followed without question by his teammates – a true immortal of Recreation rugby. He made one appearance for the West Lancashire and Border Towns representative side in 1887, against Westmorland. In the summer months, he would be seen in the whites of the Recs cricket club, where he was a more-than-capable batsman. Shortly after the photograph was taken, he received a back injury that would temporarily curtail his career until the early 1890s, although he still served for many years afterwards as a much-valued committee member.

Packing down in the scrum with Monsey was the mighty Jim Pyke, Recs' most prominent player in the rugby union era. A speedy forward with a crunching tackle, Jim played 15 times for Lancashire and became the town's first ever full international rugby player, when he was selected to play against Wales at Blackheath in 1892. His son, Jim junior also gained county honours and won a Lancashire Cup winner's medal in 1923 during the Recs' foray into the world of semi-professional rugby league.

Another well-known father and son duo were Jim and Oliver Dolan. Both were forwards, with Oliver finding fame in the front row of the scrum as a hooker par excellence and his father, Jim, who could best be described as a loose-forward in modern terms, with a roving commission around the field. A West Lancashire and Border Towns representative, Jim was also capable of getting on the scoresheet with his speed and elusiveness.

Perhaps the greatest character of them all was Albert 'Dummy' Tickle, who was deaf and dumb. This was a particular drawback, especially when playing against teams who did not know of his disability. When a player was tackled in those days, he had to yell out 'held' before the tackle could be deemed to have been completed. Needless to say, Albert got some terrific maulings, because he could not shout out the key word.

In the centre was 'little' Billy Matthews, in his early 20s, but possessing a rugby brain beyond his tender years. Although barely 10 stones wet through, he was able to hold his own against much bigger players with his speed off the mark, together with his speed of thought and possessed a convincing dummy. Such was the sporting spirit of the time that, whisper it, Billy would play the occasional game for the Saints if they were short. Likewise, Tom Foulkes, the legendary Saints full-back, was also known to turn out for the Recs. Billy formed a supreme centre partnership with Henry Gerrard, who was also speedy and elusive. A real livewire, Billy was still fit and healthy after his eventual retirement from Pilkington Brothers many years later, regularly making eight mile walks in Billinge where he lived.

One of the idols of the day was the legendary 'Barney' McGeichan, who excelled as a 220 yards specialist on the athletics track. When Recs were due to play Leigh in a West Lancashire Cup tie, Barney was inexplicably left out of the starting line-up. "No Barney... no supporters!" was the shout from the crowd, forcing the committee into an emergency about turn, with 'Barney' playing a blinder as a result.

Albert Smith nearly lost his life playing for the Recs. The team were touring the Lake District and Cumberland, staying for the weekend at Morecambe and travelling to play at Lancaster on the Monday for an evening match. Albert tackled the Lancaster full-back. There was no sign of over-aggression from the Recs player, but he lay motionless on the ground. When his teammates turned him over, he screamed in agony. He was taken to Lancaster Infirmary, where he lay for months in a serious condition, tended throughout by his devoted wife. Fortunately, Albert recovered, although his rugby days were over. He was also an old volunteer and in 1914 became an officer in the National Defence Corps, before ending his working days as licensee of the Cotham Arms in the town centre.

Another Recs' legend was Jimmy Pilkington, a supreme half-back and a prolific try-scorer, who became the club's first-ever Lancashire representative in 1890. He had an enormous hand-span, enabling him to stoop at maximum pace and pick up the ball on his way to the try-line. In one match, against Holbeck (Leeds) at Boundary Road, he did his 'party trick' so often in the first half that the opposition insisted on the ball being measured at half-time. Needless to say the ball was of standard size, unlike Jimmy's hands. He once scored a magnificent hat-trick against a powerful Wigan side at Boundary Road, whereupon he was presented with a commemorative cap by the visitors.

They were happy days for sport in St Helens. Members of the Pilkington Recreation Club, who paid a penny subscription a week, were admitted free to matches. Other spectators paid 3d and 6d according to their status. A gate of £20 was the average, but the derby match against Saints, celebrated in the photograph, pulled in a handsome return of £80.

An interview with William Monsey Parr *in The Prescot Reporter and St Helens Central Advertiser* on 7 April 1888 showed the dangers of rugby at this time and what the game was like.

Shocking accident in the football field at St Helens

"A serious accident occurred on Saturday afternoon on the Recreation football ground, St. Helens - in a match between St Helens Recreation Club and the Wigan Club, when the local captain - William Parr, better known among the admirers of football as 'Monsey', received serious injuries. Shortly after the game commenced a scrimmage took place, when Parr either fell or was thrown to the ground, several other players falling upon him. Parr was unable to rise, and although it was first thought he was only 'winded' and would recover in a few minutes, it was soon afterwards seen that he was in an unconscious state. In this condition he was carried to the pavilion where Dr F. Knowles - who was upon the ground, attended him. So serious did Parr's condition become, he having sustained internal injuries and such a shock as to be in a state of collapse, that he was taken to the Providence Hospital, where an operation was performed by Dr Knowles. The news spread through the town that death had ensued, but this was promptly contradicted; the fact being that under the skilful treatment of the medical gentleman - consciousness was restored in about an hour after admission, and it is hoped that with a few days rest and care, Parr will be convalescent. An instance of the ruling passion of football enthusiasts was given by Parr who, on recovering consciousness, and without knowing what had happened or where he was, exclaimed – 'Who's won?'"

Parr's recollections

"I'm 31 years old and not married yet, for what girl would marry such an unlucky beggar as me? You see I keep getting into the wars," sighed Monsey Parr just before he finished playing. Looking at this report we can understand how he must have felt. There was no love lost between the teams in this match. When the final whistle blew, one spectator had even struck the Wigan captain on the face with a dead rat.

In a ground-breaking interview in the *St Helens Lantern* in September 1889, Parr gave readers an insight into life with the Recreation club. He was interviewed at his lodgings in Kirkland Street, during one of his spells of inactivity following an injury on the field. "This is my 13th season as captain," he revealed, "and I think it's about time I made way for younger blood. This is the third dose of lying up I've had. But, seriously, I'm going to retire at the end of this season. I've made up my mind about it. I didn't want to be chosen captain again this present season, but they wouldn't hear of anything else. I

shall be sorry to give up for I do like the game. I'd as soon watch a football match as eat my dinner."
The article continued in question and answer format:

What is the nature of your three mishaps on the field?
The first happened three or four years ago. I was in a very tight scrimmage during a match against Aspull and got my ribs staved in. I couldn't play for seven weeks after, and even now I can feel something of it when I twist a certain way. Then last year when playing against Wigan I got a nasty kick in an awkward part, which sent me to the Providence Hospital and kept me out of the football field for five weeks [See match report]. The present accident was caused by a sprain to my ankle a few weeks ago in a practice match. It pained a good deal but I stuck to my work, though once or twice I thought of knocking off. The doctor says that there's a little bone broken just above the ankle. But it's going along nicely now, thank you.

Now, in the face of all these accidents, aren't you compelled to own that football is a dangerous game?
No. If it's played as it should be, it's not dangerous. To see Swinton and Bradford play you'd say it was as nice a game as you need wish to see. Rough play isn't football, and I think the more interest the public takes in football as they are doing, year by year, the more rough players will have to stop it off. Then if the referee would use his power, and put his foot down on all rough play it would be better. The [Rugby] Union is helping it; and there's one great advantage in having some authority like the Union. Two or three years ago, the St Helens club [Saints] went to play Warrington, and, to their surprise, got an awful thrashing. What do you think the Warrington fellows had done? They had hit on the idea of wearing jerseys made of paper or butter-rags, so as when the St Helens men caught them by the jersey the thing tore right off and they got clean away. The things cost tuppence ha'penny a dozen or something like that, I guess; and men went about the field chucking fresh 'uns to the players who'd had theirs torn off. It was a disgusting sight, and of course, St Helens paid them back at the return match; and the practice might have become general and driven all decent people from a football field; but the Union stepped in and put a stop to it. And in time the Union will do the same with rough players.

Now, in your team have you any but workingmen?
No, there's none of the clerks or such like in it. I dare say the young fellows in the office can't afford to run the risk of a broken arm or leg. And, besides, football is now very fast work and very hard work, too, and only those that are used to work hard every day can tackle it: that is, in big matches. Even we workingmen have to keep ourselves in trim by boxing with the gloves and exercising with the dumbbells, which we do every Tuesday and Thursday night during the season. I put it all down to that as we did so well last season, being beaten only once on our own ground: your muscles are all kept loose, and yet as hard as nails. This was Mr Thomson's idea, and a capital one it is.

You mean Mr W.R. Thompson, your president, I suppose?
Aye. Mr Thomson's the mainstay of our club. At every match he's there, no matter where it's played. When the ... club was first formed, he was the first captain, and used to play like a good 'un. The way I came to football was this: some time before I ever thought of playing myself, I used to go and watch some gentlemen play on what is the Recreation ground now. There was Mr Thomson, Mr Herman, Mr Martin Hammill, and Sergeant-Major Burns, and Mr Harry Varley and a Mr Jackson and – I can't remember them all. I've heard it said that Mr Herman first introduced rugby... into St Helens. I was watching these gentlemen that made me like the game. They used to play two full-backs in those days and when a man was held he waited till the rest came up, which made the game slower.

What club did you join first?
It was a club which some of us lads started, and called Eccleston Rangers, and we played on a field in Queen's Park. I think we only stayed there one season, then we changed the name to the St Helens Rangers, and played on Mrs Littler's field. Alec Borthwick was our captain and there was 'Dummy'

Tickle as well: the three of us are all still playing. I wasn't working at Pilkington's at that time. Of course, we had no enclosure. People used to come and watch us without having to pay. But after every match the hat was sent round and we thought it was good if we collected five shillings. By and by more people came to see us and we got to collect as much as a pound and 30 shillings.

How long have you been captain of the Recs?

This is my fifth season. After Mr Thomson resigned, Cunliffe who is now in France, was elected, and I succeeded him. While I'm laid up just now, Albert Smith, deputy captain, is in command. He's a good fellow and a capital half-back, playing well into Jimmy Pilkington's hands. Jimmy is a crack half-back. It was I who first got him to play football. It was once when I was short of a full team I asked him if he'd play: he said he never had played, but would try if I liked. I placed him amongst the forwards, and he played so well that I kept him as a forward for three or four matches; but he would be always handling the ball, so I made him half-back, and he's been a great success, having scored 25 tries last season. I like his play immensely: up to last season I must confess he played rather selfish, and something was said about it by the critics; but he has mended since. He's a faster runner this year by five yards in 100. He played for West Lancashire against Westmorland at Widnes, two years ago, along with Pyke and me. Pyke is a rattlin' forward, and is always one of the West Lancashire team whenever they play, which is two matches a season. Gerrard, who is known as 'Sloper,' is a good little 'un, but he got hurt last Good Friday and can't join us this season. But it hasn't stopped him from getting married, though!

You might give me a word about your team. Is it the same as last year?

There's one new man, Jackson, the full-back, who used to play for Aspull. There's young Ellison, who is a coming player. Last year was his first season with the first team. He is a good runner, good kicker and a good picker-up. Seddon is one of the finest kickers in the north. Mousedale is a good charger-down of a kick; he rarely misses. Jim Hankinson is a good runner. Compton is a good little player as centre threequarter. McGeachan is a most useful man and got into double figures with tries last year. He's good humour itself on the field, always laughing; they may knock him about like a bottle cork, it's all right. Then there's 'Dummy' Tickle, another old warhorse like myself. He is a most companionable fellow, although he's dumb, poor chap. When we're going off he keeps us alive with his mimicry and antics – holding auction sales, and pretending to sing.

The Recs don't take part in the league matches, I understand.

The masters don't like them. After that affair with Widnes two years ago when one young fellow was killed and another had his leg broken they said we'd better give up cup ties and such things. And another thing why they don't like these competitions is because they think their men are inclined to bet on them. The masters don't like us drinking and they won't allow committee meetings to be held in public houses. This year we're going to hold our meetings in a room over Mr Fothergill's shop. John Marsh's – the Sefton Arms – is our headquarters for dressing, but when we get our new ground I expect we shall have a fine pavilion and dress there.

Do the employees grumble at all at that penny a week subscription?

It's only those that get more than 10 shillings a week who do subscribe. And should they grumble? They get change for the penny in the use of the places of recreation provided. For that, they have a cricket ground, football ground and bowling greens, and all with the use of materials. They don't have to pay to go and see matches. They have reading rooms at the works which they can use at breakfast time, dinner time, in fact all day long except during working hours.

What is the record of your club as a whole?

We've decidedly won more matches than we've lost, since it was first formed. In the early days we had much difficulty in getting men to go away; sometimes we had to go with only seven or eight. Of course, every man had to pay his own expenses and find himself in rig-out. But now the club pays all fares, and gives one shilling per man for teas: and finds him in club uniform – all except shoes.

It is often remarked that it is a pity the town should be divided into two clubs, which, combined, would be so powerful. What's your opinion?
Well, of course, except for casual matches we couldn't amalgamate with any club outside the works. Ours is a works club; and the only way to bring about a combination would be for the best men in the St Helens cricket and football clubs to get work at Pilkingtons.

May I ask why you are called 'Monsey'?
When I was 13 or 14 years old I used to work at Woodhead's Flint Works on Cropper's Hill. At that time, the public houses used to open very early, and the men used to send me for beer at about half past five of a morning. But one morning, the people weren't up, and I was kept waiting for over an hour at the door with a lot of other folks. When I got back the men got on to me, and asked if I'd been asleep on the doorstep. 'Nah,' I said; 'they hadn't gotten up; and there was plenty of monses waiting there too, beside me.' They called me Monsey ever after that, and scores of folks don't know me by any other name."

Parr was a stalwart of the Recreation club for many years to come after his retirement from playing. He became a referee and filled his time in the summer months with the bat and ball.

In the pink

The first decade of rugby for the Recreation club had been extremely successful, reflected in a glowing report by the secretary, who told the 60 members present in the glassworks schoolroom that: "The club in point of wealth, strength, following and position in the football world was without parallel in the annals of the Recreation Club." The fixture card had been beefed up to include top Yorkshire sides such as Wakefield Trinity, Manningham and Leeds Parish Church, attracting large crowds to the Boundary Road enclosure. Recs' supporters also followed their team in large numbers away from home, and football specials were organised, capable of taking more than 1,500 supporters to certain venues.

As Saints moved to their new ground at Knowsley Road, in September 1890, it was the Recs who were stealing their thunder, with some impressive victories against strong Lancashire and Yorkshire combinations. More than 8,000 packed into the Boundary Road enclosure to watch the 'Good Old Rekerashun' tame the Lions of Swinton. A similar number were present for the Recs' battle against Brighouse Rangers. Little wonder – that by this time – St Helens was described as a veritable hotbed of rugbyism. Indeed, the 1890–91 campaign is regarded as perhaps the Recs most successful before the First World War. Beginning with a nine-a-side competition for the benefit of Swinton Cricket Club, in August 1890, the team played 41 matches, winning 30, losing 7, with 4 drawn; 52 goals and 62 tries were scored, with star county half-back Jimmy Pilkington notching 27 tries.

Games were played at Boundary Road and both teams went from club headquarters at the Sefton Hotel, Baldwin Street to and from the ground by horse-drawn wagonette.

Jim Pyke – the first local superstar

By the early 1890s Jim Pyke was at the peak of his powers at club and representative level. Little wonder that the journal *British Sport* added him to their series of 'Gems of the football field.' Pyke, who had been a Recs player since starting in the club's 'A' team was ideally built for rugby at 5 feet 10 inches and 12 stones 3 pounds, but one of his major assets was his speed. A former champion sprinter, Jim would break from the scrum like lightening to harass the opposition. He could also score tries as well as doing his best to stop them.

The site of Recs' first pitch off Boundary Road, now known as Queens Recreation Ground and still used for sport in the 21st century.

The Lancashire county side of the early 1890s featuring Recs' star forward Jimmy Pyke (third from right on the back row).

The England cap won by Jim Pyke in 1892.

Recs Rugby committee 1890
Back: J. Preston (PW), W. Cook (PW), Ben Holt (PW), J. Harper (SW), J. Wood (secretary), G. Hewitt (PW), L. Webster (PW), A. McLaughlin (PW), T. Holding (SW) Middle: J. Lee (SW), J. Sephton (PW), C. Etheridge (SW), Major W.R. Thomson (chairman), J. Davies (Colliery), J. McLaughlin (SW), W. Critchley (SW) Front: H. Marsh (SW), W. Parr (SW), A. Smith (PW), J. Prescott (PW), J. Parr (SW), S. Birchall (SW) (PW) – Plate Works (SW) – Sheet Works
Adam McLaughlin was involved with training both the association football team after 1898 and the Northern Union team, in its early years after the First World War.
(Courtesy Pilkington Group Limited)

The Sefton Arms, a town centre pub was the Recs headquarters in 1891.

Pyke played for Lancashire on 14 occasions and scored on his debut for the Red Rose county at Westmorland. His representative odyssey was to continue with selection for England against Wales on 2 January 1892 at Blackheath – the first St Helens rugby player to play for his country. England won 17–0 and went on to win the Triple Crown, although it was to be Pyke's only full international appearance. Indeed the tough-as-teak forward had broken his nose the previous week in a club match and did not disclose his injury to the selectors in case he should lose his place in the team.

A well-respected and unassuming character, Jim did consider retirement at the end of the 1891–92 season and for a spell his impressive assortment of caps and medals was displayed in the window of Holding's music shop in Duke Street. Yet local legend Jim played on and made one further appearance for his county in 1892–93 before eventually retiring.

In his later years he still retained a lively interest in rugby and followed the progress of his son, Jim, in the Recs Northern Union team after the First World War. For many years he was the manager of the grinding department at Pilkington's plate glassworks and was a member of the Recs cricket committee. He died after a short illness in October 1941.

A conflict of interest

When compiling their lists of matches, officials from both the Saints and Recs always tried to avoid clashes of home matches if possible. This meant improved gates and each club had the chance of catering for the other's spectators as well as its own. Yet this live-and-let-live arrangement was somewhat strained in 1892–93, when the Recs entered the Lancashire Rugby Union Cup competition, consisting of a league of 10 teams. These matches took precedence and it was more difficult for the two teams to compile home fixtures equably.

Lancashire League competition 1892–93 (Top 5 teams)

	Pts
Salford	24
Swinton	23
Tyldesley	16
Warrington	16
St Helens Recs	**15**

The fixtures were not completed. Recs played 15 matches, winning six and drawing three, scoring 81 points and conceding 67.

Although the 1892–93 season was not without difficulties, the Recs had broke even in league matches, although they did not enter the league for 1893–94 when it was extended into three divisions. Indeed, the club – and the Pilkington Company itself – always had an historic distrust of competitive rugby, ever since the tragic death of William Taylor in 1887.

Meanwhile, Saints were selected for the Second Division for the 1893–94 season and immediately had 18 Saturdays earmarked for league matches. When the Saints and Recs fixture cards were compared, it was found that on eight dates, both the first teams were out of town and on nine occasions both first teams were at home, thus dividing spectators and gates. The local press summed up the dilemma as follows: "The second Saturday in September shows that the Swinton Lions will open the Boundary Road ground, whilst Wigan are antagonising St Helens at Knowsley Road. It will be difficult to decide which to witness... on 18th November, the game between Recs and Wigan will take all the interest out of Saints' match with Tuebrook."

Those floating rugby spectators in St Helens were definitely spoilt for choice as Recs continued to play some excellent rugby and Saints won the inaugural Second Division Championship and promotion into the highest echelon of the new league structure. Yet in reality, withdrawal from the league set-up and the lack of competitive matches was to trigger the beginning of the end for Recs' golden years under the auspices of the Rugby Football Union.

1895 – Too little, too late

Rugby in the north of England was in a state of flux by the mid–1890s. Allegations of professionalism and the question of broken time payments were the battleground. This was something that was met with increasingly fierce opposition from the southern clubs. Yet the early signs for the Recs were promising. They had amassed an impressive fixture list and looked forward to the forthcoming 1895–96 season with great enthusiasm. Unfortunately, everything was to change, somewhat unexpectedly, after a meeting of leading northern clubs at the George Hotel in Huddersfield in August 1895, when a new breakaway Northern Rugby Football Union was advocated. The Recs, who were always reluctant to go down the broken time route, decided to stick with the RFU, with unfortunate results. Local rivals Saints went with the breakaway group and the die was cast.

Although outwardly optimistic about prospects for the new season, the Recs club was reported to be "sore" over certain defections from their squad to play in the Northern Union. There were accusations of dirty tricks when it was reported that half-back Jimmy Molyneux had been 'converted' and joined Leigh. The *St Helens Newspaper* spoke of the annoyance of the Recs club by what they considered to be "the improper interferences of St Helens [Saints] players" in the matter. "Four of the Leighites came over on Sunday week," the article continued. "After they had tea at the Duke Street Hotel, they persuaded the host to send for Molyneux. Doherty [Saints' winger] is understood to be the messenger and succeeded in bringing his man. The interview took place in a private room and although interrupted at least once, the important negotiations were evidently completed to the satisfaction of the visitors. Molyneux was understood to have been well-satisfied with his job at Pilkingtons, but of course, it could not be compared with the terms he was offered on Sunday evening. A regular situation at 34 shillings per week and an extra 20 shillings (£1) per match is not to be picked up any day."

The fixture list for 1895–96 was decimated, because all the clubs the Recs had worked so hard to secure fixtures with were now members of the new breakaway league and thus unavailable. Consequently crowds and interest waned considerably as a result of the watered down fixture list. Although the club was able to see the likes of James Crossley, William Pilkington and David Traynor graduate to Lancashire county honours, the Recs committee soon realised that their decision not to join the rebels had backfired.

Consequently, on 12 April 1896, they duly tendered their resignation from the Lancashire and England Rugby Football Unions and joined the new breakaway league. The decision to turn had been made several months previously, although the committee decided to wait until the end of the campaign

The *St Helens Newspaper* announced that the Recs had "left the difficult path of the pure and genuine amateur to fraternise with the 'broken-timers'." Their first game under the banner of the new organisation came on Saturday 25 April 1896, when a crowd of more than 1,500 spectators saw Recs beat Crompton in a friendly match by a drop-goal from Appleton to a try. Ironically, Appleton was a guest player from Saints. "If the Northern

Union rules will improve the play in every future match Recs play and will bring out their supporters in like manner, the club will not have cause to regret the change," added the *St Helens Newspaper*.

For the start of the 1896–97 campaign, the Recs trotted out in red jerseys to take on Walkden in the newly instigated Lancashire Second competition. Yet once again this was far from what spectators had been used to from the old rugby union days. The club's first appearance in the Challenge Cup competition was an 8–0 defeat at the hands of Rochdale Hornets in the second round at the Athletic Grounds, after a bye in the first round. To make matters worse, Saints had made considerable progress in the competition, eventually reaching the Final at Headingley, where they lost to Batley. Little wonder that interest was about to take a significant downturn.

In 1897–98 the decline was painfully apparent, with poor crowds at Boundary Road. The rugby team faced stiff competition, not just from the Saints, but from the Recs association football team. Challenge Cup hopes also evaporated after a 17–0 defeat at Halifax in the first round. By December 1897, the game against Barton had seen, according to the *St Helens Newspaper*: "A lamentable dearth of spectators, only a few hundreds being present, the assumption being that the bulk of the Recs' supporters had gone to watch the Association match at Whiston."

The Recs rugby 'A' team had been disbanded shortly after the season had started and the die was cast. The Recreation Club held a meeting on 21 March 1898, where the rugby section was told in no uncertain terms that because of wear and tear to the cricket pitch at Boundary Road and the general lack of interest, that they must cease home fixtures immediately. The Recreation Club formally withdrew from the Northern Union and went into the first of its rugby hibernations. Together with Crompton, they were removed from the Lancashire Second competition, which at the time included the likes of Barrow, Millom, Ulverston, Radcliffe, Lancaster, Barton, Birkenhead Wanderers, Walkden, Altrincham and Fleetwood. The Recreation Club would now confine their attention entirely to association football, which had been so well supported during the 1897–98 campaign.

2. 1898 to 1913: The association years

'Football' at the turn of the 19th century meant rugby or association football, and was used as a more generic term than it is today. 'Association' was what we know today as association football or 'soccer.' The Recs' new association football team, playing in blue shirts and white shorts, had begun life in the Lancashire Alliance and enjoyed a spectacular first season in 1897–98, finishing runners-up behind a powerful Haydock outfit. In the various cup competitions, the Recs were beaten 3–0 in the Final of the Lancashire Junior Cup by Skerton of Burnley at Deepdale, home of Preston North End FC. But the side did manage to lift silverware in the form of the Wigan and District Challenge Cup. Not all the matches were enthralling affairs, however. A report by 'Hawkeye' of the *St Helens Reporter* of the Wigan County Reserve versus Recs match at Springfield Park (later to become the home of Wigan Athletic FC) in February, clearly showed his frustration at the goalless draw: "All the players appeared to me, for a greater part of the time to be more or less in a comatose condition!"

Although the club's main pitch was at Boundary Road, City Road was being used with increasing frequency. The Recs' association football team had also made a new half-back signing, Oliver Ellaby, from Garston, the father of Saints' flying winger Alf Ellaby. Two players went on to gain fame in the Football League. Flint-born inside-forward William Jackson, who joined the Recs from his hometown club went on to play Second Division Football with Newton Heath FC (later Manchester United) and Burnley FC, winning a full Welsh cap in the process, while brilliant wing-half Jack Birchall, born in Prescot, joined Liverpool and had further spells at the top level with Blackpool and Blackburn Rovers.

According to the *St Helens Newspaper*, it was clear that, in the first season of the Association club, the local nature of fixtures was a huge bonus: "The committee of the Recreation Football Club may well congratulate themselves upon the fact that they decided to run an association team and they may further congratulate themselves upon the fact that the venture has been a success from every point of view. In addition to this fact, there are several clubs in the neighbourhood of St Helens, principally Haydock, Prescot, Whiston, Ashton and Earlestown, who have reason to be particularly grateful that the Recs have adopted association, a result that has brought these clubs bumper gates on more than one occasion and made them extremely pleased with themselves. During the season, the Recs played 41 matches, won 31, lost 4 and drew 6, [scoring] 117 [goals and conceding] 30 – a record for the first season of which the club may very well be extremely proud!"

Attendances were always encouraging at City Road for the association matches, comparable, in fact, with the Recs' later resurgence as a professional rugby league outfit between the Wars. Away from home, too, the Recs would be well-represented, with special trains often being arranged for their supporters – 6,000 fans were at City Road for the game against Parr in the Lancashire Alliance early in the 1898–99 season. Although the Recs finished in a disappointing third place in the league, behind Haydock and champions Earlestown, the team did make progress in the Lancashire Junior Cup. The Final was a repeat of the previous year, when the Recs once again fell to their old foes Skerton at Deepdale. They also reached the Final of the Chorley Hospital Charity Cup, only to lose 2–0 against Wigan County, at Dole Lane, Chorley – but all was not lost.

As holders, the Recs were not expected to lose their grip on the Wigan and District Junior Cup easily – especially when their opponents in the Final at Springfield Park were local rivals Earlestown, who were their biggest challengers in the league.

Wigan Junior Cup Final

St Helens Recreation 1 Earlestown 0
Saturday 8 April 1899 at Springfield Park, Wigan

It was impossible to play good football with a gale-force wind blowing across the pitch and the game seemed to consist of a series of goalkicks and throw-ins. For the whole of the first half, Chew, the Earlestown goalkeeper hardly handled the ball. Not a good game to watch, as Hawkeye reported in the *St Helens Reporter*: "The players scrambled about one end of the field making desperate efforts to stop the wind blowing the ball out of the ground and about 3,000 particles of humanity pretended they were enjoying a game of football."

Just before half-time, Jones, the Recs inside-right and captain had to leave the field after a particularly nasty injury to the groin. He returned after half-time, but could not continue. The Recs defence still managed to repel a succession of Earlestown attacks, however, courtesy of the safe hands of goalkeeper Hoy and there was soon time for a surprise counter-attack. Right-winger Dumbell took on his opposing full-back and left him for dead with a fine turn of speed. His well-judged cross into the penalty area was initially missed by William Jackson, but left-winger Davies was on hand to lash the ball into the net for the winning goal.

After the match, the Mayor of Wigan, Alderman Gee, presented the cup and medals to the Recs captain Jones and his team-mates. His attempts to make a speech afterwards were thwarted by some Earlestonians in front of the stand and following a particularly insulting remark, the Mayor advised them to "put a turnip in that calf's mouth!" which was greeted with a sympathetic round of applause.

There were often incidents of unruly behaviour at matches and City Road was no exception. After Haydock had beaten the Recs 4–2 in an Alliance match they were subjected to a hail of stones from a group of youths as they were about to board their wagonette at the end of the match. The Recs players, to their credit, chased the offenders away.

St Helens Recs: Hoy; Woodward, Monks; Hunter, Preston, Mather; Dumbell, Jones (capt), Baines, Jackson, Davies.
Scorer: Davies.
Earlestown: Chew; Williamson (capt), Heyes; Green, Parr, Lee; Harrison, Smith, Hampson, Leach, Settle
Referee: Mr Laithwaite
Attendance: 3,000

A new beginning

The forward-thinking Recs committee applied for membership of the Lancashire Combination for the 1899–1900 campaign. This was quite a big step to make, considering the relative youthfulness of the football club, and required a period of concerted team-building. Clearly, better players were needed if the Recs were to compete against much stronger opposition, including the reserve outfits of professional teams such as Bolton Wanderers, Blackburn Rovers, Liverpool, Everton and Newton Heath. In the close season, there was frantic activity as the team was virtually reconstituted, with the exception of Oliver Ellaby and flying winger Davies. Some of the new faces included goalkeeper Hunt from Skerton; full-backs Stewart (Stockport County and Liverpool) and Leigh (Parr); half-backs Taylor (Leyland) and Winstanley (Farrington). New forwards included Sanders (Skerton), Lea (Stockport County) and Allenson (Leyland).

However, according to the *St Helens Reporter* of 15 August, plans for the new season were thrown into disarray: "The suspension of the St Helens Recs Football Club so near the commencement of the season continues to excite the supporters of the club who fear it may have a disastrous effect on the club's prospects. It is understood that the suspension applies not only to the club, but to the ground and to the players individually and that no matches or practice games can be indulged in until the suspension has been withdrawn."

The reason for the suspension was a result of a 'misunderstanding' between club officials and the Football Association. A Recs player, Skepper, had appealed to the Football Association because he had not received the wages he was owed from the previous April. The FA claimed that they did not receive any explanation of the circumstances from the club, hence the suspension. But this was later cleared up when a satisfactory explanation was sent by the club.

The Recs duly opened their season against Burnley Reserves at Turf Moor on 13 August "with strange men and without practice," as the *St Helens Reporter* put it and were duly defeated 7–0. Despite a memorable first victory against Newton Heath Reserves at City Road on 21 September, the Recs found life difficult in the new division and finished bottom of the 16 clubs, with just seven wins from the 30 league matches. There were several hammerings to contend with; Newton Heath won the return fixture 7–0 at their ground in Bank Lane, Clayton and Liverpool Reserves, the eventual champions, won 5–0 at Anfield. Predictably, the reserve teams of the Football League clubs were the most successful, with both Merseyside clubs, Preston North End, Burnley, Manchester City, Blackburn Rovers and Newton Heath making up the top seven. Disappointingly, the Recs lost 2–1 to Haydock in the final of the Wigan Cup competition at Prescot.

At the Annual General Meeting in May 1900, it was revealed that Pilkingtons wanted the club to be run on strictly amateur lines, something that clearly did not go down well with the committee. A deputation was appointed to meet with the firm to see if their decision could be altered, which was successful. The team began the 1900–01 campaign in good style, with wins against Blackburn Park Road and Oswaldtwistle and there were definite signs that the players were coming to terms with the higher standards of the Combination. After a 1–1 draw with Liverpool Reserves at Anfield on 16 March, the team enjoyed some spectacular victories, especially over Easter, beating Blackburn Park Road 3–1, Burnley 2–1, and Berry's Recreation 5–1, earning them a creditable fifth place in the league. Everton were the champions with 60 points from 34 matches. Yet the Recs' transformation from the dark days of the previous campaign had been quite remarkable.

A new rival

Despite the Recs' recent success, however, things were starting to stir in St Helens in May 1901, with rumours of a proposed new football club in the town that could aspire to "a higher place in the football world than there seems any chance of the Recs doing." A specially convened public meeting was held, the results of which appeared in the *St Helens Reporter* on 14 May. The chairman, Mr Hunt, argued that football in St Helens had been "carried on under somewhat restrictive conditions" and "the only good club in the town was practically a private organisation for the benefit of the employees of Pilkington Brothers." He thought the Recs' organisation was "restricted in its advancement" and proposed that a new independent club should be formed to cater for the needs of the 84,000 people in the town, providing a team capable of taking its place among the clubs of the Second Division or even the First Division of the English League.

Over the next few months, St Helens Town AFC was floated as a company, with a pitch at the Primrose Ground, off Park Road. Captained by J.H. Wainwright, the former Stockport County player, the team took its place in the Lancashire League for the start of the 1900–01 season, together with 13 other clubs: Darwen, Southport Central, Earlestown, Workington, Rochdale Town, Haydock, Stalybridge Rovers, Chorley, Prescot, Barrow, Wigan United, Bacup and Warrington.

Meanwhile, the Recs lost their first match of the season 5–4 at Deepdale against Preston North End. In their first home match, they had to wait for the arrival at City Road of the Rossendale team who had missed their railway connection. It didn't stop an impromptu game developing on the pitch between spectators, however, starting with 20-a-side and increasing in number every minute, as described in the *St Helens Reporter*: "The side playing with the sun at their backs had the most of matters, and 40 of the forwards executed a very pretty passing movement, but in their endeavours to get the ball past the eight goalkeepers, they crowded into the net and damaged it. Then the game was stopped by one of the officials confiscating the ball."

Although the Recs eventually won the match 3–0, the team was languishing in the bottom three of the league by December. On 15 February, the unofficial 'Championship of St Helens' took place in front of more than 5,000 spectators when Recs and Town met in a friendly at City Road, which ended in a 2–2 draw. By this time, the Recs' form had started to improve and they went on to beat high-profile teams Preston North End Reserves 5–0, Everton 1–0 and Accrington Stanley 3–1 at City Road to finish seventh. The Recs had also beaten Town 1–0 at the Primrose Ground in a second friendly challenge.

The two teams were destined to meet competitively during the 1902–03 season, when the Recs left the Combination for the Lancashire League, presumably in an effort to produce more local matches. The team was entered in the FA Cup, Lancashire Cup, Rawcliffe Cup and Wigan Junior Cup competitions, just like their rivals. Fixtures were also devised to avoid home clashes – an advantage of playing in the same league competition. Other teams in the league, apart from the St Helens clubs, included Southport Central, Workington, Chorley, Barrow, Stalybridge Rovers, Rochdale, Bacup, Wigan United and Earlestown.

Recs had lost several players from the previous season, including full-back Jimmy Hodgson and former Everton centre-forward George Storey, who both joined First Division Bury. Two forwards, winger Ottey and inside-forward John Worthington, (who was on Bolton's books) were brought in. It was not long before Recs and Town were facing each other during the first part of the 1902–03 season, in an FA Cup second qualifying round match at City Road on 18 October 1902. The Recs won 3–0 at a relative canter with some brilliant football from half-back Mees. The two sides for this historic clash were:

St Helens Recs: Lee; Owens, Brown; Hunter, Mees, Ellison; Clarke, Muir, Roberts, Worthington, Banks.
St Helens Town: Halton; Parr, Watkins; Howarth Snr, Mills, Houghton; Leigh, Howarth Jnr., Savage, Howard, Money.

The luck of the draw brought Rhyl to City Road in the next round and they were comprehensively beaten 18–0. Football League representatives Burslem Port Vale were the visitors to City Road in the fourth qualifying round and the Recs were once more triumphant by the odd goal in three – a fantastic achievement. In the fifth qualifying round, however, the team lost at Glossop, despite the encouragement of more than 400 fans who had travelled by special train. The team finished fifth in the league and further changes were afoot for both St Helens clubs for the start of 1903–04. Ironically, the Lancashire League had declined as an attraction and several clubs began to look for an alternative competition, so a Second Division of the Lancashire Combination was formed, with many former Lancashire League clubs, including Recs and Town, becoming members.

Golden years

The Recs enjoyed only a moderately successful campaign in the new division in 1903–04, finishing 11th out of 18 clubs. St Helens Town, however, were fifth and were invited into the First Division. The Recs responded in supreme fashion, by becoming Second Division Champions in 1904–05, with their neighbours, who finished bottom of the First Division, being relegated. It was the start of a golden era of football for the Recs, but at the start of the 1905–06 campaign, they joined their rivals St Helens Town at Park Road, because their own ground at Windle City was being redeveloped.

The Recs made a superb start to the 1905–06 season, with four wins and two draws from eight matches, putting them in second place by the middle of October. St Helens Town – complete with former Rec Oliver Ellaby – were beaten in the FA Cup, only for the Recs to lose 5–1 to Earlestown, on the day their new ground was opened by Colonel Pilkington.

A description of the improved enclosure appeared in the *Reporter* on 24 November: "The new ground is by far the best in the town from every point of view. The spectators will be more comfortable and will have a splendid view of the playing pitch which has been sodded and laid out specially. The playing pitch measures 115 feet by 75 feet and the sodded portion is 125 feet by 85 feet, thus leaving plenty of margin all round the field. In addition to the embankment comprised of ashes, round the rails the ground will possess two admirable stands. The one on the Popular Side, which is already erected, is set back about ten yards from the rails and is 60 feet long. It will provide standing accommodation for close on 800 spectators. The chief stand which is not yet erected is to be a most elaborate structure and will seat 800 comfortably. The front of the stand will be raised to a height of 9 feet and underneath the back position, dressing rooms and rooms for the use of the secretaries and referee will be constructed and fitted up on the latest principles. The ground when finished will accommodate about 20,000."

As far as their supporters were concerned, it was no surprise to see the team riding so high in the league. They showed that they could compete against the cream of the best reserve outfits of clubs in the north west.

Their defence was reliable, with Ed Roughley in goal, a trustworthy keeper, who later joined Hull City where he plied his trade for five years in the Second Division. Full-backs Burden and Clegg, who was the captain, were as good a combination as any in the league; Martin, Patten and 'Wick' Hunter formed a formidable half-back line. Hunter enjoyed a successful benefit match against Everton Reserves in February, with the Recs winning 2–1 in front of more than 5,000 spectators.

Up front 'Juddy' Roberts was a consistent goalscorer, while Prescot-born Walter Dagnall provided much-needed guile, spending a season in the Second Division with Hull City in between his two spells with the Recs. 'Ned' Neve was another player who was to enjoy a successful league career, with Hull City and Derby County. Another star was former Blackpool inside-forward Alfie Kearns, an Irish international who enjoyed a brief spell with the Recs before returning home to join Distillery.

A 4–0 thumping of Southport at City Road took the Recs to the top of the table, but the other title chasers had games in hand and it was a short, yet glorious reign for the City Road club.

Lancashire Combination table on 20 February 1906 (top three)

	P	W	D	L	Pts
St Helens Recreation	**27**	**13**	**8**	**6**	**34**
Accrington Stanley	23	13	7	3	33
Manchester United	28	12	7	9	31

The team went on to draw 5–5 with Manchester United Reserves at City Road in a marvellous contest, while Liverpool were thrashed 5–1, courtesy of two goals from Dean, Roberts with one and one each from full-backs Burden and Clegg. Unfortunately, the Recs could not quite maintain this terrific mid-season form and finished fourth out of 20 – a fantastic achievement nonetheless. Accrington Stanley were champions, one of the rare occasions that a reserve team from a Football League club did not take the honours.

A red letter day

It was a great occasion for the Recreation Club on Thursday 6 September 1906, when Colonel Richard Pilkington opened the new grandstand at City Road before the Combination match with Bolton Wanderers Reserves. Although Bolton won 1–0, the new building was to be very important over the next half century for the club. According to the *St Helens Reporter*, the new stand had "ample provision for the press," and included underneath its seating "dressing rooms, with bathrooms for both home and visiting teams, secretary's office, referees room and a room for drying the players' costumes in wet weather."

The new developments made the Recreation Club a self-sufficient outfit and one step ahead of Saints, who still used a public house, the Talbot Hotel in Duke Street, for bathing and changing – something that would continue until the building of the pavilion at Knowsley Road in 1920. Looking to build on their growing status, the Recs committee were confident that their team would top the Lancashire Combination by the end of the 1906–07 season. Unfortunately, their predictions did not quite come true. The Recs finished rather disappointingly in lower mid-table – although the club had signed a rising star, Harry Lee, from Leyland, a winger-cum-centre forward, who was to join Fulham in the Second Division after his short spell at City Road.

The 1907–08 Recs were buoyed by the return of Walter Dagnall from Hull City, together with two signings from Blackburn Rovers, winger Tommy Cunliffe and Herbert France, a centre-forward. Crowds were still encouraging and the team could still pull off unexpected results against sides above them in the league. Yet it was a return to the status quo of the previous campaign – 14th position, although the team embarked upon a memorable run in the FA Cup, ending in a 4–1 reversal at Chesterfield in the fifth qualifying round. The team also achieved a memorable 4–0 victory over Blackpool in the Lancashire Senior Cup at Bloomfield Road, before bowing out at Oldham Athletic in the third round. Yet there was still plenty of interest to come for Recs' fans over the next few years, as supporter Jack Potter explained: "I lived in Argyll Street, so it was easy for me to go to City Road. I watched the team play in the Lancashire Combination and they signed the famous goal-keeper Teddy Doig from Liverpool. He was a really big signing for the club at the time."

Teddy Doig – capital custodian

For two memorable seasons, 1908–09 and 1909–10, Recs supporters could watch their club's biggest name signing - a Scottish goalkeeper who had become a legend at club and international level, with Sunderland and Liverpool. Born in Letham, Forfarshire, Teddy Doig began his career with Arbroath before moving south to Blackburn Rovers and then joined Sunderland in 1890. He proved to be a reliable and durable goalkeeper, ever-present in seven out of the 14 seasons he spent with the Wearsiders, making 456 appearances in all, and a member of the 'Team of all the Talents' that won four First Division Championships – 1892, 1893, 1895 and 1902. He played for Scotland against England on four occasions and left Roker Park in 1904 for Liverpool, where he played a major role in helping his new club gain promotion to the First Division in 1904–05, once again as an ever-present. Teddy went on to play 53 matches for the Reds before he was released by the club at the age of 41. He is still the oldest first team Liverpool player. Ironically, his last game for Liverpool in April 1908 was a 3–3 draw at Anfield against the team that would eventually sign him – St Helens Recreation, whom he had encountered on several occasions when playing for Liverpool Reserves.

Doig's full debut for the Recs came in a 2–2 draw against Bolton Wanderers Reserves, on 5 September 1908 and with the veteran keeper in inspirational form, the side made excellent progress in the league in the first part of the campaign, including a famous 1–0 victory against previously unbeaten Oldham Athletic on 24 October. The Recs saved their best performances for the two Merseyside clubs, however, with a storming 3–1 win at Everton on Boxing Day, followed by a resounding 3–0 success against Liverpool at City Road in February, with Doig saving a penalty. Despite the backing of a huge crowd at home to Everton on Good Friday, the Recs lost 1–0, yet still managed to finish the season in fourth place, with their famous goalkeeper yet again ever-present in 46 matches overall. A typical goalkeeper of the times, Teddy wore a cap to hide his receding hairline. Once when it fell off during the heat of a match he was more anxious to find his cap than the ball.

Doig's experience was once again vital in the 1909–10 campaign, with the Recs covering themselves in glory with a fabulous run in the Lancashire Senior Cup, including an astonishing 4–4 draw against Liverpool's first team at Anfield. Seven days later, despite conceding home advantage in the replay, St Helens Recreation achieved a memorable 3–1 success – arguably the club's greatest achievement in association football. Despite conceding an early penalty, the Recs took the lead with goals from Holden and young forward Fairclough to lead at the break. According to match reports, Teddy Doig faced several hot shots from the Liverpool forwards, which he dealt with admirably. In a highly-contested second half, Fairclough netted a third, with the Recs in total command. Accrington Stanley fell 3–0 in a replay before the great run came to an end with a 2–0 loss in the semi-final to another virtually full-strength Everton side at Goodison Park, who went on to beat Blackburn Rovers in the Final. The Recs team at Anfield was:
Doig; Evans, Dalton; Holden, Ryder (capt), Patten; Williams, Lees, Chorley, Fairclough, Cunliffe.

The Recs showed indifferent form in their league campaign, however, although there was a distinct improvement in the new year, with Doig once more showing his penalty-saving ability in the 1–0 victory over Preston North End at Deepdale. He also kept a clean sheet against a strong Everton reserve team at City Road in March, but the Recs finished rather disappointingly in 16th place. Teddy played in more than 40 matches, his last being a 2–2 draw against Manchester United Reserves on Saturday 30 April 1910. He then announced his retirement from competitive football just before his 44th birthday, after an incredible career. He remained a fine athlete for his age and such was his agility that he could jump backwards over a dining room chair even at the age of 50.

Sadly, in the autumn of 1919, Britain was in the clutches of a virulent virus, 'Spanish flu' and Teddy became seriously ill. All local hospitals were full and he was taken to Rainhill Hospital, near St Helens, where he died on 7 November. "A splendid fellow, everyone will miss the cheery Teddy ... a most estimable man," wrote the *Liverpool Echo* the next day. "He was 52 years of age last week and his last playing club was St Helens [sic]. Our sympathy goes out to his wife and family of eight."

From Recs to Rio

Hooker Oliver Dolan's famous rallying call during the 1930 rugby league Lancashire Cup Final against Wigan, "All local lads and proud of it," could not be applied to the Recs during their association football years. In the Lancashire Combination, the team would not have competed against the top reserve sides relying only upon local talent. Although many of the squad were signed from other West Lancashire non-league clubs, some were 'journeymen' professionals, who, like Teddy Doig, were near the end of their careers.

It is indeed an interesting exercise to look back at some of the colourful characters signed by the Recs during this time. Cornelius Hogan, a dashing centre-forward who played for the Recs in 1905 was born in Malta and had played in the league for New Brighton Tower and Burnley.

Born in the Bridgetown district of Glasgow, Tommy McDermott was a fiercely competitive inside-forward, who began his career with non-league Rutherglen Rosebank before becoming an Everton regular, from 1903 to 1905. He continued in league football with Chelsea, Bradford City and Gainsborough Trinity, before embarking on an end-of-career odyssey that included Dundee Hibernians, Anfield Royals, Wirral Railways, Vale of Leven and Broxburn Shamrocks, with St Helens Recs thrown in for good measure.

Among local lads who were to make good as professionals were Peasley Cross-born Jack Bamber, a more-than-useful half-back, who started at City Road in 1911 and joined Liverpool from St Helens Town, where he was a first team regular before joining Leicester City and Tranmere Rovers. Centre forward Albert Fairclough played for both St Helens clubs before playing for Manchester City, Bristol City and Derby County, and inside-forward Harry Woods starred for Newcastle United and Arsenal after beginning his career at City Road.

But perhaps the most amazing story concerns Liverpool-born Harry Welfare, initially a wing-half, who began with the Recs and eventually joined Liverpool, where he made four appearances in the First Division in 1912–13. Harry went to Rio de Janeiro shortly afterwards, to take up a teaching post at the Anglo-American school in the city. He continued to play football and became a veritable legend, first with Corinthians of Rio and later Fluminense – two of the greatest clubs in Brazil.

Playing as a goal-scoring centre forward, South American defences were not used to his bustling style and the 'English Tank' began to score goals almost for fun in the Carioca Championship. Up to 2006, he still held the record for goals scored for Fluminense against Botafogo with 17. Harry stayed in Brazil, becoming equally famous as a coach for Vasco da Gama, from 1927 to 1930 and again in 1940, before his death in 1966.

As for what was possible – Tommy Magee played rugby for the Recs just at the end of the First World War and then switched to football, where he was signed by West Bromwich Albion. The Widnes-born full-back went on to win five full caps for England during his 15 years at the Hawthorns – becoming a real legend of Midlands football.

The Recs' Junior team for 1904-05 line-up at City Road.
The names are lost in the mists of time, except that the man on the far left on the back row resembles secretary Joseph Wood.

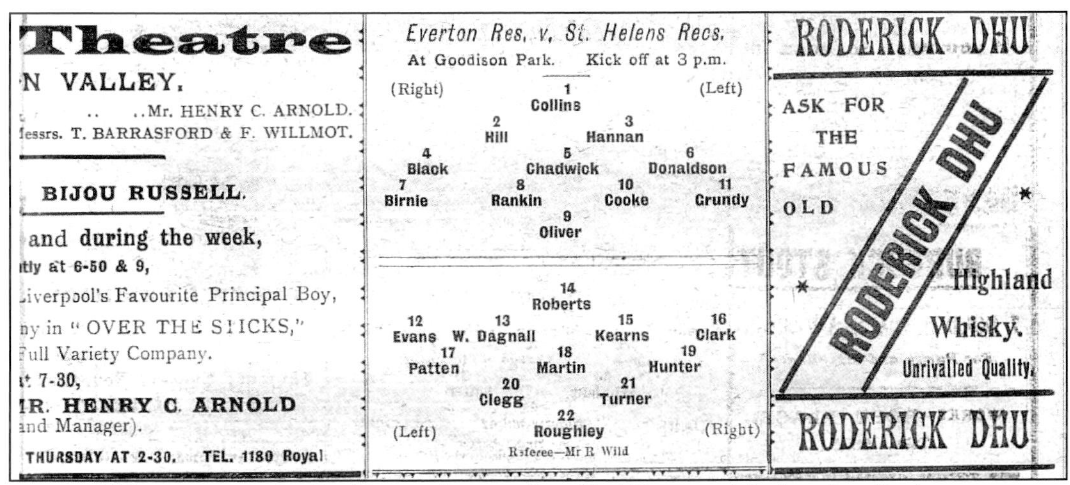

Theatre
'N VALLEY.
..Mr. HENRY C. ARNOLD.
lessrs. T. BARRASFORD & F. WILLMOT.

BIJOU RUSSELL.

and during the week,
ıtly at 6-50 & 9,
Liverpool's Favourite Principal Boy,
ny in "OVER THE STICKS,"
Full Variety Company.
ıt 7-30,
IR. HENRY C. ARNOLD
and Manager).
THURSDAY AT 2-30. TEL. 1180 Royal

Everton Res. v. St. Helens Recs.
At Goodison Park. Kick off at 3 p.m.

(Right) (Left)
1 Collins
2 Hill 3 Hannan
4 Black 5 Chadwick 6 Donaldson
7 Birnie 8 Rankin 10 Cooke 11 Grundy
9 Oliver

14 Roberts
12 Evans 13 W. Dagnall 15 Kearns 16 Clark
17 Patten 18 Martin 19 Hunter
20 Clegg 21 Turner
22 Roughley
(Left) (Right)
Referee—Mr R. Wild

RODERICK DHU
ASK FOR THE FAMOUS OLD
RODERICK DHU
Highland Whisky.
Unrivalled Quality.
RODERICK DHU

This programme for the Liverpool versus Bury First Team match also gives the teams for the Everton Reserves versus St Helens Recreation clash at Goodison Park.
Everton won 3-1 in front of 5,000 fans. (Courtesy Bill Bates)

Left: George 'Juddy' Roberts was a big favourite with Recs' football fans. He worked at BICC in Prescott for 50 years and died in 1955 aged 82. (Courtesy Curtis Johnstone). Centre: Goalkeeping legend Teddy Doig in his Sunderland kit before he joined Recs. (Courtesy Eric Doig)
Right: Tommy McGhee, played rugby for Recs and then switched to football, joining West Bromwich Albion. (Courtesy Bill Bates)

The 1907-08 St Helens Recreation team and officials at City Road.
Back: Joseph Wood (secretary), E. Hunter (assistant secretary), Adam McLaughlin (trainer), James Hunter, R. Sidler, John Grimshaw, H. Alcock, John Dougherty, Peter Fairclough, Charles Turner, Thomas Cunliffe, T. Fildes, D. Johnson, T. Davies; Middle: H. Roberts, George Welding, John Martin, John Patten, H. Lee;
front: Walter Dagnall, George Roberts, Herbert France, H. Logan.
(Courtesy Curtis Johnstone)

Football action at City Road in 1959 in the Pilkington Works Challenge Cup as Plate Works Maintenance 'A' take on Ravenhead Fitting Shop 'A.' Plate Works centre forward Tom Connelly just fails to connect with a left wing cross. Notice the wooden stand in the background, built in 1905-06 and now dilapidated. (Courtesy Pilkington Brothers Ltd)

Joseph Wood was the secretary of the St Helens Recreation Club during their association football and Northern Union ventures. He was also chairman of the club for a spell. (Courtesy Curtis Johnstone)

Decision time

It is interesting to note that Liverpool Reserves, featuring squad members such as Robbie Fowler and Steve McManaman, played several matches at Knowsley Road, during the depths of winter in the early years of the 21st century, sparing the wear-and-tear of their own pitch at Anfield. Yet during the 1910–11 season, the reserve teams of Liverpool, Everton, Blackburn Rovers, Blackpool and Manchester City would be regular visitors to City Road to play against the Recs. Despite a poor first half to the campaign when relegation was a distinct possibility, the team rallied in the New Year to finish in a respectable mid-table position, including a memorable 2–0 victory at Anfield – Liverpool Reserves' first home defeat of the season. The final home game of the campaign saw Burnley blitzed 5–0 at City Road, with centre-forward Ouseby scoring a wonder goal for Recs' second. Charging down a pass in his own half, he dribbled away at top speed towards the Burnley goal and completed his near length-of-the-field run by lofting the ball over the Burnley keeper Tillotson, who had no chance of stopping it. It was a superb victory and something that Recs' supporters would look back on somewhat ruefully, given the circumstances of the next few months.

Storm clouds were brewing ominously by the end of May, with the Lancashire Combination in crisis. The majority of Lancashire's Football League clubs transferred their reserve teams to the newly-formed Central League in 1911–12, with obvious implications for clubs like St Helens Recreation – and neighbours St Helens Town. Both clubs had called meetings as soon as the proposals were mooted by the 13 breakaway clubs. St Helens Town met at the YMCA on Friday 9 June 1911, presided over by chairman Peter Phythian, with some members of the Recreation Club.

There were several options open to the club members in their search to get first-class football in St Helens, yet there was the rather crucial question of finance. Phythian explained that owing to the split that had occurred in the Lancashire Combination, the Town club would be placed among teams of only moderate abilities. The first alternative proposal was that the club should seek to join the new Third Division of the Football League. This was seen as viable, although travelling expenses would be higher. It was stated that many more than 1,000 football fans from St Helens watched Liverpool and Everton each week and the town, with a population of 96,000, could support a first-class team, especially when Bury had only a population of only 50,000.

The second option was an amalgamation with the Recreation club, yet when the Recs contingent at the meeting was asked about this matter, they were, quite understandably, non-committal.

In light of the changes, and in order to boost the Town club financially, it had been hoped that 1,000 shares could be sold at 10 shillings each. Up to the night of the meeting, only 40 had been taken up. Yet there was still enthusiasm for the move forward. There were clubs like Cardiff, Portsmouth, Hartlepool and Croydon who were also looking at entering the new Third Division and it was generally thought that if these clubs were playing in St Helens, the extra attraction of a higher standard of football would increase the receipts to more than the extra cost of travelling. What the committee wanted was "a good team at a reasonable price". But it was accepted that the chances of getting into the league depended on the support of the businessmen of the town. According to Councillor Phythian: "If the present opportunity was lost there would never be another chance of a St Helens team getting into the League." These were prophetic words indeed.

The Recreation club met at the Grove Street Dining Room the following night, with the meeting chaired by Wilfred Ellison. Their options were somewhat less expansive – join the Central League, if accepted, or retain the status quo in the Lancashire Combination. The committee realised that the Lancashire Combination would become watered down with the withdrawal of the 13 clubs, although their players were always going to struggle in the previous competition. The club had spent every penny it was allowed to on professional players – £16 a week during the season. That amount did not seem to have acquired sufficient talent for them to win matches and thus appeal to the public. The 1910–11 season had been a strain financially and the club had not actually made a profit for many years. Indeed, making a profit was virtually impossible because members of the Recreation club were admitted to matches at half price. Everyone connected with the firm paid a penny a week to the Recreation section. Yet that money was not used for the football club. Mr Ellison realised that the situation was a quandary for club members: "The only proposition is whether we join the Central League, or stay in the Lancashire Combination. If we joined the former, we will be going into a class of football that we have been accustomed to. If we remain in the Combination we would be much better than the majority of clubs who would be left in the competition and we might be assured of winning."

Finance was, once more, the crucial factor. As a club they had no money. They had overspent their income year after year and at the present time they owed Pilkington Brothers a considerable sum. On those grounds alone, they had no right to go into a higher class of football, which would mean higher expenses. Indeed, there was a groundswell of opinion that questioned the very existence of the association football team itself. The chairman himself was in favour of the Central League option, however, rather than a proposal to join the Third Division, because there was no guarantee that the loss would not be greater than it had been in the past. The application for membership of the Central League would be looked at favourably because of the ground itself, which was one of the best-appointed outside the Football League. It was considered that the Third Division 'experiment' would lead to several defunct teams as a result of the extra finance required.

It came to pass that the St Helens Town application to the Football League was turned down, together with the Recs' hopes of a place in the Central League. Both teams were to square up to each other in the revamped First Division of the Combination, together with local rivals Earlestown, who disbanded after just a few matches of the 1911–12 campaign and were replaced by Heywood United. The Recs finished runners-up in the First Division of the Combination, six points behind champions Rochdale; St Helens Town were fifth from the bottom. There was a noticeable decline in 1912–13, with the Recs finishing eighth and the die was cast. The *St Helens Reporter* on Friday 11 April gave notice of yet another change of direction: "The existence of the St Helens Recreation Football Club under the association code has not been quite the success it was hoped to be; in fact it has in late years involved the club in a loss of something like £500 a year. Compared with this state of things the financial side of the club in its rugby days was bright indeed and there are many among the club's supporters who would welcome a reversion to the rugby code. The weight of this opinion is now making itself felt and the committee are considering the question in all its bearings. The latest development is the decision to take a vote of the members as to whether the club shall cease to be an association club and go back to the rugby code."

For the record, the Recs' last appearance at City Road for an association football match was on 19 April 1913, when the team thrashed Altrincham 5–0 in a benefit match for winger Tommy Cunliffe, who scored two goals himself. The team was:

Mercer; Hulme, Williams; Meadows, Corfe, Platt; Dagnall, Bradley, Sherratt, Chorley, Cunliffe.

Oliver Ellaby, one of the City Road football pioneers, started following rugby league and was elected president of Saints' Supporters Club in the late 1920s. The landlord of the George Hotel in St Helens town centre, which was later run by Recs' legendary loose-forward Bill Mulvanney, Oliver passed away in 1930 and left a widow and eight children, including Saints' winger Alf Ellaby, who would himself make many appearances on the City Road turf just like his father – but in the handling code, which was to become prevalent at the Recreation club once more.

St Helens Town FC lasted until 1923, but were then reformed in 1946. Famous German goalkeeper and former prisoner of war Bert Trautmann started his football career in England with the club before joining Manchester City. In 1987, they beat Warrington Town 3-2 in the FA Vase Final at Wembley. Today they play their matches in the North West Counties League at Knowsley Road.

The Birth of the Babes: St Helens Rovers
Greenall Whitley Cup Winners 1912-13
This is the junior club that meant so much to the future development of the St Helens Recreation club, featuring, in particular, legendary scrum-half Johnny Greenall (front row, far right) and tough-as-teak loose forward Bill Mulvanney (middle row, first left). Captain Peter Corns, who played and scored the first try in the Recs' return to the Northern Union fold against Pemberton Rovers, is with the trophy. Stand-off Peter Marr is holding the ball, with ferocious forward Peter Cartwright, wearing a somewhat patched-up jersey, second from right in the middle row.

3. 1914 to 1923: The Babes come of age

The annual meeting of the St Helens Recreation Football Club was held in late May 1913 at the works cafe and was, according to reports "attended very sparsely." Over 4,000 of the workforce engaged at Pilkingtons glass works and collieries had recently voted that the club should return once more to rugby, their first love, hence the meagre turn-out. The 'people's game' had run its course. Secretary Joseph Wood reported that the balance sheet showed a loss, although this had been less than the previous season, owing to the transfer fees received for Edelson, who joined Hull City, and Lofthouse, who moved to Reading.

The committee argued that there were a large number of junior association football players employed by the company and that they should be catered for, but it was to no avail. One decision was that the new team – whatever code – would have amateur status, which would be a tough proposition for a football team in the First Division of the Lancashire Combination.

By early June, the die was cast and there would be no association football at City Road for the 1913–14 season, although rivals St Helens Town continued at Park Road. The only element of doubt concerned the nature of rugby football provided by the Recreation club – whether it would be under the auspices of the Rugby Union or the Northern Union. Either way, only out-of-pocket expenses would be paid to players. Northern Union was the unanimous choice, however, as members recalled the dark days of 1895 when the club refused to join the new organisation – with catastrophic results.

Three weeks later, a meeting was held to form a new Northern Rugby Union club. Application for membership of the Lancashire Combination – the same competition as the 'A' teams of the first-class clubs played in – was made. There was also to be a second team, playing in the St Helens Junior League. Once again it was stressed that both teams would be composed of amateurs. Joseph Wood, who had been secretary of the association football club, was elected secretary of the new club and a new committee elected: D. David, S. Bevan, C. Porter, J. Marsh, J. Rigby, J. Williams, A. Brown, K. Farringdon and T. Ashcroft.

Wood later attended the meeting at the Grosvenor Hotel in Manchester on 17 June 1913, when the Recs were duly elected to the Lancashire Combination. At the same time, Brighouse Rangers and Castleford were elected to play in the Yorkshire competition. A major advantage for the Recs was that they would be playing neighbouring clubs, which would maintain interest. This was one drawback of the football team, with most clubs a greater distance away, apart from the 'derby' clashes with St Helens Town. The possibility of big money gates against the likes of Saints' 'A' team was certainly another major attraction that promised to equal, if not beat, any attendance of recent years. Expenses would be significantly reduced and it was the intention of the club officials to run the club with local talent.

Joseph Wood had made the transition from football to rugby and was an experienced official, although many of those who acted as committee men for the football team did not put their names forward. According to the *St Helens Reporter*, "The only aspirant for a new position was rejected!" The club's fixture list was not confined to Lancashire – the Combination stipulated that home and away fixtures had to be taken with at least four Yorkshire clubs.

A new recruit proved to be a crucial signing. Saints let one of the game's greatest scrum-halves slip through their fingers and unknowingly provided the Recs – soon to be their deadliest rivals – with the core of their great side of the 1920s. Johnny Greenall played for local junior team St Helens Rovers and was invited for trials with several of his team-mates, including Bill Mulvanney, Peter Corns, Peter Marr and Peter Cartwright. Johnny was thought to be too small and was told to come back in a year's time. Although his friends had impressed, they refused to sign on without him. The following week the Recs committee snapped up the lot of them. It proved to be a masterstroke and one reason why the Recs were to become such a force to be reckoned with in the game. Other Junior League stars who Saints missed include Joe McComas, Tommy Smith and Frank Bowen. Little wonder that Saints eventually turned to South Wales to sign rugby union players to bolster their playing ranks in the early 1920s.

The Recs had also done well to acquire the services of Alf Glover, formerly a trainer with Saints' 'A' team, who certainly knew his stuff. A former champion athlete, Alf held the position for the next 16 years and his brother, Richard, was the club's captain in 1915. Early indications were promising, with a well-attended practice match and the Recs duly made their debut on 6 September 1913, with a win against Pemberton at City Road in the Lancashire Combination. They wore jerseys of green with narrow chocolate brown hoops and white shorts – the corporate colours of Pilkington Brothers. Results were encouraging for the new outfit, as were crowds, although before the end of the campaign sport was about to take a back seat as Europe was dragged into the confrontation that became the First World War.

As for Pilkingtons, continental trade had virtually dried up during the conflict and several tanks for making glass were closed down. Part of the Cowley Hill works next to the City Road ground was adapted to manufacture shells and some of the profits from this were used to fund an emergency hospital for the wounded at nearby Ravenhead, which opened in 1917. The firm's close connection with the Territorial Army resulted in hundreds of employees, including members of the Pilkington family, being mobilised, leading to a shortage of labour, partly overcome by employing an increasing number of female workers.

Rugby continued almost on an *ad hoc* basis, although even finding friendly fixtures was problematic. During the winter of 1915–16, Recs played Saints on seven occasions. The nucleus of the first Recs side consisted of players who had been exempt from service in the forces. Several happened to be very talented players indeed. They knew each other's game inside out and the committee had made some astute signings.

The team gained valuable experience during the war by playing against the senior clubs and in January 1919, they were admitted to full membership of the Northern Union, taking part in the abridged Lancashire League and Cup competition, before 'normal service' could be resumed in the 1919–20 season. Many of the bigger, established clubs took time to recover from the effects of the First World War. By the time they had done so, the Recs were well-established themselves and were not 'Babes' in the strictest sense, although this became their nickname.

The club had also changed its playing strip to the famous red, amber and black hoops that soon struck fear into their opponents – colours that still remain to this day.

The march of the Babes

What a start they had. The Recs celebrated their first home game of the 1919–20 season at City Road with a 54–0 drubbing of Bradford Northern in a 12-try spectacular. After the narrow defeat at Salford seven days later, 'Observer' in the *Daily Dispatch* could see that they were going to be a force to be reckoned with: "It is a strong, healthy 'baby' that the Northern Union has adopted; an infant that thus early has made its presence keenly felt among its new family circle. Unless I am grievously mistaken, St Helens Recs will be more than a match for most of the clubs in the league." Loose forward Bill Mulvanney also made an impact in representative rugby, making his county debut for Lancashire against Yorkshire at the Cliff on 24 September 1919, scoring a try in the Red Rose county's 15–5 victory. The main highlight for Recs' supporters, however, came with a convincing 21–6 victory over the old enemy, Saints, at City Road on Christmas Day.

The team finished 11th in the Northern Union, five places above Saints and blazed a trail in the Challenge Cup, beating Hunslet 9–0 at Parkside in the first round. The Recs were drawn at home in the second round, where a huge City Road crowd of 11,900 produced record receipts of £650 and saw Recs defeat Barrow 9–2 with relative ease. Yet the club's biggest challenge to date lay ahead, when they were paired with mighty Huddersfield, the 'Team of all the Talents', in the third round. This was to be the supreme test of the new boys' mettle, after all, the claret and gold outfit had not been beaten on the Fartown ground since 1914, a point emphasised in a letter to the *St Helens Reporter* from Huddersfield's captain Harold Wagstaff, just after the draw was made: "My wish for the draw last Monday was that we should meet the Recs at St Helens. The first part of my wish was granted, but as you know, the game has to be played at Fartown. You will no doubt ask my reason for wanting to visit St Helens. I will tell you. I remember my first visit to St Helens a few years before the war, when our team received the finest reception they have had on any ground since they achieved their greatness. This event is still talked about in Huddersfield today, both by supporters and players who took part in that sporting game. So once again I felt I would like to play before the magnificent spectators of St Helens."

"We have heard a great deal of the 'Babes of the League' and I may say that we are not underrating them at all. In fact I have heard them described as the nippiest team in Lancashire. Anyway, I think, of course, that we shall win and we have not been defeated on our own ground since September 1914. However, if luck should go the Recs' way, the first congratulations would be from – Yours sincerely, H. Wagstaff."

Indeed Wagstaff had lunch with the Recs players and officials beforehand 'Just to see that they did not wander off to play Huddersfield Town by mistake!' Approximately 1,000 Recs supporters travelled across the Pennines on the morning of the game, mostly by special train. It had rained heavily before the match and the players had difficulty, initially, in keeping their feet on the sodden Fartown turf. Yet the pitch would be a terrific ally for the Recs in their game plan, which included keeping the ball in the forwards and marking their opponents tightly.

Joe Bates, at full-back, was prominent early on and handled the heavy, greasy ball superbly in the most trying of conditions when put under pressure. After a superb passing move instigated by Johnny Greenall the Recs forwards continued to press their opponents. For a few fleeting moments, Grundy and Wagstaff ran neck-and-neck for the ball as it ran towards the try-line. The Recs man claimed to have got a sensational touchdown before Wagstaff, but referee Mr Eddon signalled that the ball had gone over the dead-ball line, much to the relief of the home crowd.

Huddersfield then took the lead from a drop-goal by Gronow set up from a free-kick. Meanwhile Gwyn Thomas, the Huddersfield full-back, dived at the feet of the onrushing Recs pack and kept his line intact.

At half-time, the score remained 2–0 to Huddersfield, although after the break the Yorkshiremen were decidedly second best as the Recs forwards out-played their opponents. Their tackling, typified by Leyland, was all-embracing, with scrum-half Johnny Rogers unable to produce his usual brand of magic.

St Helens Recs at The Willows, Salford 30 October 1915. Back: Dick Silcock (F), Patrick Downey (F), Gartland (F), Bill Ashall (LC), Frank Bowen (F); middle: Billy Marr (SO), Joe McComas (RW), Thomas Hardman (FB), Bill Grundy (RC), Johnny Greenall (SH); front: Albert Simm (F), Dickie Glover (LW), Berlin Barnes (F). (Positions in brackets)

The Recs team and officials at City Road on 1 October 1921. Back: Adam McLaughlin (trainer), Tom Ashcroft (c), W. Bradbury (c), Saltz (guest – Pittsburgh PA USA), R. Powell, R. Large (c), J. Williamson (c), Bill Ashall, James Glen (c), T. Fairclough (c), Joseph Wood (secretary), James Rigby (chairman), Berlin Barnes, J. Prescott (c), Joe Bates, C. Porter (c), Alf Glover (trainer), middle: Tommy Smith, Albert Simm, Tommy Dingsdale, Jimmy Owen, Johnny Greenall (capt), Tom Ainge, Joe McComas, Harry Grundy; front: Dick Ramsdale, Peter Cartwright, Fred Leyland, Frank Bowen, Bill Mulvanney. (Courtesy Ian Cartwright)

City Road Legends 1922. Back: Adam McLaughlin (trainer), Harry Grundy, Frank Bowen, Tommy Smith, Fred Leyland, Jimmy Pyke, Bill Mulvanney, Joe Bates, Alf Glover (trainer); front: Albert Simm, Bob Hull, Joe McComas, Johnny Greenall, Joe McNulty, Jimmy Owen.

Middle: Bill Mulvanney and Jimmy Pyke
Bottom: Jimmy Owen and Joe McComas

After a scrum under the home posts, the referee awarded a penalty to Recs, which was promptly converted by McComas. "This equaliser was like wine to the weary," wrote 'Spectator' in the *Reporter* and the rest of the game was played out with Huddersfield's passing game versus the Recs' tackling – a tremendously exciting encounter with the 10,000 crowd roaring most of the time. In the final minutes, Wagstaff went on a mazy solo run, beating half a dozen Recs' tacklers with typical strength and swerve, but the cover came across and the danger passed.

At the final whistle, Wagstaff went towards Greenall to congratulate him on a magnificent performance, a difficult task indeed, considering it was hard to tell the two sides apart by this stage. "The Greatest Achievement of the Season... the Recs startle the Northern Union," trumpeted the *St Helens Newspaper*. The Babes had nearly succeeded where so many others had failed. Now it was back to City Road and part two of this incredible Roses battle.

Challenge Cup Third Round replay
St Helens Recreation 6 Huddersfield 8
Wednesday 17 March 1920 at City Road, St Helens

The replay, which kicked off at 4pm on the following Wednesday, St Patrick's Day, was one of the greatest rugby league occasions enjoyed in St Helens. Such was the desire to see this mouth-watering clash that people would do anything to get a vantage point, climbing up trees, onto railway wagons and anything they could think of. Jack Potter, who attended the game, recalled the huge interest generated by the match and the prospect of seeing one of the greatest teams of all time: "The boards were bulging and thousands couldn't get in... they were sitting on the houses at what they called 'Bug Row'. (City Gardens) They paid money to go in and watch the match through the upstairs windows." A total of 20,000 people paid for admission, while an estimated 3,000 got inside when the gates were rushed, with Recs officials allowing the crowd in rather than have the barriers smashed. Over 3,000 actually went away, unable to get anywhere near the terraces. Receipts were £1,560, beating the previous record from the Barrow match several weeks before.

Huddersfield skipper Wagstaff won the toss and decided to play against the wind and sun in the first half. It was clear that Huddersfield would again prove to be formidable opponents, characterised by some brilliant play from full-back Gwyn Thomas, who ran the ball out superbly. After six minutes play, however, Joe McComas booted over a penalty after a botched play-the-ball from the visitors. Recs failed to capitalise on this early advantage, when Fred Leyland found himself with just the full-back to beat and four men in support. Unfortunately he lost control of the ball and a crucial chance was gone.

It was then that McComas used the wind to its full advantage by slotting over a penalty goal from fully five yards inside his own half. In a fiercely competitive match, first Huddersfield's Thomas and then Billy Ashall and Owen of the Recs left the field. Ashall in particular remained a passenger for the rest of the match with his arm hanging limply by his side. Mulvanney took his place in the backs for threequarters of the game.

Huddersfield made use of their scrum-dominance, 21–15 in the first half, with a try from Ben Gronow, which reduced the deficit to a single point. Yet McComas astounded the huge crowd shortly after with another magnificent long-range penalty goal.

After half-time the end-to-end play continued, with centre McNulty bluffing and swerving through several defenders only to be tackled just short of the line. It needed a touch of class from Harold Wagstaff to change the course of the match, with just eight minutes to go. The legendary centre made ground expertly before firing out a wide pass for scrum-half Habron to touch down. Much to the disappointment of the crowd, Gronow's conversion sailed between the posts for a two-point lead that was never relinquished, but it was close. In the last minute, McComas attempted another shot at goal from just over half-way. He got the range and elevation, but the ball sailed agonisingly wide.

"The better team won on the day," wrote 'Spectator'. "The home team did all that was expected of them, bar one thing. They dribbled, packed, fielded and kicked delightfully and their tackling was an object lesson. But they lost the game by weakness in attack - their penetrating power was bad."

After the final whistle, the crowds swarmed onto the pitch and applauded Huddersfield skipper Wagstaff from the arena. Johnny Greenall and his men received similar treatment. Defeated but certainly not disgraced, they had given everything and the result could have gone either way. In a promotion reminiscent of the famous film-makers Mitchell and Kenyon, Glover's Picture House in Baldwin Street advertised highlights of the *Great Football Match* as a special feature twice weekly, which was a huge success.

This particular match remains one of the most famous and talked-about occasions in St Helens' sporting history and helped to enhance the burgeoning reputation of the 'Babes' as a team to be reckoned with throughout the league.

St Helens Recs: Joe Bates, Joe McComas, Bill Ashall, Joe McNulty, Jimmy Owen, Tommy Smith, Johnny Greenall (capt), Fred Leyland, Winstanley, Harry Grundy, Bill Mulvanney, Dick Silcock, Bob Hull
Scorer: Goals: McComas 3.
Huddersfield: Thomas, Rosenfeld, Gleeson, Wagstaff (capt), Todd, Habron, Rogers, Swinden, Naylor, Fenwick, Gronow, Clarke, Sherwood
Scorers: Tries: Habron, Gronow. Goal: Gronow
Half-time: 6–3
Attendance: 23,397; *Receipts:* £1,560

Everything else was an anti-climax after the Huddersfield match, with the completion of the league campaign and some extra friendlies thrown in for good measure. The team finished 11th in the league, with a 51.79 per cent success rate, five places above their local rivals Saints. The Recreation club had certainly proved that so far it could more than survive in the competitive world of top-flight rugby league and supporters were delighted by the never-say-die attitude of the players every time they put on the red, amber and black strip. Were the Babes just one-season wonders? Could an essentially locally-produced team continue to be sustainable and begin to challenge for the game's top honours? The next few years would be crucial.

Bill Ashall – One that got away

Over the past few decades in rugby league, where the average height and weight of players has increased dramatically, huge 16 stone plus centres like Gene Miles, Mal Meninga and Paul Newlove have used their powerful frames to wreak havoc among opposing defences. How different it was in the early 1920s, when the Recs provided one of the biggest centres in rugby league – Bill Ashall, who weighed in at 13½ stones. Bill, together with his winger Joe McComas, formed a deadly partnership during the Recs' formative years in the Northern Union after the First World War.

Although Billy was born and bred in St Helens, he was definitely one that got away – and came back. A former junior with Sherdley Athletic around 1912, Bill was asked to go to Knowsley Road for a trial. The Saints were keen to sign him, but baulked at the £5 fee that

Bill wanted. One of the Sherdley committee had links with Hunslet and recommended young Ashall to the Yorkshire club, who promptly paid out the five gold sovereigns to sign him.

Bill spent seven seasons at Parkside, playing alongside the legendary Billy Batten, but found the travelling to and from his St Helens home a real bind. In 1919, he returned home to the Recs and established himself as a fans' favourite. Throughout the early 1920s he occupied the right centre position with Joe McComas outside him. Although selected to play for Lancashire, Bill missed out as a result of injury and was subsequently overlooked. But his most memorable game was that fantastic Challenge Cup tie at City Road described above, against Huddersfield. It was not just the 8–6 defeat that was painful for Bill, because he was forced to leave the field with a chipped shoulder bone. "I think we could have beaten them if we'd had 13 men on the field," he recalled later.

Huddersfield's captain, Harold Wagstaff, remained the player he most admired and always quoted his words when describing the ideal situation for a centre: "Give me six good, heavy forwards, between 15 and 16 stones, with one just a bit faster than the others for loose-forward. Let them get the ball out to us and we'll do the rest." Bill made the most of his opportunities with the ball on Christmas Day 1919, when the Recs defeated Saints 21–6 at City Road, with Bill scoring two tries and making one for his buddy Joe McComas.

An electrician's mate at Pilkington's Plate Works, Bill was alter to become assistant trainer of the Recs with the legendary Ted Forber until their withdrawal from the league in 1939. He then moved to Knowsley Road in a similar capacity until 1941. Bill became, like many of his former team-mates, a licensee, running the Owl's Nest Hotel in Haydock.

Town's top dogs

Pilkingtons employees received increased benefits in the early 1920s with the formation of the company's welfare department. Dental and medical facilities were provided, and optical, chiropody, physiotherapy and rehabilitation services were added later. The 1920s would also see the work's team, St Helens Recreation, develop into a side capable of challenging for major honours in rugby league's top flight. Their rivals, Saints, began the decade with high hopes and a new pavilion at Knowsley Road. Yet before too long, as the Recs began to enjoy hitherto unparalleled success, Saints were literally facing a fight for survival.

There were regular five-figure crowds at City Road as the Recs began the 1920–21 campaign in fine style. Although home defeats ensued against Wigan, Swinton and Broughton Rangers, the team reached the Lancashire Cup semi-final, only to lose 9–3 in a titanic battle at Leigh in front of more than 16,000 fans. The disappointing run coincided with an injury to star scrum-half Johnny Greenall. "The Recs without Greenall are like a ship without a rudder," wrote one critic.

Northern Union match

St Helens Recs 39 St Helens 0
Saturday 1 January 1921 at City Road, St Helens

The captain was back for the new year clash against the Saints at City Road, a match that became embedded in the folklore of the Recreation club, just like the clash with Huddersfield 12 months before. It was a one-sided affair for the 13,000 spectators, but for those who supported the red, black and amber, it was 80 minutes made in heaven. The Recs, in second-place in the league table and consisting of wholly St Helens-born players, inflicted a 39–0 drubbing over their great rivals. Although Saints lost two players through injury during the match, the damage had already been done in the first quarter.

The Babes were far and away the better team in every department and after the first score within five minutes of the start there was never any doubt as to the result. Their forwards got possession almost as they pleased and the St Helens backs spent most of the 80 minutes chasing their opponents, who threw the ball around with great freedom.

Billy 'Wee' Pierce was the outstanding player in the team. The young Recs stand-off gave a delightful exhibition and besides cutting through splendidly on numerous occasions, did some very fine tackling. Bustling Billy Ashall was the best of the threequarters, with McComas responsible for 14 of his team's points. Frank Bowen was the pick of a dominant set of forwards, his second try being a brilliant individual effort. Recs supporters always had this result up their sleeves to wind up their rivals. Little wonder that passions occasionally boiled over on the terraces on derby day.

St Helens Recs: Joe Bates, Jimmy Owen, Jim Pyke, Bill Ashall, Joe McComas, Billy Pierce, John Greenall (capt), Albert Simm, Oliver Dolan, Harry Grundy, Bob Leyland, Bill Mulvanney, Frank Bowen.
Scorers: Tries: Ashall 2, McComas 2, Bowen 2, Pierce, Grundy, Leyland; Goals: McComas 4, Dolan, Mulvanney.
St Helens: Charles Collins, John Molyneux, Thomas Gormley, Charlie Crooks (capt), Michael Hanley, William Hankinson, Edward McLoughlin; Peter Molyneux, Harold Heaton, William Jackson, Harold Bradbury, Thomas Durkin, George Farrimond.
Referee: Mr R. Jones (Widnes)
Half-time: 14–0
Attendance: 13,000; *Receipts:* £1,030

As a result of an injury crisis, the team finished the campaign in a rather disappointing 15th position in the league table, with a 51.67 per cent success rate. But in the Challenge Cup, the Recs enhanced their burgeoning reputation still further when Wigan came to City Road in the first round. There was a huge crowd of almost 20,000, with a large contingent cheering on the visitors. According to the local press, "The row of charabancs was half a mile long," as the crowd eventually began to encroach on the inside of the surrounding fence. Wigan played some classy rugby, with their threequarter line getting clean possession from star halves Sid Jerram and George Hesketh. Yet the Recs had a tactical plan up their sleeve, with Frank Bowen selected in the centre who did a great destruction job on his opposite numbers Danny Hurcombe and Tommy Howley.

The Recs led 4–0 at half-time, courtesy of two Pyke penalties, but the Cherry and Whites fought back after the interval, when Hurcombe walked over the line to score. The conversion was inexplicably missed by Howley and it was Bowen who became prominent, this time in attack, as he fed Joe McComas for a sparkling try that was converted by Pyke. Although Hesketh created a try for his winger, Smith, the Recs doggedly held their three-point lead for the last quarter. It was a good day to be a Recs' supporter, as the Parr Temperance Band played *The end of a perfect day*. What's more, at Knowsley Road in the same competition, Saints slumped to an ignominious 7–0 defeat at the hands of Bramley.

In keeping with the up-and-down nature of the season, the Recs endured a shock 7–0 defeat at home to Widnes in the next round. 'Overcome by Chemicals', was the headline in the local press. Secretary Joseph Wood told 800 supporters at the club's AGM in June that injuries were to blame for the mixed bag of results.

In July 1921, City Road played host to royalty, with the visit to St Helens of the Prince of Wales (later King Edward), who met First World War veterans on the pitch. This included the two St Helens VCs, Sergeant J. Molyneux and Corporal J.T. Davies, and Sergeant Oliver Dolan of the 64th Field Ambulance, who had won the DCM with Bar at Passchendaele. Dolan was, of course, the Recs' hooker and lived virtually next door to the ground in Wellington Terrace.

In the driving seat

Saints' supporters were aghast that the Recs had stolen their thunder in such devastating fashion. In the days before the First World War, Saints had made strenuous efforts to develop local talent. First of all, the Junior League was formed and put on a sound footing. Then Tom Phillips – Saints' chairman and headmaster of Rivington Road School – began a schoolboy competition. A potential pipeline of talent had been established, but it was not to bear fruit for Saints. The astute Recs committee rubbed their hands at the many errors of judgment made by their Knowsley Road counterparts. The Recs signed just one 'outsider,' at this time – Dick Ramsdale, a veteran front-row forward who had won every honour in the game with Wigan, including two Great Britain tours to Australia.

Saints looked to Wales for their team-building, a policy that almost rendered the club bankrupt, so much so that by the 1923–24 season, with the club over £1,000 in debt, they were only saved by a last-ditch 'Save our Saints' fund-raising campaign in the town, organised by committeeman Frank McCormick, who was also a local councillor. They were given a £20 donation from their greatest rivals at City Road – a tremendous gesture indeed.

Although the Recs, too, were hardly operating at anything like a profit, the 1921–22 and 1922–23 campaigns saw them consolidate their position in the professional rugby league ranks. Finishing just outside the top 10 on both occasions, progress in cup competitions was largely disappointing. Yet in terms of representative rugby, several Recs players were selected against the visiting Australians in 1921–22, a measure of the club's advancement in such a short time: Jimmy Owen played on the left wing for England versus Australia at Highbury; Jimmy Owen (right wing), Joe McComas (left wing) and Johnny Greenall (stand-off) all played for Lancashire against Australia at Wilderspool; Johnny Greenall (stand-off) and Frank Bowen (second row) played for the Lancashire League against Australia at Goodison Park, while Johnny Greenall played at stand-off for the Northern Union versus Australia at The Willows in the third test match.

The Recs committee and supporters looked for further improvement as the 1923–24 season beckoned. Modern Super League players – especially those who have international commitments – have a relatively short pre-season break. In the 1920s, however, the long summer enabled rugby players to indulge in other sports. Full-back Tommy Ainge was a star cricketer with the Recreation team; some took part in athletics, with the Pilkington Recreation Sports held annually at Denton's Green. Others, like winger Jimmy Owen and half-back Jimmy Lawrenson, played tennis on a regular basis. Both missed the pre-season trial as a result of their involvement in a particularly important tournament.

The Recs squad, with the exception of the old warhorse Ramsdale, had an average age of 26 and was fully battle-hardened for Northern Union. At full-back, Tommy Dingsdale looked as though he was going to make the position his own, with his safe handling, the ability to clear danger with his clever side-stepping and a sure kicking game. In the threequarters, Jimmy Owen was an international class finisher; Joe McComas was a vastly experienced player who could play at centre or on the flanks; Jim Pyke was a stylish rugby player, capable of some sublime moments in possession, while Tommy Gormley and former

Wigan flyer E.L. Smith gave the backs extra pace and penetration. Bill Ashall's speed and physique would also be invaluable.

At half-back, skipper Johnny Greenall was entrenched in the number seven jersey – the mastermind of the side – and he would be partnered, initially by Lawrenson, a diminutive, yet elusive performer, with a superb pair of hands. Fred Halton waited in the wings as cover at stand-off. The forwards continued to be a major strength within the team. Ramsdale had been a superb signing for the club. "He is a deadly tackler," wrote one critic, "and his weight and great strength in the scrum are invaluable. You never see the Recs pack being turned on Ramsdale's side." He was joined in the 'engine room' by Fred Leyland and Harry Grundy, who had great strength and pace. Hooker Jack Hughes was capable of supplying a steady stream of ball to the threequarters on his day.

The back three were gaining a fearsome reputation for themselves. All were capable of destroying the opposition's attacks, with Smith possessing the mobility that saw him operate in the centre or at stand-off when the need arose. One of the major concerns, however, lay in goalkicking. The Recs were never able to recruit someone like Jim Sullivan, who could boot over a century of goals with regularity each season. At any one time, Dingsdale, McComas, Pyke and Grundy were given the responsibility. It was Dingsdale who became the most accomplished, reaching his own century for the season during 1926–27.

Almost 1,000 fans went to The Willows for the first game of the 1923–24 campaign, against Salford, where the Recs opened their account with a creditable 8–2 success. Missed goalkicks proved costly at home to Broughton, however, on a pitch that showed signs of drainage work during the close-season, with a distinctive herringbone pattern clearly visible.

Johnny Greenall was outstanding in the 13–0 victory over York. "He initiated every single combined movement which ran through the Recs back division," wrote 'Nemo' in the *St Helens Newspaper*. "Then on top of all this, Greenall scored his splendid single-handed try which introduced a splash of excitement into a rather sombre game." Yet the burgeoning partnership between Greenall and Lawrenson was cruelly shattered in the return match against Salford at City Road, when the stand-off broke his collar bone. He was later described as "comfortable" at the Pilkington Special Hospital, one of the special privileges of being an employee of the firm.

It was in the 1923 Lancashire Cup that the Recs really came of age. After enjoying a bye in the first round, two specially-arranged afternoon training sessions were organised before the second round clash at home to Rochdale Hornets. The Recs, with Fred Halton excelling at stand-off smashed their hapless opponents 21–0. Bill Mulvanney scored the first try, with Greenall, Smith, Pyke – with a sublime interception – and Gormley further scorers. Dingsdale's three goals completed the rout.

Another fortunate home draw saw Oldham visit City Road in the semi-final and an incredible atmosphere was generated by more than 15,000 fans, paying £690 for the privilege. This was a real nail-biter, with the Recs never able to pull away from the visitors convincingly. Once more, lacklustre goalkicking was a factor, with two goals kicked by Dingsdale and six missed, including two attempted drop-goals. Scrum-half Greenall had a hand in all three tries, with his mastery of the scrum-base, in the 13–11 success, although his dominance would have unexpected ramifications later on in the week. Just when the pressure was on, the Recs could rely on the experience of Ramsdale, who battered back about half-a-dozen opponents to clear his lines when danger threatened.

All hell broke loose just seven days before the final against Swinton with the publication of a letter in the *St Helens Newspaper and Advertiser* from Jim Pyke's father, the former

Recs and England international, who took exception to a certain section of the Oldham match report by the correspondent Nemo:
"Dear Nemo – I have read your report re. Recs v Oldham match on Saturday. Anyone reading your report and not having seen the game, would come to the conclusion that it was a game between Oldham and Greenall, plus a couple of forwards.

Judging from your remarks, the threequarter backs particularly the centres, were next to useless, but do you ever ask yourself whose fault it is? If you did, I don't think all your praise would fall on the redoubtable Greenall

I notice in your report you remark 'Pyke missed a pass from Halton.' Did you notice that this was the only pass he got all through the game and this happened in a game that the Recs got the ball four times to their opponents once, and this with a great scrum-half like Greenall playing. Surely the master-mind could find some way of getting the ball to his backs more than once in a game?

Have you ever noticed how often the Recs' centres get the ball from the scrum except when they are hemmed in? Do you ever see Greenall throw the ball out without trying to burst through himself first?

In my humble opinion, this latter is the cause of the centres not showing to advantage – and if I were one of them I am jolly well sure they would want one fresh one.

I have no doubt you will be going to the final. Keep your eye on the Swinton scrum-half and you will see the half-back game played as it should be played, and the centres given a chance i.e. a chance to play, not a chance to be knocked into the other world as they are catching the ball by the on-coming forwards.

So – the Recs haven't got a good centre, not even Owen, although you do your best to boost him up each week. I would go further and say they never will have until Greenall gives them a chance. I could do all that's required of a centre for the Recs and I shall soon have seen 60 summers. Yours faithfully, James Pyke."

There was wide debate about the team, and the most erudite response came from 'Premier' in the *St Helens Newspaper*, who put the whole thing into perspective: "I too saw the Oldham cup-tie. Johnny Greenall and the forwards won it. If a scrum-half can win a game by his own efforts, why should he pass on the task to his centres? Greenall, as a captain, used the brains of a captain. He directed the team's greatest force (himself) into Oldham's most vulnerable spot. He penetrated that spot and Oldham mourn in consequence."

Lancashire Cup Final
St Helens Recs 17 Swinton 0
Saturday 24 November 1923 at Central Park, Wigan

Excitement was at fever pitch for the Final, generating incredible interest from the sporting public - a virtual full house of almost 26,000, at Wigan's Central Park, with an estimated 9,000 fans journeying to the town by train from St Helens and district, including more than 7,000 from Central Station alone. The Recs team travelled to the match in a new and luxurious coupe charabanc, which, according to the local press, had electrified door handles and outside metallic parts, "so as to prevent the meddling of children".

It seemed as though it was the Recs themselves who were electrified, as they tore into their opponents with great enthusiasm. After seven minutes, Tommy Dingsdale banged over a penalty to give the Recs the lead, with Jimmy Owen slotting over an astute drop-goal midway through the half for his side to lead 4–0 at the break. In the second stanza, the

Recs emphasised their dominance, when Pearson, the Swinton full-back, was carried off the field. After a period of intense pressure, Halton delivered the ball to Pyke, who steadied himself and kicked a superb drop-goal for the Recs. From a scrimmage in midfield it was Pyke again who caused the damage, with a brilliant break and kick over emergency full-back Halsall's head and a superb follow-through to touch down. Another great try was soon to follow, when Gormley broke from halfway, kicked over the defence, picked up and raced along the touchline. Jimmy Owen ran along in support and received a well-timed pass on the Swinton '25' to finish off the move under the posts. Pyke converted and at 14–0 the silverware was clearly destined for City Road. Virtually on the final whistle, Greenall stole the ball at the base of the scrum and sidled over in the corner for the final score of a memorable day for the Recreation club.

After the final whistle, Johnny Greenall and the team were presented with the trophy by Mr H. Rebbitt, the President of the Lancashire County Union, as hundreds of caps were thrown into the air out of sheer jubilation.

Dense fog delayed the return of the team to St Helens, but on their arrival they proceeded to the Town Hall, where a large crowd assembled in Victoria Square to give them a rousing welcome. The players were conducted to the Mayor's parlour where they were received by the Mayor and plied with light refreshments. They then came out onto the steps where the cup was again handed to the skipper Johnny Greenall by the Mayor, Alderman Peter Phythian. After leaving the Town Hall, the players and officials moved on to the sheet works dining room where dinner was served. There were the usual congratulatory toasts and Colonel Norman Pilkington congratulated the team on its great success. At the end, the Mayor presented the team with the medals they had won.

"Greenall and Pyke in Excelsis!" trumpeted Nemo in the *St Helens Newspaper*, as the pre-match controversy appeared to evaporate. "I saw Greenall do all that Bryn Evans did and on top of it all he added his own opportunism and individual ability. Compared to the Oldham game, the centres did get more opportunities and they took advantage of them," he maintained. "Each dropped a goal and each scored a try and in addition, Pyke improved a try, so that he distinguished himself to the tune of seven points."

The Recs had come of age in spectacular fashion, by beating their rivals Saints in the race for silverware – a fantastic achievement in such a short time. Although all was doom and gloom at Knowsley Road, the club would increase in strength over the next few years.

St Helens Recs: Billy Dingsdale, Tommy Gormley, Jimmy Owen, Jimmy Pyke, Joe McComas, Fred Halton, Johnny Greenall (capt), Dick Ramsdale, Jack Hughes, Harry Grundy, Tommy Smith, Albert Fildes, Bill Mulvanney.
Scorers: Tries: Owen, Pyke, Greenall; goals: Pyke 2, Dingsdale, Owen.
Swinton: J. Pearson; F. Evans, H. Halsall, J. Evans, C. Brockbank; A. Jenkins, B. Evans; M. Strong, H. Blewer, T. McCormick, H. Worsley, S. Howarth, H. Powell.
Referee: Mr H. Horsfall (Batley)
Half-time: 4–0
Attendance: 25,656; *Receipts:* £1,450

Eleven years at the top

Seven days later, the game against Rochdale Hornets at City Road had all the appearance of a gala occasion, with both the British Legion Band and the Bert Hughes Prize Jazz Band in attendance, as the team was photographed with the coveted Lancashire Cup. It had also been designated as Johnny Greenall's benefit match. Greenall had been a Rec for 11 years and captain for six, taking over when fellow scrum-half Dickie Glover retired from the game.

Despite receiving 'special attention' from his opponents over the years, Johnny was never cautioned or sent off in his career and remained a role model for others, including younger brother Billy, who followed him into the Recs team. "He was a great player," remembered Billy "and I tried to model my game on him. It was such a pity that he never went on tour. He looked set to go to Australia in 1924. He was in the squad and they gave him a list of what he needed, but at the last minute there was a change, when they decided to take Walter Mooney from Leigh instead. Apparently one of the Leigh committee had a big influence on international selection."

Despite being well protected by one of the fiercest loose-forwards in the game, Bill Mulvanney, Johnny had another 'guardian angel' who looked after his interests on – and off – the field. His mother, Hannah, watched every match and woe betide anyone who had the temerity to rough up her son. The chances were they would get a good thrashing with her umbrella, which was used almost exclusively for that purpose – very rarely to keep the rain off. She is immortalised by Gus Risman in his book *Rugby Renegade*. The minutes of the Saints club committee, after a recent derby clash in the late 1920s said: "Ernie Shaw had reported to the secretary that Mrs Greenall had accosted him in the public street and attributed to him Johnny's injury, Shaw being much upset in consequence. The regrettable incident was fully discussed and secretary was instructed to write to Mrs Greenall." Never mind the likes of Smith, Fildes and Mulvanney – hell hath no fury like a woman scorned.

Pride of the Red Rose County: St Helens Recs - Lancashire Cup Winners 1923
Back: Tommy Smith, Bill Mulvanney, Albert Fildes, Dickie Ramsdale, Jack Hughes, Harry Grundy; front: Joe McComas, Jim Pyke, Johnny Greenall (captain), Colonel Norman Pilkington (president), Jimmy Owen, Fred Halton, Tommy Gormley, Tommy Dingsdale.

Despite the murky day and a nation facing growing unemployment, the mood was one of celebration at City Road when the rampant Recs, clad in the famous red amber and black strip, proudly paraded the Lancashire Cup, which they won for the first time by defeating Swinton 17–0 at Wigan in November 1923. Over 80 years have passed since the Lancashire Cup was brought back to town for the first time, but the memory still lingers on for that ever-dwindling band who can recall the original City Road enclosure with its all-wooden stand, which would scarcely meet present-day safety criteria.

This was a time when rugby league rejoiced in its cloth-cap image, with the occasional homburg, fedora or trilby the choice of the more fashion-conscious and, as the picture confirms, dapper Recs official Colonel Pilkington was something of a trend-setter with his natty bow tie, kid gloves and peaked headgear. A member of the local glass manufacturing family, William Norman Pilkington was a noted athlete in his Cambridge University days, played rugby union for England before the turn of the century, and won the DSO with the 5th South Lancashire Regiment in the First World War. On demobilisation he switched his allegiance to the professional code with St Helens Recs on their elevation to the senior Northern Union in 1919, and gave great service to the City Road cause before his death in 1935 – just four years before the demise of the club itself.

It is absorbing to reflect on the 13 warriors who gave the Recs their first item of silverware. Skipper Johnny Greenall was the elder brother of Billy, who also donned the Recs shirt. Then there was the legendary back three of Tommy Smith, Albert Fildes and Bill Mulvanney. Greenbank-born Smith was the father of Wilf, a Saints star of the 1950s and 1960s, while Fildes and Mulvanney entered the licensed trade on hanging up their boots with Albert - who later joined Saints - dispensing drinks at the White Lion Hotel, Church Street, as Bill slaked the thirsts of elbow-benders at the George Hotel in the town centre.

Prop Dickie Ramsdale was signed from Wigan and was a member of the first Great Britain squad to tour Australasia in 1910, and went again in 1914. Platt Bridge-born, he won three Lancashire Cups, a League Championship medal and two Challenge Cup runners-up medals with Wigan, for whom he made 313 appearances from 1905 to 1920. Jim Pyke was the son of St Helens first rugby union international of the same name. Jim junior worked in the home sales department at Pilkington's and also became assistant secretary at City Road. As for half-back Fred Halton, he was persuaded to try his luck at Recs by his elder brother Jack, who then lost his place to him. Fred was eventually transferred to Rochdale Hornets in 1929, went to live there and captained the Hornets. Jack Halton's sons Fred junior and Ernie also played at professional level, the former with Salford and the latter with Liverpool City, with Ernie also starring as a winger with Ruskin Park rugby union club. Rough-and-ready centre Tommy Gormley was born in the Park Road end of Pocket Nook, and joined Saints after kicking off his career with Warrington, while hooker Jack Hughes also worked for 'the Firm,' which Pilkingtons was dubbed colloquially. Hughes later suffered a neck injury that ultimately finished his career, paving the way for Oliver Dolan to take possession of the coveted number nine jersey.

Winger Joe McComas was another member of the Recs trophy-winning squad to be called to the bar with playing days over, and he was the jovial mine-host of the Queens Arms, Fingerpost, which was still dubbed 'McComas's' long after Joe had placed the towel over the pumps for the last time. Haresfinch-reared forward Harry Grundy was followed into the professional ranks by his son Jack, who played with Saints and Barrow and became the first St Helens-born star to win the Lance Todd Trophy while a member of the Shipbuilders' side which defeated Workington at Wembley in 1955. Harry's other son Ken, incidentally, rendered yeoman service as secretary/treasurer of Liverpool City. Sidestepping full-back and goal-kicker supreme Tommy Dingsdale later joined York, and subsequently died in a road accident. He was the brother of Billy, who reached international status with Warrington and was a popular publican at the Stanley Arms at the corner of New Cross and King Streets in St Helens.

'The Recs without Greenall is like a ship without a rudder.'
Johnny Greenall was a brilliant scrum-half, who played for the Northern Union against the Australians in 1922 but was never selected to tour down under.

4. 1924 to 1927: Recs in Excelsis

Rugby and glass were certainly making the headlines in 1924. Pilkingtons produced the largest sheet of plate glass ever made, 288 inches long and 168 inches wide, weighing 1,700 pounds, for the Window of the Empire display at the British Empire Exhibition in London. Meanwhile, Recs supporters dearly hoped that the Lancashire Cup success of the previous campaign was the springboard for further honours, because their team looked to be more than capable of maintaining a place in the rugby league elite. Their major challengers would come from Lancashire – Swinton, Oldham and Wigan – with any victory over the powerful Cherry and Whites from Central Park being particularly well-received by the City Road supporters.

The rivalry between Saints and Recs supporters was increasing in intensity, because the men from Knowsley Road were themselves climbing the league ladder. There are numerous reports of fist-fights on the terraces on derby day as supporters' emotions invariably spilled over. Perhaps the most unusual tale is of a Saints' supporter who went on a coach with Recs supporters to a game in Yorkshire. At Blackstone Edge in the Pennines, a place akin to Siberia in winter, someone recognised him as a fan of the enemy team. The coach promptly stopped and he was duly dispatched into the freezing cold to fend for himself.

Despite their increased success, the Recs were one of three teams to show a substantial loss from the previous campaign in their balance sheets, £100 higher than the Saints, where Councillor McCormick was still asking for final donations towards the club's appeal fund. The key accounts are shown below:

Profit		**Loss**	
Wigan	£2,843	Hull	£1,293
Leeds	£2,800	St Helens Recreation	£1,000
Hunslet	£1,346	St Helens	£900

The Recs began the 1924–25 season at home to Salford, with the British Legion Band entertaining the 6,000 fans before Colonel Norman Pilkington performed the kick-off. It was a sign of things to come at City Road, as the visitors were totally outplayed, Recs winning 25–4, including seven sparkling tries. Seven days later, there was a much harder assignment, at Swinton, one of the strongest sides in the competition, where the Recs were unlucky to lose by just a single point in a game that had the critics in ecstasy. "Hat's off to Johnny," was the call in the local press, as Nero hailed him as the complete scrum-half, adapting his play and tactics according to the situation. The 21–20 reversal gave the squad great confidence overall, leading to just one loss and draw in the next 11 league and cup matches. Early season expectations naturally centred around the defence of the Lancashire Cup. A home draw with mighty Wigan at City Road proved to be Recs' first real test. Could they rise to the challenge?

On the silver trail

Meanwhile, following a long-term injury to star winger Jimmy Owen, the Recs had acted swiftly to reinforce their back division with the signing of Jack 'Tot' Wallace from Barrow. The possessor of a beguiling two-footed sidestep, Wallace had scored 81 tries in 165 games for the Shipbuilders and made a successful debut for the Recs in a 2–2 draw at Warrington

St Helens Recs (left) and Oldham at Weaste (Salford) before the 1924 Lancashire Cup Final. Referee Frank Renton is far right; Recs president Colonel Norman Pilkington is one of the touch judges (far left) (Courtesy Robert Gate)

on 27 September. More than 19,000 fans packed into City Road to see if the Recs, without the influential Greenall, could put up a good fight against the old enemy Wigan in the quarter-final. The spectators certainly could, with an unseemly scrap in the paddock just before the teams took to the field.

Acting captain McComas won the toss and from the start Wigan, without stars Ring and Howley put their opponents under terrific pressure, but the Recs line held firm. Jim Sullivan, who looked rather stale after his exertions on the recent Australasian tour, gave Wigan the lead with a penalty, but it was Recs who took the lead 10 minutes before half-time. A break by Tommy Parker and Attie van Heerden broke down. Jim Pyke picked up the ball and sped away, putting a kick over Sullivan's head. Van Heerden got back and regathered, but was tackled by Pyke and the ball broke loose for stand-off Halsall, a pre-season signing from Saints, to touch down. Pyke added the conversion.

Skipper McComas produced an exceptional piece of skill after the interval, by skipping past van Heerden and putting Jim Pyke away under the posts with a gem of a pass, and he once again added the conversion. Midway through the half, Wigan were a beaten side, especially when Tot Wallace zoomed into a yawning gap down the middle and put Tommy Smith in under the posts. Pyke's conversion sealed a fantastic 17–2 success. "It was a splendid triumph for home-grown production," trumpeted Nero in the *St Helens Newspaper*. "Along comes a team which represents the cream of the rugby league talent of at least two continents and is soundly beaten by 13 players who almost to a man are purely local."

The final could well have been an all-St Helens affair. The Recs triumphed 7–5 in front of 4,581 fans at Little Park, Barrow in their semi-final, while a near 20,000 crowd at Knowsley Road saw the steadily improving Saints lose 16–9 to a powerful Oldham side, who then faced the Recs in the Final at Salford on 22 November. The Willows was not a popular venue as far as Recs fans were concerned. It was a difficult place to get to by train and there was a lack of proper banking or terracing, making viewing the match quite an ordeal for some. Despite this, more than 4,500 fans made the journey with many employees of Pilkingtons starting work an hour early to enable them to catch one of the many special trains. They were greeted with heavy rain and a pitch resembling a quagmire – bare of any turf down the middle. Prospects for a fast, open game were non-existent.

Lancashire Cup Final
Oldham 10 St Helens Recs 0
Saturday 22 November 1924 at The Willows, Salford

The first real chance fell to the Recs, when Wallace rounded Rix and passed to Halton, who just failed to gather. It was a game where scoring opportunities had to be taken and Oldham right centre Alan Woodward held the ball with several players in support and decided not to pass, when a try looked odds-on. Then, it was the Recs' turn once more, as Tommy Dingsdale embarked upon a mazy, side-stepping run through the Oldham defence. He kicked over his opposite number Ernest Knapman, but couldn't re-gather the greasy ball! Shortly after, Woodward scored Oldham's first try, which was converted by Knapman.

Despite heavy pressure on the Oldham line early in the second half, the Recs' attack lacked its normal penetration. A Knapman penalty increased Oldham's lead to seven points and the Roughyeds clinched the silverware when the greasy ball eluded Halsall's grasp and Ambrose Baker – one of many forwards who had followed up – got the touchdown. Although the conditions had not helped, Wallace and Dingsdale were not at their best and skipper and 'Commander-in-Chief' Greenall had been marked out of the game for most of the time. Ironically, the Recs gained some revenge seven days later in a league match to the tune of 22–9, in much drier and firmer conditions.

Oldham: Ernest Knapman, Albert Brough, Alan Woodward, Evan Davies, Sid Rix, George Hesketh, Alf Bates, Rod Marlor, Alf Tomkins, Herman Hilton, Bob Sloman, Ambrose Baker, James Fisher.
Scorers: Tries: Woodward, Baker; Goals: Knapman 2.
St Helens Recs: Tommy Dingsdale, Fred Halton, Joe McComas, Jimmy Pyke, John Wallace, Jack Halsall, Johnny Greenall (capt), Dick Ramsdale, Jack Hughes, Harry Grundy, Tommy Smith, Albert Fildes, Bill Mulvanney.
Referee: Rev. F. Chambers (Dewsbury)
Half-time: 0–5
Attendance: 15,000; *Receipts:* £1,116

In the New Year the Challenge Cup provided another route for silverware for the buoyant Recs. The first round of the competition became etched into sporting history, with Wigan's crushing 116–0 defeat of hapless Flimby and Fothergill, which included 22 goals from Jim Sullivan. Little wonder the Wigan marksman ended up with a staggering 138 by the end of the season. The Recs swatted aside the challenge of Hull in the first round at City Road before enjoying their own points bonanza in the next round, when another amateur outfit, Dalton, surrendered home advantage and were duly thrashed 74–0. Dalton had reached the second round after a replay against Barnsley United. The third round saw the Recs go down 9–5 to Rochdale Hornets at the Recreation Ground – a tremendous disappointment, with memories of the county cup successes still fresh.

By the end of the gruelling league campaign, the Recs had, in many ways, exceeded expectations, finishing fourth – their first in the coveted 'top four'. Swinton were league leaders, winning 30 out of 36 matches for a record of 83.33 per cent, followed by Hull KR, Wigan and the Recs. The Saints nudged themselves into 10th position, above Batley. The Recs finished their league campaign with a 7–5 victory at home to Swinton and travelled to Manchester to face the Lions in their first-ever Championship semi-final four days later. Although the result failed to live up to expectations – Swinton winning 20–2 after a particularly brilliant second half performance – the general feeling was that the best side had won and the Recs had been well-beaten, especially in the key area around the scrums. Despite a scoreless first half, in which Albert Fildes tackled everything that moved and rookie winger Durdock Wilson constantly troubled the home defence with some gutsy running, Swinton's classy passing game, producing six tries, won the day.

One of the most pleasing aspects of the season, however, had been the three victories over Wigan, making it four consecutive losses against the Recs for the Cherry and Whites. The Recs triumphed 10–3 in the Central Park mud on 31 January in front of just 7,000 fans who braved the atrocious conditions. At City Road on 21 March the Recs beat their opponents 12–4, with a terrific try from Jim Pyke and an equally sensational effort from Tot Wallace in the last minute, when he managed to score in the corner, despite the efforts of Jim Sullivan. "This destroys a legend," wrote Nemo, "which was getting a hold in St Helens that we could produce nothing which could overcome the Wiganers!"

New signing Tot Wallace had certainly made his mark during the season, with 26 touchdowns, with Tommy Smith scoring 21 tries in second place. Jim Pyke became the first 'Rec' to kick more than a half-century of goals with 52, but was way behind Jim Sullivan's 138. Tommy Dingsdale and Tommy Smith had helped Lancashire to the County Championship during the season.

However, at the club's annual meeting in the Volunteer Hall in June, a working loss of £190 was reported, as a result of setting aside gate receipts from the Hunslet game (£400) and Broughton match (£300) for the benefit of Jimmy Owen and Joe McComas respectively – two marvellous servants of the City Road club.

Joe McComas – Recs' pocket battleship

One of the greatest players to grace the red, amber and black colours for nearly 20 years, Joe McComas was a member of the team that rose from Lancashire Senior Competition status to become a real power in rugby league. He first joined the club with the likes of Bill Ashall, Johnny Greenall and Frankie Bowen, when Dickie Glover captained the side. For 10 seasons after the First World War he was nearly always there, mostly as a winger, but at centre or full-back he was just as effective.

He was tricky rather than speedy, but in defence he was a pocket battleship and before Tommy Dingsdale came on the scene, his low, raking kick planted many a goal between the sticks from the touchline. Joe never let the side down and reached the peak of his career in conjunction with Jimmy Owen, Jim Pyke and Billy Ashall. The first time the Recs won the Lancashire Cup in 1923, Joe was one of the outstanding performers; four seasons later, when the club finished at the top of the table, losing only six matches, he was one of the most consistent players.

Joe was never the easiest player to handle from a management point of view, but on the field he never played within himself. Recs fans recalled with relish the occasion when, with a strapped-up shoulder, he was deliberately switched from his wing to deal with the threat of Wigan's Attie van Heerden. The way that the South African could score tries by leaping over his immediate opponent was rarely seen. His aerial adventures came to an abrupt end when Joe merely seized his ankles and flung him over the touchline.

Joe was reluctant to end his career and, after leaving City Road, had a few games with Broughton Rangers. Later, because rugby was such a big part of his life, he turned out with Uno's Dabs in the local Junior League, to give them the benefit of his experience. A Lancashire county player, he became a licensee in St Helens – like so many of his former team-mates and passed away in his early 50s after a long illness.

The Recs' success in the mid-1920s was the result of acquiring the best local talent, sustained by occasional forays into the transfer market, bringing the likes of Dick Ramsdale and Tot Wallace into the squad. Another major reason was the fitness regime operated by legendary trainer Ted Forber. The team always seemed to have the edge on their opponents in fitness and stamina, if not rugby ability. In the summer months before the start of the 1925–26 campaign, Forber organised extra training sessions at City Road to keep his boys one step ahead of the opposition. Ted also trained sprinters for professional races and Tot Wallace was one who benefited by joining them and putting on an extra half yard of pace. The diminutive flyer went on to score 24 tries during the campaign, making representative appearances for Lancashire and England as a result.

The strength of the squad suffered a double blow before the season, however, with a serious head injury ruling out hooker Jack Hughes more or less indefinitely and the puzzling retirement of international winger Jimmy Owen. A Recs icon, Owen had hardly played for the past 12 months as a result of a leg injury. He had taken part in the extra summer training sessions at City Road, but by the time of the final trial match at City Road he was reported as being on the way to Canada. By October, he was living on a ranch in Calgary, but the Recs had replaced him with another nugget from the local conveyor-belt of rugby league talent. Jack Durdock Wilson starred in the team's impressive 13–0 success in the first match at Leeds. Although considered too small for a centre berth, he simply could not be dropped on current form.

The Recs certainly felt the benefit of all the summer track work as they sat proudly at the top of the table by the end of October – having played nine, won eight, with a double defeat at the hands of rivals Swinton, in league and Lancashire Cup the only disappointments. In front of more than 7,000 fans, Tot Wallace soared in for the first four-try haul of his career against Hull KR as the Recs maintained their title aspirations. However, a mid-season slump saw eight matches lost from 12, with one draw, leaving the side barely in touch with the top four places. The dip in results corresponded with an injury to skipper Johnny Greenall and it was only when he returned in February that any further impetus was renewed.

County Championship Match
Lancashire 26 Yorkshire 10
Saturday 12 December 1925 at City Road, St Helens

The Recs' standing in the higher echelons of rugby league was recognised when the prestigious Lancashire versus Yorkshire County Championship clash was staged at City road on 12 December, in front of a bumper 13,000 crowd, which produced receipts of £630 – double the total from the last county match in Lancashire. There was much local interest, with Tot Wallace and Tommy Dingsdale from the Recs and Leslie Fairclough from the Saints in the Red Rose line-up. Fairclough, in particular, delighted the crowd with a superb performance at stand-off. Full-back Dingsdale kicked two goals, although Wallace got relatively few opportunities to shine during the game.

Lancashire: T. Dingsdale (St Helens Recs), J. Wallace (St Helens Recs), J. Evans (Swinton), C. Carr (Barrow), S. Rix (Oldham), L. Fairclough (St Helens), W. Evans (Swinton), J. Bennett (Wigan), W. Burgess (Barrow), W. Cunliffe (Warrington), A. Brough (Oldham), R. Taylor (Hull), J. Price (Wigan).

Scorers: Tries: Rix 3, Carr 2, Evans; Goals: Dingsdale 2, Carr 2.

Yorkshire: L. Osborne (Hull KR); J. Denton (Featherstone Rovers), F. Dawson (Hunslet), J. Hirst (Featherstone Rovers), G. Austin (Hull KR); Pearson (Keighley) J. Parkin (Wakefield Trinity); A. Thomas (Leeds), H. Smith (Bradford Northern), E. Barraclough (Featherstone Rovers), W. Clements (Featherstone Rovers), W. Cooper (York), F. Gallagher (Batley)

Scorers: Tries: Hirst, Denton; Goals: Osborne 2.
Referee: Mr F. Peel (Bradford)
Half-time: 13–7
Attendance: 13,000; *Receipts:* £637

Meanwhile the festive derby fixtures against the Saints produced some dour rugby, with a 3–3 draw on Christmas Day 1925 at City Road, in front of a 14,000 crowd and a 4–2 win for Saints in the return on New Year's Day.

A morale-boosting home victory against Swinton put the Recs in the top four once more on 16 January, but Challenge Cup hopes evaporated in a second round defeat at Warrington, where there could have been a major disaster when a terrace wall collapsed. Fortunately, injuries were slight, apart from on the field, when loose-forward Bill Mulvanney's season was ended with a broken fibula.

Down to the wire

Just when hopes for a top four finish looked decidedly rocky, the Recs pulled off a magnificent victory at Hull KR in early March to keep them alive. After three sparkling victories, the Recs went to Oldham on 17 April needing a win to secure a play-off place. Although the Roughyeds could not get into the top four, they still provided formidable opponents for the visitors. After a try apiece in the first 15 minutes, the game developed into an end-to-end contest, with neither side seemingly capable of making the breakthrough.

After half-time the struggle continued, until the Recs were awarded a penalty well inside the Oldham '25'. Tommy Dingsdale took the kick and miscued badly, with the heavy ball barely rising 10 feet from the ground before sailing wide of the target. Although both teams continued to fight the game out to the bitter end, the result was 3–3, the chance had gone and Hull eventually secured fourth place with 67.10 per cent to the Recs' 66.66 per cent. "With the winning post in sight, the Recs cleared the last hurdle," wrote Nemo, "but stumbled and were beaten by a short head."

Despite the best training and preparation, a season's success can always depend on one defining moment. In this case, the luck had gone against the Recs, although the loss of Greenall before the match was another crucial factor.

Colonel Norman Pilkington presided over the club's AGM in July 1926 and announced a working loss of more than £300 from the last campaign. Gate receipts were largely disappointing, given the club's relative success, with three matches bringing in particularly poor revenue – Barrow, Broughton Rangers and Wigan Highfield. "It was somewhat of a disappointment," added the Colonel, "that the Recs did not reach fourth position in the Northern Rugby League, but we have the consolation that we failed to reach this position by decimal points."

However, the Recs committee was confident that their team would continue to improve and become genuine contenders for silverware. Over at Knowsley Road, Saints, with the emergence of superstar winger Alf Ellaby, shared their optimism of challenging for major honours. One thing was certain, the local battle for supremacy – the 'Championship of St Helens' – would be keenly contested.

The Recs began their preparations for the 1926–27 season with the usual practice match at City Road, between the first and 'A' team, although this time receipts were given directly to the Miner's Relief Fund – a grim reminder of the strike that had affected the coal-mining industry since the early summer following the General Strike in May. Club colours were to be red, amber and black hoops, with a change strip of royal blue. A stand season ticket for City Road cost 25 shillings, with 15 shillings for the popular side. Indeed, regular patrons were delighted with early progress in the league campaign, as the team hit their straps with a sensational 58–0 thrashing of Salford in the first match. "Recs' Field Day – who walked in the procession," was the headline for the match report in the *St Helens Newspaper*.

Two hard-fought matches in Yorkshire, at Halifax and Leeds, brought in maximum points, with left-winger Durdock Wilson excelling at Thrum Hall, running the Halifax defence ragged with a fantastic hat-trick. In the first 14 matches, Recs' colours were only lowered twice, at Swinton and Hull KR, which also included a drubbing of hapless York – "All Out 63 – Recs' cricket score!" trumpeted the match report – and a storming 28–14 victory over the visiting New Zealanders. The latter achievement was particularly impressive given that Greenall, Wallace, Dingsdale and Fildes were playing elsewhere for Lancashire on that day.

However, it was the Lancashire Cup that really captured the imagination of the St Helens sporting public. Both teams were at home in the first round, with Saints overcoming junior club Pemberton Rovers 51–8 and Recs disposing of Leigh 21–3 at City Road. In the second round there were favourable home draws, with Saints disposing of a powerful Swinton side and the Recs overcoming Rochdale Hornets 26–2. Both semi-finals were drawn, initially, with the Saints beating Widnes 17–0 at Knowsley Road and the Recs rendering Salford pointless at the Willows in a dogged 14–0 success.

Lancashire Cup Final
St Helens 10 St Helens Recs 2
Saturday 20 November 1926 at Wilderspool Stadium, Warrington

The all-St Helens cup final was to be played at Wilderspool, with the LMS railway offering special excursions to Warrington for one shilling and threepence. Admission to the terraces ranged from one shilling to one shilling and threepence, with boys charged just threepence. Grandstand tickets for Recs' supporters were available from secretary Tom Ashcroft at three shillings and sixpence. It seemed unfortunate that the two teams could not be allowed to toss for the choice of home ground to save their followers a lot of trouble and expense. After all, times were hard, and many regular supporters just had not got the money to make the 'trip over the wire.'

Needless to say, there was a mass exodus of more than 12,000 'Sintelliners' to Warrington on Cup Final day, creating a unique atmosphere. At the outset, the normally reliable Tommy Dingsdale failed to find touch and a scrum was formed on his own '25'. Sparks flew immediately as the front-rows greeted each other in customary, explosive fashion, with the referee giving a stern lecture to both sets of forwards. The scrum had hardly been reformed when Mr Horsfall penalised the Recs pack. George Lewis made no mistake with the resultant penalty and registered the first points after only a minute's play.

Saints put their opponents under relentless pressure during the opening exchanges and a tremendous handling movement among the forwards saw the ball whipped out to second-rower Lou Houghton, who kicked over the defence only for winger Tot Wallace to touch down and save a dangerous situation. A well-judged free kick by Dingsdale put the Recs into their first real attacking position of the match. The ball was fumbled behind the Saints pack and scrum-half Greenall got his men moving. A scramble ensued in the Saints 25 and things looked dangerous when Groves was penalised for offside. Unfortunately, Tommy Dingsdale sliced the place kick and lost the chance of levelling the score.

It was a costly miss. After 15 minutes, Saints right-centre Alf Frodsham caught the ball from loose play and put in a tantalising grubber kick which caught the Recs defence flat-footed. Stand-off Les Fairclough picked up the ball cleverly on the bounce, beat Albert Fildes with a beautiful swerve and shot under the posts for a typical opportunist try. Lewis converted and Saints continued to enjoy most of the territory and possession. After 31 minutes they increased their lead, courtesy of Alf Ellaby. Receiving the ball from Lewis's well-timed pass, he put in a short kick over his opposite number Durdock Wilson. Full-back Dingsdale was caught out of position, and Ellaby, more akin to the association football code he left behind, dribbled over to score an un-converted try in the corner.

The Recs, roared on by their supporters, made a desperate attempt to get back into the game as half-time approached. From a scrum, Shaw was penalised for offside. Pyke took the kick and reduced the lead by two points, as half of Wilderspool roared with delight.

Back in St Helens many supporters who had been unable to get to the match had gathered in Hardshaw Street to follow the progress of the game by means of the scoreboard outside the *St Helens Newspaper's* offices. The scores were relayed from Warrington every 20 minutes, and when the 10–2 half-time score was given, a huge roar went up from the Saints supporters. Recs supporters could be heard saying "Wait 'till the second half – we'll show you!" Saints supporters predicted another 10 points from their favourites. "Ellaby gets two tries every second half," they replied, as Hardshaw Street echoed to the sound of largely good-natured banter.

The teams began the second half in rapidly deteriorating light. This time it was the turn of the Recs forwards to take the initiative. Yet they struggled to make an impression, with both the atrocious conditions and Saints' man-and-ball defence effectively putting the game increasingly beyond their reach. Welsh centre George Lewis got the Saints out of a tight corner with another fine touch kick. His skill and coolness was most valuable at the time when the Recs threw everything into the assault on the Saints line.

By the last quarter, the players were hardly distinguishable owing to several coats of mud and the rapidly gathering gloom. Wallace could be excused in the circumstances from giving a pass to a Saints' player by mistake. Six minutes to go and the cup seemed destined for Knowsley Road. Full-backs Crooks and Dingsdale had a brief kicking duel, after which the Saints pack dribbled up-field for Wallace to come to the rescue once again. The last few minutes were characterised by a magnificent catch by Greenall in the failing light as controlling the ball became a near-impossibility. Meanwhile, in Hardshaw Street "10–2 – three minutes to play" was shown to cheers from the Saints supporters.

On the final whistle, the cheering was deafening. Thousands jumped over the barriers intent on congratulating their mud-splattered heroes. Fairclough and Crooks were hoisted shoulder high and carried through the sea of ecstatic St Helens spectators to the grandstand where the presentation was to take place.

Mr Rebbitt, the Lancashire County secretary, handed over the cup to Saints skipper Fred Roffey amid thunderous applause. After the presentation, a bitterly disappointed Johnny Greenall sportingly acknowledged the Saints victory. "No use beating about the bush," he said, "the best team won on the day."

Both teams later returned to the Town Hall, where a large crowd had assembled to see the gleaming trophy. The Mayor, Alderman Richard Waring, seemingly went to the Final as a neutral. He bought the Recs colours and then the Saints and kept them in his pocket. At the reception he revealed his true feelings, as he joined in heartily when the Saints' players

Cartoon previewing the 1926 Lancashire Cup Final.
The cup did come to St Helens, but to Knowsley Road, not City Road.

sang their victory song *Praise God from Whom All Blessings Flow* in the Mayor's parlour. Needless to say, celebrations were somewhat muted in the Recs' camp. They realised, however, that with more than half of the season remaining, they were in a strong position in both the Northern Rugby League and Lancashire League tables. The battle was lost, but not the war. At least the miners' strike, which lasted 30 weeks in all, was terminated several days later

St Helens Recs: Tommy Dingsdale; Jack Wilson, Albert Bailey, Jim Pyke, Tot Wallace; Johnny Greenall (capt), Harold Halsall; Tommy Higgins, Oliver Dolan, George Highcock, Tommy Smith, Albert Fildes, Bill Mulvanney.
Scorer: Goal: Pyke.
St Helens: Charlie Crooks; George Cotton, Alf Frodsham, George Lewis, Alf Ellaby; Leslie Fairclough, Walter Groves; Bob Atkin, Albert Simm, Lou Houghton, Bill Clarey, Fred Roffey (capt), Ernie Shaw.
Scorers: Tries: Ellaby, Fairclough; Goals: Lewis 2.
Referee: Mr Horsfall (Batley)
Half-time: 2–10
Attendance: 19,439, *Receipts:* £1,192

Unfortunately, there was a much sadder postscript for Johnny Greenall. He missed the home match against Barrow at City Road two weeks later to attend the funeral of his younger brother Albert, who had died of pneumonia in the Providence Hospital. Both teams lined up for a minute's silence in front of the main stand as a mark of respect. Albert had been confined to bed with flu for almost two weeks before the final, but was told by the doctor that he could go and watch the match. The cold, wet conditions brought on a relapse, from which he never recovered and he died the following Monday.

Albert was a promising footballer, who played in the Junior Recs Rugby League competition. The Pilkington Company was so expansive in the town that individual factories and departments were able to field their own teams. Albert was a member of the Stables and Transport XIII, who would pit their sporting wits against their fellow work colleagues representing the likes of Grinding and Polishing, Drawn Glass and Rolled Plate. The league, together with numerous inter-works medal competitions, was an important source of talent for the professional club.

Durdock's match

Recs winger Jack Wilson, who was employed at the plate works in Watson Street, was a tough-as-teak winger, with a direct running style. The youngest of 13 children, he once went to a local shop for a bottle of pop and got his words muddled. They had Dandelion and Burdock, but not the 'Bandelion and Durdock' he requested, and the nickname 'Durdock' stuck with him for the rest of his life. After playing three strenuous county cup ties and one league match, the Recs took on mighty Wigan at City Road. Sheer exhaustion could have been an excuse in the circumstances, but the home side thrilled the large crowd with a fine 10–5 success over their neighbours. Although Wigan scrum-half Syd Abram opened the scoring with a converted try, Durdock soon squared matters with a devastating solo effort from half-way. "Wilson must have learned his Euclid well at school," wrote Rex in the *St Helens Newspaper,* "for he has a sound knowledge of the definition that a line is the shortest distance between two points. Wilson goes straight for his objective with a determination, without any measure of side-stepping and twisting." For the greater part of the second half, the visitors were down to 11 men, when Wilf Hodder was sent off for

Left: Feisty winger Jack Durdock Wilson.
Right: Durdock Wilson's medals: (left) Lancashire League Champions 1926–27 (right) Lancashire Cup Winners 1930–31. (Courtesy Margaret Whittle)

persistent scrum infringements and Tommy Dingsdale smashed winger van Heerden over the touchline with such ferocity that the South African badly dislocated his shoulder. A Dingsdale penalty gave Recs the lead, before Durdock finished off a move in rather more orthodox fashion to seal a famous victory.

Seven days later at City Road, he was once again the hero of the piece, with a brilliant run down the left, past several hapless Barrow defenders, before flying over for the winning try with just two minutes to go! "A particularly bright gleam in a rather mediocre afternoon's play" wrote one critic.

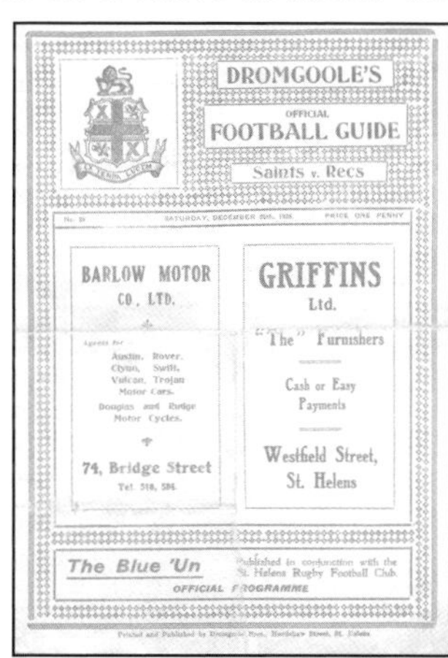

The 1926 Christmas match

In the Christmas Day derby, however, Durdock got a little carried away and punched his opposite number, Alf Ellaby, causing great uproar. This uncharacteristic behaviour received a stern lecture in the local press from legendary journalist Tom Reynolds, alias 'Premier': "I should like to advise him to let his first offence be his last. Wilson is a very clean player. He can well afford to leave the fisting business to those who fancy it." Seemingly with a reference to recent industrial disputes, he added: "Striking – apart from all other considerations – does not pay."

Durdock took the advice and stuck to what he did best – scoring tries and stopping his opposite number from scoring. In their many duels along the touchline, Ellaby only scored two tries when he and Durdock were in direct opposition. Although representative honours were denied him, unlike his partner Tot Wallace on the other flank, he roared in for 33 tries during the 1926–27 campaign, putting him in third place behind Ellaby with 55 and Wigan's Johnny Ring who scored 49. Durdock's 37 touchdowns in 1928–29 were the most scored by a Recs player in a season. The only player to come close to his achievements was 'young gun' Albert Pimblett, who scored 33 in the 1935–36 campaign. Durdock also made the most appearances, 46, missing just one match in the Recs' greatest-ever season, 1926–27.

4504

RUGBY LEAGUE FOOTBALL

OWEN'S BENEFIT

at CITY ROAD, OCTOBER 18th, 1924,

RECS v.
HUNSLET

KICK-OFF 3 O'CLOCK.

GROUND - 1/- INCLUDING TAX

Reporter Ltd., Printers.

Left: Jimmy Owen was sadly missed at City Road after his premature retirement from injury. (Courtesy Pilkington Brothers Ltd). Right: Ticket for Jimmy Owen's benefit match. (Courtesy Curtis Johnstone)

Middle left: Mercurial full-back Tommy Dingsdale in his England jersey and cap.

Middle right: Formerly a centre and occasional stand-off, Tommy Smith scored tries as a second-rower and won county honours with Lancashire. (Courtesy Ian Cartwright)

Bottom left: Pendleton-born, John Tot Wallace was signed from Barrow.

The battle of City Road

Although the free-scoring (and much-targeted) Ellaby kept the Saints in contention, it was the Recs who set the pace in the league competitions. At the year's end, they finished proudly in first place in the Northern Rugby League, beating their strongest rivals, Swinton, into second place by a single point. Indeed, a place in the top four was assured courtesy of a fantastic 19-match unbeaten run after the Lancashire Cup Final. Yet they lost or drew five out of their last seven matches over the Easter period. There were no other distractions, with the Recs, like Saints, falling out of the Challenge Cup at the first hurdle, 6–5 at Hull.

There was another twist, however, as the Saints won their last seven matches, to climb into fourth place in the table. The subsequent pairing of Recs against Saints at City Road in the Championship semi-final thus created intense interest in the town. Saints fans were quick to argue that their rivals had gone off the boil, while Recs supporters countered that their team would show the quality that had seen them top the league and win the coveted Lancashire League title for the first time in their short history. Not only could their team gain suitable retribution for their county cup demise, but a Championship 'double' was a real possibility. Bragging rights in the town would be assured for quite some time.

Championship Semi-final
St Helens Recs 33 St Helens 0

Saturday 23 April 1927 at City Road

Almost 20,000 fans packed into City Road for the second instalment of the 'Championship of St Helens'. There was a distinct air of tension as the two captains, Johnny Greenall of Recs and Fred Roffey of Saints led their respective teams onto the field. Recs won the toss and faced a strong wind with the sun in their eyes. Instead of playing their usual open game, Saints made the mistake of kicking far too much. Had they taken a leaf out of the Recs' book in keeping the ball down and not kicking wildly, it would have been to their advantage. The Recreation forwards kept the ball close and were far superior in the scrums and in open play. The back three, alias the Three Musketeers – Smith, Fildes and Mulvanney – were very much in evidence early on, yet every forward revealed a willingness to back up in the loose. Skipper Greenall was outstanding and dominated the battle of the half-backs, scoring the first try of the match after half an hour, with Dingsdale converting. Just on half-time Greenall once more made the running, before putting Tommy Smith over with a well-timed pass. A second Dingsdale conversion gave the Recs a 10–0 advantage. The Saints faced an uphill struggle with the elements against them after the interval.

The atmosphere in the ground remained extremely tense and feelings ran high. The game had not been in progress 10 minutes before supporters were fighting like fury behind the goalposts at the top end, and a few minutes later below the stand. The players, as might be expected, were too impetuous, and the undisciplined crowd made them worse. Eventually tempers snapped on the pitch and there was a flurry of fists. The second half had been in progress about eight minutes when Saints' Bill Clarey and Recs' Tommy Smith traded blows in the middle of the field. Smith struck Wally Groves several times. Groves retaliated and Houghton and Recs loose-forward Bill Mulvanney barged into the fray. The referee, Reverend Frank Chambers, following the play 15 yards away missed it, and a touch judge ran 30 yards onto the field to grab as many participants as he could reach. He got Groves, Mulvanney and Houghton - while Smith did a vanishing act. Groves tried to follow suite, but not quickly enough. Referee Chambers came running up and though still 10 yards from the touch judge signalled to all three – Groves, Mulvanney and Houghton – to get off.

'Premier', the Saints correspondent in the *St Helens Newspaper*, was most critical of the handling of the incident: "If the game had been out of hand, if the players had been warned of their conduct and had been threatened with expulsion, one could have understood the outbreak of the referee; but there had been fewer warnings than usual in any game. Without warning there came the drastic expulsion of three players from the game, and subsequent ruin of everything from a sporting point of view."

Three minutes later Ellaby was carried off the field after receiving a nasty kick on the head. From that moment play was farcical. The Saints had a three-man pack, with second-rower Fred Roffey on the right-wing and loose-forward Ernie Shaw on the left. The Recs went on the attack and the traffic towards the Saints goal was pretty heavy. Recs scored five more tries and matters might have been worse if the Recs had not sportingly withdrawn a forward to play in the threequarters, and refrained from pushing in the scrums. St Helens actually got more of the ball from the scrums with their three men than before. After the triple dismissals, the Recs were well and truly in command, with skipper Greenall the keystone of the team. "The Recs were simply coldly calculating and forceful. Football was never intended, nor was it played and the Saints were not only beaten, they were mopped up," wrote Tom Owen. The Recs never allowed the star Saints' threequarter line to show their paces. True grit had won the day.

After the final whistle, the Recs' players made their way towards the main stand where they received a rousing ovation from their fans when the Lancashire League trophy was presented to the team by chairman Major Guy Pilkington. This was indeed, Recs in Excelsis! Whatever the outcome of the Championship Final, this defeat of the old enemy was always the one that Recs supporters would always have ready when their rivals got argumentative.

St Helens Recs: Tommy Dingsdale, Jack Wilson, Joe McComas, Bob Innes, Tot Wallace, James Honey, Johnny Greenall (capt), George Highcock, Robert King, Frank Bowen, Tommy Smith, Albert Fildes, Bill Mulvanney.

Scorers: Tries: Smith 2, Wilson 2, Wallace, Honey, Greenall; Goals: Dingsdale 5, Greenall.

St Helens: Charlie Crooks; Alf Ellaby, George Lewis, Teddy McLoughlin, Alf Frodsham; Leslie Fairclough, Walter Groves; Bob Atkin, Albert Simm, Lou Houghton, Bill Clarey, Fred Roffey (Capt), Ernie Shaw.

Referee: Rev. F. Chambers (Huddersfield)

Half-time: 10–0

Attendance: 19,000, *Receipts:* £1,058

Wilderspool revisited

The Recs committee picked the same team that had defeated the old enemy to play in the Championship Final, as Warrington prepared to play host to almost 25,000 rugby fans, with local licensees allowed to open an hour early, at 4.30pm, in anticipation of bumper takings. The Wilderspool pitch was hard and dry, with only the sides and ends covered with grass.

Championship Final

St Helens Recs 8 Swinton 13

Saturday 30 April 1927 at Wilderspool Stadium, Warrington

The hard ground and new ball initially made handling difficult in the opening exchanges. The Recs adopted a spoiling game, realising that Swinton would dominate scrums and possession overall. Early pressure by the Recs' pack saw Swinton centre Jack Evans make a hasty clearance, straight to Tommy Dingsdale, who was just wide with an adventurous drop-goal from all of 45 yards. But Swinton registered the first points with a penalty after Honey fell on the ball to counter a Swinton rush and was penalised for not playing it properly. Bert Morris kicked the goal.

After 20 minutes, there was a stroke of luck for the Recs, as Mulvanney charged down a kick from Swinton's Hector Halsall and ran for the ball as it rolled over the line, with Swinton full-back Elwyn Leigh in hot pursuit. Somehow, both missed the ball and Frank Bowen made a successful grounding, over which referee Horsfall saw no problem. Although Tommy Dingsdale failed with the conversion, the larger part of the game was being played just outside Swinton's 25 yard line. Mulvanney smashed full-back Leigh into the ground – and cloud cuckoo land – with one of his famous 'heaves' and the Recs threequarter line refused to let their opponents settle, despite Swinton dominating possession from the scrums. Just before the interval, Joe McComas darted through from half-way and kicked through, whereupon he was smashed to the ground by desperate cover defenders. Tommy Dingsdale's successful penalty gave the Recs a crucial three-point advantage at half-time.

Swinton full-back Leigh was once again pummelled, this time by Albert Fildes, as the tempo of the game rose considerably. But scrum-half Bryn Evans was becoming a key figure for the blue-and-whites. He took the ball from a scrum 12 yards from the Recs' line, where he shot away from the pack and beat James Honey. Looking round for support he was tackled by Tommy Smith "as a terrier would seize a rat", according to one correspondent. Unfortunately, the tackle was rather mistimed and Evans was flung half-a-dozen yards through a ruck of defenders, where he was able to skip past Dingsdale for a rather fortuitous try. Morris missed the kick and the chance of a crucial two-point lead.

During one particularly vigorous passage of play, Mulvanney and Henry Blewer slugged it out in the centre of the field. Apparently, the Swinton forward was hard of hearing and the value of referee Horsfall's subsequent lecture would seem to have been questionable to say the least. Swinton were countering their opponents' spotting tactics by pushing grubber kicks through and following up swiftly. Soon it was Mulvanney's hearing that came into question as he bludgeoned Chris Brockbank after he attempted a drop-goal, but shortly after, a grubber kick from Morris near the corner flag was gathered over the try-line – and promptly spilled – by Dingsdale, leaving Beswick with the easiest of tasks to touch down.

It was a cruel twist in what was becoming a classic cup final. In the 73rd minute, Bryn Evans once more darted round the pack and put in another tantalising grubber kick, which was followed-up by his namesake Jack. He picked up, drew the cover and fed Bryn who ran over from close-range. Morris's conversion looked to have sealed victory for the Lions, although Bob Innes reduced the deficit with a splendid try in the last three minutes after good work from Mulvanney and Fildes.

Recs' supporters bemoaned their luck afterwards, a point emphasised by Premier in the press afterwards: "An unlucky team never won a cup final. And on the whole, it must have been Swinton's lucky day, best team or not!" Yet he thought it a better spectacle than the semi-final: "There was no personal feeling between the players, which seem inevitable when players all reside in one town, divided into two camps." The scrum possession was 27–13 to Swinton in the first half, and 28–8 in the second.

The gleaming trophy was presented to Swinton captain Hector Halsall by Mr Wood, the Rugby League chairman, who paid tribute to both teams in "the best final he had ever seen." Johnny Greenall and the boys were later given a civic reception at the Town Hall, where Recs' Chairman Mr Joseph Rigby said that the club's success was only just beginning after such a tremendous season.

St Helens Recs: Tommy Dingsdale, Jack Wilson, Joe McComas, Bob Innes, Tot Wallace, Jim Honey, Johnny Greenall (capt), Albert Fildes, Frank Bowen, George Highcock, Bob King, Tommy Smith, Bill Mulvanney.
Scorers: Tries: Innes, Bowen; Goal: Dingsdale.
Swinton: E. Leigh, F. Evans, H. Halsall (capt), J. Evans, C. Brockbank, W. Rees, B. Evans, M. Strong, H. Blewer, H. Morris, T. Halliwell, E. Entwhistle, F. Beswick.
Scorers: Tries: B. Evans 2, Beswick; Goals: Morris 2.
Referee: Mr Horsfall (Batley)
Half-time: 5–2
Attendance: 24,432; *Receipts:* £1,803

Despite their second loss in a Final at Warrington, it had been a sensational season for rugby league in St Helens and the future looked bright indeed. Both Recs and Saints players figured heavily in representative rugby during the campaign, with the selection of four from City Road (Dingsdale, Wallace, Greenall and Fildes) and two Saints (Ellaby and Fairclough) in the Lancashire team that beat Yorkshire 18–13 at Wakefield, and won the County Championship for good measure. Fildes, Wallace and Fairclough had also figured in the test series against New Zealand, won 3–0 by Great Britain. There was a feeling that the composition of the squad to tour Australasia at the end of the 1927–28 season should certainly reflect the strength of the game in the famous glass-making town.

At the AGM at the Town Hall in June, Major Guy Pilkington commented favourably on the team's success on the field and the increase in season ticket sales. Once again, however, the club reported a working loss of £373, its fourth successive one – an endemic problem in the club's time in professional rugby league. The losses were underwritten by Pilkingtons, but with the depression years of the 1930s on the horizon, things were looking ominous.

5. 1927 to 1933: Local lads and seven stars

The financial loss from the previous campaign was clearly a source of concern for the Recs committee and certain economy measures proposed for 1927–28 were not well received by the players. At one stage, no one had signed on for the club and the annual trial match was in jeopardy. "Those who came up were given a game," wrote the *St Helens Newspaper* and it was not possible to charge spectators for entrance – a disappointment – as proceeds normally went to local charities. Fortunately, the issue was resolved before the long trip to Hull KR for the opening match of the season, although Wallace and Mulvanney were the last two to sign on, much to the alarm of the committee.

Another bone of contention was an amended play-the-ball rule, whereby only one player from each side was to stand at the play-the-ball with one other player from each side immediately behind. This led to much confusion during the City Road opener against Salford, although the Recs managed a convincing 37–3 victory. The side was quite capable of repeating the successes of the previous campaign, yet early results were mixed. Deadly rivals Wigan ended Lancashire Cup hopes with a hard-fought 10–7 success at City Road – but then the Recs, powered by their formidable pack and the back three of Smith, Fildes and Mulvanney began to find the consistency that was such a feature of the previous campaign.

Visitors Wigan were beaten in a league fixture four days later, when the Recs exacted due revenge in the blinding rain. Given the forward domination, it was a day on which the threequarters could shine. The centre-wing partnership of Albert Bailey and Durdock Wilson produced the first try, while on the other flank, centre Jim Pyke scored his side's second try, with his outside partner, Tot Wallace putting in a strong defensive display, belying his slight build. The two outstanding men on the field, however, were the two full-backs – Jim Sullivan and Tommy Dingsdale, with Tommy just coming out on top. "He caught the wet, slippery ball from all lengths and angles," wrote Rex in the *St Helens Newspaper*, "and found touch with amazing accuracy almost every time." Sullivan saved his line on a number of occasions as the Recs swept to a resounding 8–0 triumph.

Success bred success – Broughton, Oldham, Rochdale, Swinton, Hull and Bradford (including a stunning Wallace hat-trick) were all put to the sword. By Christmas, the Recs were third in the table, behind Leeds and Swinton, with their rivals Saints desperate for a top four spot.

A Christmas cracker

The successful rise of the Recs in the professional game over the past few years had bred much resentment among Saints supporters. It was a true derby rivalry, akin to the Saints-Wigan fervour of today, but on some occasions with considerably more spice! Before the first clash of the season, on Christmas Eve at City Road, Colonel Norman Pilkington opened the new stand at City Road, giving additional covered accommodation for 8,000 spectators. However, the aggressive nature of the rugby spilled out onto the terraces, with a huge disturbance in the paddock in front of the main stand, which was quelled by the local constabulary. "Last season we had community singing and most people thought it a success. They said it brought people close together," wrote one correspondent. "This season we have community fighting and it brings people closer still!" There was further trouble when one spectator made an attempted lunge at Alf Ellaby and was restrained by the police. Alf was already well-shackled by his opposite number the pocket-dynamo Wallace. A Tommy Smith try in the last few minutes helped the Recs to a 5–2 victory and in the return fixture at Knowsley Road he helped himself to two more as the Recs swamped the home side 22–5. Albert Fildes raised the temperature with a late hit on Saints' full-back Graham, who was knocked clean out, but overall it was a day when the Recs' splendid rugby took the plaudits. The rampant Recs climbed to third place in the table as a result of the festive matches, although such intensity could not quite be maintained.

The ferocity of the games was reflected in a story told at the time:

A man was walking along Baldwin Street towards Church Street.
"Am I right for the slaughter house?" he asked a bystander.
"You are walking the wrong way," was the reply.
"Wait until you see a Windle City tramcar. Ride on it until you come to an enclosure with boards around it. Pay a shilling at the turnstiles, and you'll then be in the slaughter house."

The winning run came to an end with a shock 9–8 reverse at home to Hull KR and a further run of defeats in late February and early March meant that the Recs finished in fifth place in the table, just outside a play-off position, with 48 points from 36 matches and a 66.66 per cent success rate. Saints finished a disappointing 11th. The Recs finished runners-up, three points behind Swinton, in the Lancashire League and the committee looked towards a lengthy run in the Challenge Cup to bring in much-needed extra revenue.

Recs make history

The Recs beat Wakefield Trinity 17–0 in the first round of the Challenge Cup at City Road on a real gluepot pitch and faced the daunting prospect of a trip to Leeds in the second round. Such a tasty Roses clash drew 22,400 fans to Headingley, including four special trains booked by Recs' supporters, although some did not make kick-off time as a result of the congestion. It was to be a game that would stick in the memory of every Recs supporter that day, as the team almost overcame near-impossible odds to bring off an amazing victory. "A performance never surpassed in the history of the game," wrote Premier in the *St Helens Newspaper*. "The Recs made history last Saturday and I am glad I was there to see it."

Despite losing by a single point, 13–12, Recs had covered themselves in glory. They had lost two men and had another virtually incapacitated yet led by three points at half-time against one of the strongest teams in the league. There was disruption to the Recs' preparation even before kick-off, when Albert Fildes was taken ill on the train to Leeds, Frank Bowen's brother Alf deputising in the second row.

It was the Recs who threatened early on, with a promising move by Frank Bowen, Jimmy Pyke and Tot Wallace brought back by referee Jack Edden for a forward pass. Durdock Wilson made a timely interception to nullify a dangerous Leeds attack near his own line and team-mate Joe McComas pulled off a magnificent last-ditch tackle on Leeds' centre Desmond as a try looked an absolute certainty. Enter the skipper, Johnny Greenall, who broke the deadlock with a tantalising grubber which was spilled by Leeds full-back Jim Brough. Jim Pyke received and threw out a wide pass to Tot Wallace who scored in the corner. Dingsdale failed with the conversion – a potentially costly miss even at this stage.

It was then that the problems began for the Recs, when Wilson was tackled heavily and subsequently knocked out in front of the Popular Side. He was carried to the touchline and never returned. This was a real full-blooded cup-tie at this stage, just 15 minutes before half-time and even Jack Edden, a most difficult referee to upset, was finding the match hard to control. Suddenly tempers boiled over on half-way, when a Recs forward went down as if poleaxed. Bill Mulvanney, with a quick glance to the left and right, and assuming that the referee was elsewhere, gained due revenge for his stricken team-mate with a booming right hook. Referee Edden tapped him on the shoulder immediately afterwards, however and pointed the way to the dressing rooms. Mulvanney departed with his head down, looking as if he wanted the earth to open up and swallow him. He knew full well that such a rush of blood was not what was required in the circumstances!

After half-time, with Wallace now a virtual passenger, Leeds threw everything at the visitors. Williams put in a short kick for his winger, Andrews to pick up in a suspiciously offside position, before passing to Brough who scored in the corner. Ten minutes later, a Dingsdale penalty saw Recs regain the lead, yet it was short-lived, as Andrews scored past the depleted Recs threequarters for Thompson to convert. Then came the incident that eventually cost the Recs the match. Tommy Dingsdale waltzed through the Leeds cover in a mazy, sidestepping run, before kicking over full-back Brough, who promptly obstructed him. Dingsdale's subsequent penalty was scant reward for such a dazzling piece of invention and still left the Recs trailing by a point and just after the hour Andrews scored his second try of the afternoon, with Thompson converting, to increase Leeds's advantage to 13–7.

There were two minutes remaining when Jimmy Honey scooted over for the visitors, Dingsdale's goal separating the sides by just a single point - but it wasn't quite enough. Johnny Greenall and the boys left the field to a rapturous reception from both sets of supporters. It was a moral victory and the large contingent from St Helens in the huge crowd realised that, given the circumstances, their team had shown unbelievable grit and determination and were unlucky to lose.

Premier argued that a performance of this nature should transcend the differences between supporters in glass town: "We may have our little differences owing to the spirit of local rivalry that binds one man to the Recs and one to the Saints, mainly by reason of accidental circumstances giving the choice of club. But the strength of local rivalry would be merely local bigotry if it prevented any man from giving just appreciation to a team sent out from St Helens after that team had written one of the most glowing pages in the history of cup warfare and had brought back from foreign soil a defeat that was a greater triumph than a full team's victory could ever have been."

A good man never looks behind him

Legendary Recs trainer Ted Forber was one of the best in the business and had the reputation for getting a player fit for action in considerably less time than medical opinion estimated. He had to work overtime during the Headingley cup-tie, trying to patch-up players and keep them on the field in those far-off days without substitutes. Durdock Wilson's cause was futile, given the terrific battering he had received, although Tot Wallace managed to stay on until the final whistle, following some of his expert treatment. He was, of course, powerless when Bill Mulvanney saw the red mist and was dispatched for the proverbial early bath. One of Mull's favourite sayings was 'A good man never looks behind him,' a point not lost on Ted, given the circumstances. The Leeds forward who had begun the ruckus had not noticed that Mulvanney was behind him. Ted summed it up fittingly at the finish. "I should have looked before I hit him," said Mulvanney. "You should," Ted replied, "but you always said that a good man never looks behind him."

After the end of the season, the fearsome Mulvanney could be seen in another guise as a defender in his own association football team, billed as a Saints-Recs XI, who took on The Police Association team in aid of the Police Clog and Stocking Fund. There were 5,000 people in attendance at the Peasley Cross Athletic ground, with Tommy Dingsdale 'a rare battler at centre half' for Mull's team, who lost 2–1.

Not Recs – nor Saints, now – 'For England and St Helens'

Saints' James Foster May was a great administrator and a member of the Rugby League Appeals Committee. In December 1927, he was elected as a member of the special committee to select players for the Australian tour at the end of the season, together with Recs chairman Joseph Rigby. Both chairmen believed that there were a number of players in St Helens who deserved the chance of finding fame on two continents. Despite the intense rivalry there had been between the two local teams, all was put on one side when they examined the claims of players for the tour. They selected on merit.

The selection process had begun on 1 February, at Headingley, when the Whites, including Alf Frodsham and Ben Halfpenny from the Saints, took on the Reds, who had Tommy Dingsdale, Oliver Dolan and Frank Bowen in their ranks. Ellaby and Fairclough (Saints), Jim Sullivan (Wigan) and Jonty Parkin (Wakefield) were spared the trial process, as the selectors were satisfied with their capabilities. The tour selection committee met again at the Victoria Hotel in Manchester to select the teams for the second trial at Rochdale on 27 February. Dolan and Bowen were the only representatives from the town of St Helens, although on opposite sides, watched by an incredible 9,000 crowd at the Athletic Grounds.

Seven players from the town were picked to go 'down under' for the first time – Alf Ellaby, Les Fairclough, Alf Frodsham and Ben Halfpenny from Saints; Frank Bowen, Oliver Dolan and Albert Fildes from the Recs. In fact, it was nearly four from each team. Only one vote prevented Bill Mulvanney from making the trip with his Recs colleagues.

The St Helens Seven Stars reflected the strengths of their respective clubs. Ellaby, Frodsham and Fairclough were among the most dangerous backs in the game. Ben Halfpenny – a snip at £250 from Widnes at the start of the season – was a running forward ahead of his time. Weighing over 13 stone, he could do 100 yards in less than 11 seconds. All the Recs selections were from their formidable pack. Runcorn-born Albert Fildes was a big brainy footballer and a deadly tackler. Oliver Dolan was a reliable hooker and Frank Bowen another big bustling forward who would add much-needed power up front.

The decision to include the St Helens stars caused some controversy in rugby league, and a letter in the *St Helens Newspaper*, reprinted from the *Leeds Mercury*, emphasised the depth of feeling in Yorkshire over the squad selection and "the preponderance of players" from the two St Helens clubs. The letter concluded: "I do not wish to suggest that the two St Helens selectors have used their powers of selection unfairly, but, as long as human nature remains what it is, one's geese are always prone to assume swan-like proportions."

Jim May was quick to reply, giving an insight into the selection procedure: "It may interest the public to know how the voting went with regard to the St Helens players who are chosen for the tour. Halfpenny was the first forward chosen... selected unopposed without a dissenting voice from anyone. The three St Helens back players, Ellaby, the leading scorer of the game, Fairclough, English international half-back, and Frodsham, St Helens captain and test trial team captain, were all selected in the same way. The Rugby League selection committee chose these three men for themselves entirely on their merits as the outstanding players of the rugby league game today. Dolan, the Recs hooker had been a success in the trial and with only three men to back him up in the cup game against Leeds actually was a success there. The only two St Helens players who were not elected by consent were the other two Recs men Bowen and Fildes. These were voted upon and were carried in the proper way."

A huge crowd gathered at St Helens Central Station to bid farewell to the Seven Stars, who wore their light grey hats, adorned with the gold emblem of the Rugby League. As the guard's whistle blew, final hand clasps were made and the men jumped into the carriages. The on-lookers bowed their heads and gave an impromptu rendition of the old hymn *Praise God From Whom All Blessings Flow*, a simple act, yet fitting in its own way. As the train moved out of the platform, four fog warning explosives were detonated for a final farewell.

The party left from Tilbury on 25 April for their marathon adventure in the southern hemisphere and were given little chance of success by friend and foe alike, especially when the tourists won only two of their opening six matches. Yet as the tour went on, their team work and confidence improved enormously. Both series against Australia and New Zealand were won by two tests to one. The tourists won the first two tests against the Kangaroos, at Brisbane and Sydney – with Alf Ellaby scoring vital tries in both of them. The pack was the mainstay of the side however, and only eight forwards were used in the six tests. Despite some initial misgivings regarding his selection, Albert Fildes played superbly in every test, with Frank Bowen appearing in all the New Zealand internationals. The *St Helens Newspaper* carried weekly bulletins from the St Helens contingent during their long trip.

The 1928 Rugby League Lions had made the critics eat their words and they returned home in triumph, via Fiji, Hawaii and Canada. Financially the tour had been a roaring success, earning the players a well-deserved bonus of £136 per man. The jubilant party landed at Liverpool on 28 September – suitably refreshed for their own domestic season which had just begun. They were met by a crowd of 14,000 cheering fans when they reached the Town Hall, before being entertained to dinner by the Mayor, Alderman Waring.

Saints' Leslie Fairclough later revealed that he had been offered an astronomical £15 per week to play for a leading Sydney club, plus his own pub to run. Albert Fildes, meanwhile, outlined what the tour had meant to him: "First: I shall never forget the artistry of little Leslie Fairclough, the cleverest little man I've seen. Second: I shall never forget the wonders of a tour that I would be glad to repeat some day again. Third: I shall ever remember what really fine fellows footballers can be when they are given a chance to develop their best qualities on the field and off. We have been a very happy band, but we are all happier still because we are home again."

Later the following month, all the Seven Stars paid their own tribute to J.F. May – the main 'mover and shaker' in terms of selection – as Les Fairclough presented him with a magnificent silver trophy with the inscription 'Presented to J.F. May by the St Helens Tourists of the 1928 Australian Team'. No one had deserved it more. As one of the speakers said, the players all realised that Mr May was an approachable friend for all players.

1928 Seven Stars to Australia

All matches:	Apps	Tries	Goals	Pts	Test matches: Apps	Tries
Frank Bowen	16	2	0	6	3	1
Oliver Dolan	7	0	1	2		
Alf Ellaby	14	20	2	64	5	4
Les Fairclough	12	11	0	33	4	5
Albert Fildes	13	3	0	9	6	0
Alf Frodsham	17	15	0	45	2	0
Ben Halfpenny	10	8	0	24		

The touring seven stars in 1928. From the left: Alf Ellaby (SH), Albert Fildes (Recs), Alf Frodsham (SH), Ben Halfpenny (SH), Frank Bowen (Recs), Oliver Dolan (Recs), Leslie Fairclough (SH). (Courtesy Brian Potter)

The following article was written by Recs' hooker Oliver Dolan, and appeared in the first edition of Pilkingtons company magazine, *The Cullet* in October 1928:

The Tourists by Henry O. Dolan, the Recs 'Striker'

"A treat of a lifetime commenced when we left our homes on the 19th of April last. A crowd of friends, amongst whom was our highly-esteemed Secretary, Mr T. Ashcroft, bid us bon-voyage on the 20th as we left Tilbury Docks for Australia and New Zealand. The voyage was enjoyed by everyone until we reached the Bay of Biscay, when after a seemingly ravenous desire for food, we took a sudden dislike to it, owing to its being too "choppy" (the sea - I mean).

We began to find our sea-legs on nearing Gibraltar, and on entering the waters of the Blue Mediterranean the voyage became a real pleasure. A stay of 15 hours at Marseilles gave us sufficient time to have a good look round. Then between the islands of Corsica and Sardinia, through the Messina Straits and on to Port Said where a tour round the Arab "quarters" was convincing proof that there's no place like home." 13½ hours down the Suez Canal brought us to Port Sudan and incidentally into the hot zone, bathing becoming the most popular pastime.

Colombo in Ceylon was our next calling place, much amusement being caused as we mounted the rickshaws for conveyance to the Cinnamon Gardens. Cocos Islands (with their coconut groves and coral reefs) of Emden and war fame, was the next and only place sighted for the next 8 days, after which we arrived at Fremantle. Round the coast to Adelaide and Melbourne, stopping at both places but not sufficiently long to get in touch with Mr Mees and the Firm's other Representatives. Sydney was reached, the world-famous harbour presenting a wonderful spectacle in the rising sun.

The Town Hall here was the scene of our official reception, which was well attended. Training commenced in the afternoon in front of an army of photographers,

Here we had the pleasure of meeting Mr G. Scott, who later introduced Fildes, Bowen, and me to Mr J.C. Goodwin, a valued customer of our firm and the kindest of hosts, who spared no effort to give us a good time. Amongst many other interesting and memorable sights in Australia, three, to my mind, stand out alone. They are the Bulli Pass, the Blue Mountains, and Fildes' last-minute tackle which saved England from defeat at Toowoomba.

On arrival at Auckland we had waiting for us our old club-mate and international, Jimmy Owen. It will interest his many friends here to know that he is quite well and has a good position. Whilst he is still unable to play football owing to the injury that necessitated his retirement, he keeps himself fit by playing basket-ball and "surfing", the latter being a very popular sport out there.

On reaching the South Island of New Zealand we were met by Mr J. Pinnington, Representative for the Firm at Dunedin, and had the pleasure of travelling a few hundred miles with him, for he was returning "home" after having completed his 'round'. This was a double pleasure, for, apart from knowing Jim before he went to New Zealand, we had the advantage of his interesting comments on the different places en route. On reaching Dunedin he very kindly invited us St. Helens boys round to his house, where we spent a most enjoyable evening. On leaving New Zealand our route was via Fiji and the Hawaiian Islands, Suva and Honolulu being the calling places, after which we arrived at Vancouver, where we were received by another of the Firm's Representatives in the person of Mr H. A. Anderton, who had drawn up a programme of entertainment that could not be carried out owing to the disappointingly short duration of our stay. We afterwards crossed the Rocky Mountains and enjoyed some wonderful scenery as we travelled through the mountains.

Toronto was our next place of call and there we were met by still another representative, Mr J.E. Harrison, but our very limited time was fully occupied in a visit to Niagara Falls. Montreal was our last place of call before leaving Canada for Liverpool. Here we met the last link in the chain of representatives in the person of Mr 'Reg' Harrison who laid himself out to entertain us.

Our arrival at Liverpool, where we were welcomed by the Rugby League officials, including our secretary, Mr T. Ashcroft, completed a journey of... 33,000 miles, and it was pleasing to know that on nearly the whole of the route we could stop and have a chat with, or be entertained by, one of the firm's representatives – "one of us". It was indeed a great help to us St. Helens boys to grasp their hand of welcome, and we felt distinctly proud of our connection with this world-famous firm."

Departure of legends

At the annual meeting at the Town Hall on 19 June 1928, one thing certainly had not changed. The Recs announced a loss of £411, which was partly blamed on exceptionally bad weather at certain times during the season, cutting down some gates markedly. There were also other factors to contend with, such as the shock news that trainer supreme Ted Forber was joining rivals Saints as successor to Ted Smith and would be replaced at City Road by former Recs forward Dick Silcock. Forber was considered to be a vital cog in the City Road success story of the past decade. Formerly the assistant trainer at Blackpool FC, he then came to prominence by training sprinters for big money handicap events before joining the Recs. He held certificates for 'medical electricity' (presumably somewhat different to the famous 'magic sponge') and Swiss massage and fitted perfectly into the Recs mindset: "I am a great believer myself in making rather than buying players so far as is preferable." he once remarked. "I think there is plenty of really good material round about if we only develop it properly through the summer season as well as during the playing season." Forber had made a huge impression with the players at City Road. One marvellous tribute was paid to him by full-back Tommy Dingsdale. When presented with his international cap, and asked to make a speech he simply said: "Gentlemen, I owe all this to our trainer, Ted Forber!" and immediately sat down.

There was further disappointment for Recs supporters in October 1928, when Johnny Greenall – the scrum-half and captain of the team since its early days in the Northern Rugby Union – announced his retirement. Johnny gained international honours for the first time against the Australians in 1922 and played for Lancashire on many occasions. He also cited his new role as licensee at the Black Bull Hotel in Knowsley Road as a factor in calling it a day. "I have in mind the many splendid players who have received very little respect from crowds as their powers began to diminish," he remarked. "I do not want to play beyond my time and would rather retire as I am, still young enough to enjoy life and in possession of a reputation, I hope, that I have always tried to keep clean."

His final derby appearance against the Saints was summed up by Premier in the *St Helens Newspaper:* "Greenall was the inspiring force. He was the coolest man on the field. He never got flustered. He saw his openings and went through them alone as only 'Johnny' can do. When faced with an inevitable tackle, he went down without losing his head. When he was more keenly tackled than he deserved he did not push the other fellow for it; he accepted it with a shrug and waited for the referee's whistle." That was Johnny Greenall to a tee – a fantastic player and a genuine all-time great for the City Road club.

So near and yet so far!

What better replacement for Johnny Greenall than younger brother Billy? A real pocket dynamo who could tackle well above his weight, he would dart around the pitch like a firefly in mazy, dummying runs, causing total confusion in the opposition. The young scrum-half was one of the real successes in the Recs' ranks during a rather disappointing league campaign during 1928-29, with the team finishing eighth in the Northern Rugby League. Lancashire Cup hopes evaporated at the hands of Warrington and it was left to the Challenge Cup to stir the imagination of the City Roaders. There was a big plus for the finalists – they would play at the Empire Stadium, Wembley, for the first time.

The Recs began the cup trail with two exceptional victories, against Broughton and Featherstone, with Halifax put to the sword 21–0 at home in the third round. Mighty Wigan waited in the semi-final, the first-ever at Swinton's new ground at Station Road. Although the Recs' famous fighting spirit was much in evidence in a terrific cup-tie, there were extenuating circumstances, according to Billy Greenall: "I had broken my ankle two or three weeks beforehand and they patched me up to play. I had so many bandages it looked as though I had gout. The referee was Mr Peel, who refereed the first round tie between Saints and Wigan and robbed Saints to death. They drew at Knowsley Road and Wigan won the replay. When Wigan played us in the semi-final, we scored three tries and he disallowed two. He couldn't disallow the other one because I gave Mulvanney the pass on the line. It got to the last minute and we were leading 5–3. The Wigan forwards tried to dribble the ball through and I dived on it. One of them hacked out and caught my bad ankle and I just lay there. The referee blew for a penalty to Wigan. Mulvanney asked him what it was for and he said that I had not got up to play the ball. I couldn't – I was unconscious. Sullivan kicked the goal from the touchline and it was 5–5. We replayed the following Wednesday. In the meantime I stayed in bed until the morning of the match and they still patched me up to play in the afternoon. At half-time they were leading 10–0 and Wigan kicked off to restart and one of our forwards hacked it straight into Jim Sullivan's hands. He came through and gave it to one of his threequarters, who scored. It wasn't one-way traffic by any means – they beat us 13–12 in the end. Yet the feeling was that the referee had done us out of the game at Swinton. I heard later that he had got suspended for three matches for the following season as a result of the way he handled our semi-final." The semi-final and replay, at Leigh's Mather Lane ground had been watched by more than 52,000 fans.

On the day of the big match, the Recs team and their supporters travelled down to London with heavy hearts for the Final between Dewsbury and Wigan in the special train they had hired beforehand, just in case they had been playing instead. It was the nearest the Recs got to a Challenge Cup Final in their 20 year history as a professional club and what would have been a fantastic achievement.

On 10 May, the fans were able to pay tribute to one of the most valued servants at City Road, Frank Bowen, who was one of the Seven Stars in 1928. 'Bowen's Team,' including Saints' stars Ellaby, Mercer and Fairclough in the famous red, black and amber jerseys, took on an International XIII, with Jim Sullivan of Wigan and George van Rooyen of Widnes, at City Road and won 43–21. A terrific forward, from a famous rugby family, Bowen became an expert on the blind side of the front row after many years as a utility member of the pack. "I was with the Recs when they joined the Northern Rugby Union after the War," he said, "And I may claim to have grown up with them and shared in all their successes and steady rise to fame in the league."

George 'Jumbo' Highcock - giant in performance – if not poundage

Another key Recs player from this time was George Highcock. Dictionary reference reveals that 'jumbo' simply means very large, so why was legendary Recs' prop George Highcock dubbed with that elephantine sobriquet? For, although of military bearing and a ramrod six feet tall, George tipped the scale at no more than just over 13 stone, but he was nonetheless rated as being among the toughest forwards ever to don the famous red-amber-and-black jersey. So why 'Jumbo'? The explanation is almost surreal in that he was named this by the City Road fans from the moment he signed for the club in 1924. The inspiration came via the team's number one fan who was also nicknamed 'Jumbo,' and whose stentorian roar of 'come on the Recs!' reverberated throughout the time-honoured stadium. Consequently when the highly-respected Highcock made his debut bemused supporters thought he was a relative of the vociferous man on the terraces and – to coin a phrase – the name stuck.

To give him his full title George Alban Highcock was born in 1903 and was the son of Peter and Mary. His father was killed in action during the First World War. The youngster was raised in Atlas Court, Fingerpost, and attended Holy Cross and St Vincent's schools before working at Pilkingtons. Having begun his rugby league career at schoolboy level and with amateurs Shamrock Rovers and Gerards Bridge, the rising star found his way to City Road, where he was to become the cornerstone of a pack which often read George Highcock, Oliver Dolan, Frank Bowen, Tommy Smith, Albert Fildes and Bill Mulvanney. George eventually hung up his size eleven boots in 1938 following more than 300 incident-packed appearances.

In the meantime he had married his sweetheart Mary, and the devoted couple became parents of a bumper crop of three sons - inevitably one named after his dad - plus seven daughters. The grandfather of George junior's wife Sheila, Harry Colwell, was Recs' coach in 1908, while the extended family included 35 grandchildren.

Highlights of George's oval ball odyssey included being in the Recs' side which won the Lancashire Cup at Swinton in 1930, playing for Lancashire in 1932, and narrowly missing out on Australian tour selection in that same year.

Despite being 35 years old, George enlisted in the Royal Marines on the outbreak of war in 1939, and was bracing himself for action with the British Expeditionary Force only to be taken ill with stomach ulcers, which rendered him unfit for further military service. He loved to regale his family about what might have been in France.

Partial to the occasional Woodbine and pint of 'flat rib', more commonly known as mild beer, tales abound about George, some apocryphal or embroidered, but all etched in rugby league folklore. In particular when he was 'banjoed' by Wigan's Welsh heavyweight boxer Lew Stephens at Central Park. George was on the receiving end of a real hay-maker which called for 'raw plastic surgery,' Said a rueful Highcock: "We were packing down so tightly that I couldn't move my head one road nor t' other, and I saw Stephens' fist coming up but I was ambushed."

As a result of the unprovoked assault, Highcock's nose was symmetrically flattened, with both nostrils spread across his face and similar clearance on each side. Off went 'Jumbo' for a nose-plugging repair job with strong arms holding him down such was his distress. Vowing vengeance, Highcock returned to the fray but Stephens obviously thought discretion was the better part of valour, and kept out of the wounded prop's way for the rest of a torrid afternoon. However, as philosophical George put it: "I might have missed Stephens but I thumped one or two others instead."

George Highcock passed away in 1969 at the age of 66. The Recs were well represented at the funeral with Oliver Dolan, Jimmy Honey, father of the Saints star of the 1950s, and Joe McNulty all present. The one-time City Road warhorse would have liked that.

Left: George 'Jumbo' Highcock (Courtesy George Highcock jnr).
Right: proud legacy - George Highcock (jnr) and wife Sheila with Jumbo's portrait and county cap.

Left: 'Jumbo' at work. Like all his team-mates, George Highcock worked at Pilkingtons. He is featured on this 1964 photograph from the *Pilkington News*, testing glass cutters used in the CH3 warehouse at Cowley Hill.
(Courtesy George Highcock jnr)

Enterprise unlimited

There were unexpected repercussions at the next Recs' AGM at the Town Hall, when Joseph Rigby was ousted as chairman of the club, a post he had held for the past 12 years. He had been a committee member since the Recs' return to rugby in 1913. The Recs still remained outside the top 10 in the Northern Rugby League in 1929–30, finishing in 13th place. To the disgust of their fervent supporters, it was Saints who were the dominant force in the league for most of the season. Despite finishing top of the league, however, they lost in the Top Four play-offs to Leeds and were beaten by un-fancied Widnes at Wembley. The Knowsley Road club had reinforced their ranks with the signing of three New Zealanders, Lou Hutt, Trevor Hall and Roy Hardgrave, which had given them a considerable 'edge' in the search for honours – 'Enterprise Unlimited' the local press called it. This is something that would have been alien to a club like the Recs, who could not have afforded such a deal in the first place. Indeed there was much criticism by supporters early in the new year when negotiations to sign Saints' unsettled international threequarter Alf Frodsham broke down as the committee refused to match the Knowsley Road club's £450 valuation for the player, offering only £400. Thankfully, the committee bowed to pressure from disgruntled fans and brought the 1928 Great Britain tourist to City Road, where his experience and try-scoring ability was a much-needed addition to the threequarter line.

Spectator interest had been revived by the visit of the touring Kangaroos to City Road on 14 December 1929, with 9,000 coming through the turnstiles to see the visitors win 24–8 in what was a spirited performance for the Recs, who were without hooker Oliver Dolan for the majority of the match. Despite losing 8–3 to deadly rivals Saints on Christmas Day at City Road, the Recs retaliated with a single-try victory at Knowsley Road on New Year's Day 1930. The game held special memories for Saints' scrum-half Frank Jones. After the teams had gone at each other hammer and tongs for 80 minutes, they shook hands and 'Happy New Year' was said all round. After changing, Frank walked home with Recs' full-back Tommy Dingsdale – doughty foes walking and laughing side by side. Yet when turning into Boundary Road they were greeted with the sight of two spectators, one Saints, one Recs, trading punches over the result of the match.

There was extra spice for the fans with the first round of the Challenge Cup pairing the two sides together, at Knowsley Road once again on 8 February. Supporters talked in the local hostelries about possible match-winners. Would it be Ellaby for the Saints? What about the Recs' formidable pack? Maybe the tie would be settled with a Durdock Wilson special? Despite all the predictions, the match-winner came from an unexpected source! More than 17,000 fans packed into Knowsley Road to see the latest clash of the Titans. It proved to be a struggle of epic proportions along typical cup-tie lines.

The order of the boot

The undoubted highlight of an even first half was the kicking duel between Tommy Dingsdale – the Recs shooting star and a comparatively untried performer Jack Arkwright. On a real glue-pot pitch, normally reliable George Lewis failed with several attempts at goal early on, but full-back Dingsdale gave the Recs an early lead from a penalty. After 13 minutes, St Helens were awarded another kickable penalty, albeit from an awkward angle. Lewis handed the ball to Arkwright who fancied his chances even though he had never before kicked in a competitive match. The big prop gave the leather an almighty thump and watched it sail between the posts to equalise the scores.

The former Sutton Commercial forward kicked another two penalties to Dingsdale's one to give Saints a 6–4 lead, but just before half-time there was a ray of hope for the Recs. Somewhat against the run of play, Albert Fildes worked a try along the blind side of the scrum to regain the lead for the visitors.

In the second half, however, the Recs pack, which used to be the great strength of the team, was beginning to buckle under the increasing weight of the St Helens attacks. The younger Saints forwards such as Halfpenny, Hall and Harrison were seemingly more suited to the furious pace of the match than their counterparts and gradually gained the upper hand. It came as no surprise when Alf Ellaby scampered over to register the Saints' winning try after a particularly crisp passing movement from the backs. Arkwright hit the upright with his conversion, but his emergency place kicking had been an inspiration to his team-mates at such a critical stage of the game. So Saints went through 9–7.

Albert Fildes – double agent

Unlike rivals Saints, with their clutch of overseas stars, the Recs persisted with the home-grown talent that had served them so well during their first 10 years in professional rugby league. One of the latest local lads to make the breakthrough was Albert Bailey, a fast and powerful threequarter, who notched 26 tries in the 1930–31 season. Tommy Dingsdale also regained his shooting boots during the campaign, finishing fourth in the kickers' chart with 93 goals. Alf Frodsham and the evergreen Durdock Wilson starred in the back line, with former Rochdale Hornets' half-back Pat Martin forming a formidable combination with Billy Greenall. In the pack, Frank Bowen, Jumbo Highcock and Oliver Dolan were the stalwarts of the front row, with Jimmy Jennion, Tommy Smith and captain Bill Mulvanney completing a powerful back row. But where was the third member of the famous trio, Albert Fildes?

Unfortunately, Fildes, the landlord of the White Lion Hotel in Church Street, had experienced some difficulties at City Road at the start of the 1930–31 season and had not signed on again. Needless to say Recs' fans hoped that their star packman would resolve his differences with the committee as soon as possible, but it was not to be and he was placed on the transfer list at £850 on 14 August 1930. Albert was a county and international representative and the Recs committee needed to bring in much-needed revenue should he choose to leave, after a record loss of more than £1,000 from the previous season. Fildes himself made a request a week later to the Rugby League Management Committee for a reduction in the fee, which was set at £600. Much to the chagrin of the Recs supporters, Fildes signed for Saints. The Saints' committee had long admired his terrific tackling and were delighted to see him in red and white. "Yet when they got him, they were soon proudly boasting that they had taught him to play football," remarked one Recs' die hard, caustically. "Yet his trump card was how to stop it."

Not everything was doom and gloom at City Road, however. Ironically, the legendary trainer Ted Forber came back to City Road after his brief sojourn with Saints. Perhaps the good days would soon be making a return to City Road – yet the break-up of the famous Three Musketeers, Smith, Fildes and Mulvanney – the trio that struck fear into the hearts of the opposition – was a bitter pill for Recs' fans to swallow. This was compounded when

Fildes was selected for his second tour down under in 1932, with his new team crowned Rugby League Champions for the first time.

County cup kings

The Recs got a bye in the first round of the Lancashire Cup in 1930–31 and beat Leigh in the second convincingly 24–7. Oldham were defeated 6–4 in a dour encounter at City Road in the semi-final to give the Recs arguably their greatest challenge. Wigan, with their all-star line-up were their opponents in the Final at Station Road, Swinton and provided a chance for the Recs to avenge their defeat in the Challenge Cup two years before. Local pride was the key here. The Recs' line-up for the Final all had one thing in common – they were St Helens born and bred. Conversely, Wigan were able to scour the world for rugby talent and their team consisted of six Welshmen; one Scot; one Cumbrian; one New Zealander and four Lancastrians. Only three of the successful squad from 1923 remained – Mulvanney, Smith and Dingsdale – but the team had been well-prepared by Ted Forber and could always be relied upon to give their wealthier opponents an uncomfortable 80 minutes.

Lancashire Cup Final
St Helens Recs 18 Wigan 3
Saturday 29 November 1930 at Station Road, Swinton

On a bright, blustery day, the new ground at Swinton throbbed with activity during the hours before kick-off, with thousands of supporters streaming off the special trains onto the station behind the grandstand. Wigan fans, who seemed to be in the majority, wore their usual cherry and white colours, despite their team playing in a change strip of blue jerseys and white shorts. Many of the Recs' fans sported berets in their famous red, amber and black colours. When Mulvanney and Sullivan led out their troops, there was a real air of expectancy in the crowd. Just before referee Robinson blew for the kick-off a Recs fan with an old army bugle on the Popular Side sounded the military 'fall in'.

Right from the start, the mighty Recs pack worked to gain the ascendancy and Dingsdale was just short with an attempted penalty into the wind. The first real chance came Recs' way, when stand-off Pat Martin charged down a clearance kick from Jim Sullivan and lost the race to touch down by inches. Then it was scrum-half Greenall who put in a clever grubber, only for the Wigan defence to scramble the ball clear once more. The little scrum-half was in superb form and had a major hand in the first try. Following a scrum near the Wigan '25' he shot round the blindside, dummied a pass to Durdock Wilson, drew Roy Kinnear and Sullivan and released a brilliant pass inside to Bill Mulvanney, who went over unopposed. Dingsdale's conversion was another huge boost for the forwards, who harried and hounded their opposite numbers. Oliver Dolan indulged in what would be 'sledging' today by shouting "All local lads and don't forget it!" in scrums and melees.

It was not long before the Recs extended their lead, but not without controversy. Wigan centre Gwyn Davies lost the ball, which was picked up by Albert Bailey who streaked for the line. Syd Abram, Sullivan and Johnny Ring joined in the chase, but Bailey managed to fling himself over the line. Gwynne Davies seemed to snatch the ball just as he was grounding it, but the referee gave the try. The big screen technology of modern-day Super League would doubtless have solved the conundrum. Dingsdale's goal gave the Recs a vital 10-point cushion, especially when winger Johnny Ring scored a try in the corner 10 minutes

St Helens Recs – Lancashire Cup Winners 1930. Back: George 'Jumbo' Highcock, Albert Bailey, Oliver Dolan, Jimmy Jennion, Frank Bowen, Tommy Smith; front: Ted Forber (trainer), Billy Greenall, Pat Martin, Billy Bowen, Colonel Norman Pilkington (president), Bill Mulvanney (capt), Alf Frodsham, Tommy Dingsdale, Jack Durdock Wilson, Joe Carson (assistant trainer).

after half time. Although Wigan won the scrums by a ratio of 2–1, the Recs were quite content as long as they dominated the territorial battle. Whereas Wigan's wingers Kinnear and Ring had few chances to shine, Greenall and Martin tried to open up play in the loose.

The ever-alert Billy Greenall sent the Recs supporters wild with delight when he completely bluffed the opposition to send strong-running second-rower Jennion over for the Recs' third try, which was un-converted. The little master completed a brilliant exhibition by creating the fourth and final Recs' score, although not without incident: "I remember we were leading 13–3 and there was a scrum near the line" he recalled. "We got the ball and I went between the Wigan half-backs up to half-way. Sullivan was waiting and there was no fooling him. I gave the ball to Tommy Smith, who had come up with me, but he was a bulky forward, not a sprinter. As I went past Sullivan he grabbed my wrist. Tommy Smith just kept on running and as their winger came across, Smith passed to Jimmy Jennion who scored. I waited until he put the ball down and Sullivan was still holding my wrist. When I saw his face over my shoulder, he was just my height, so belted him as hard as I could. He gave me concussion for three matches on the trot after that. When I woke up I used to think that perhaps I might have deserved it anyway."

There was a huge roar in the main stand as the red, black and amber ribbons were placed on the gleaming trophy and the unheralded scenes at the end were captured in print by 'Colonel' in the *St Helens Reporter*: "The kettle of enthusiasm boiled over at Swinton when the final whistle sounded. Excitement ran riot. Thirteen Recs players jumped in the air and shouted their whoops of victory. Thousands of Recs spectators climbed over the barriers and swept onto the field, surging around the thirteen victorious gladiators, slapping them on the back and cheering them until they were hoarse."

There were several superb performances to admire from the Recs, including the form of Jimmy Jennion, one of the fastest men on the field, who seemed to fill the void left by the departure of Albert Fildes. Billy Greenall was the undoubted mainspring of the attack for the backs, although Mulvanney looked after him like a daddy round the scrums, increasing his effectiveness in the process. It was the 37-year-old veteran who stood side-by-side with rival captain Jim Sullivan during the presentation, and the cup was presented by G.F.

Hutchins, the joint manager of the 1928 tourists. 'Mull' gratefully accepted the trophy and gave a rather muffled speech: "Brevity is the soul of wit and this is going to be the record short speech for the Rugby League. I am sorry for Wigan for they have played a downright hard game, but I'm delighted our team has won." He then called for three cheers for Jim Sullivan and the two protagonists shook hands. There was some consolation for the Wigan team – it was the first county final that runners-up medals were awarded.

It was non-stop celebration for the Recs as they returned to St Helens by coach, with the cup sitting prominently on the front seat. Then, they were received by the Mayor Alderman Rudd on the Town Hall steps, before retiring to the Raven Hotel in Church Street for a special victory dinner, where the theme of 'thirteen St Helens-born lads' ran like a recurring tune in a symphony, following speeches from club president Colonel Pilkington, and chairman James Glen. At the end, Tommy Smith and captain Mulvanney joked about not leaving 'bald-headed forwards' out of the team, sentiments echoed by the chairman.

St Helens Recs: Tommy Dingsdale, Jack Wilson, Billy Bowen, Alf Frodsham, Albert Bailey, Pat Martin, Billy Greenall, George Highcock, Oliver Dolan, Frank Bowen, Tommy Smith, Jimmy Jennion, Bill Mulvanney (capt).
Scorers: Tries: Jennion 2, Bailey, Mulvanney; Goals: Dingsdale 3.
Wigan: Jim Sullivan (capt), Johnny Ring, Gwynne Davies, Tommy Parker, Roy Kinnear; Frank Jones, Syd Abram, Tom Beetham, Jack Bennett, Hal Jones, Wilf Hodder, Len Mason, John Sherrington.
Scorers: Try: Ring.
Referee: Mr R. Robinson (Bradford)
Half-time: 10–0
Attendance: 16,710, *Receipts:* £1,030

Recs supporters argued that this was the club's greatest-ever victory, and with good reason. Yet the report in the Pilkingtons works magazine *The Cullet* commented about poor crowds up to the Final: "No gate so far has reached £200. It is a pity that the efforts of the committee in trying to encourage local talent is not more appreciated."

The end of an era

The great days of the mid–1920s, when the Recs were indisputably top dogs in the town had started to disappear by the 1931–32 season. Supporters of the famous red, amber and blacks now had to be accustomed to life outside the top 10, with their deadly rivals Saints finishing as League Champions for the first time. Warrington knocked the Recs out of the Lancashire Cup at Wilderspool and all three St Helens' representatives in the Challenge Cup - Recs, Saints and junior side Unos Dabs – lost at the first hurdle. Unlike the heady days of 1928, no one from City Road was selected for the Australian tour, although Tommy Dingsdale, Jumbo Highcock, Albert Bailey and Bill Liptrot were involved in the tour trials. It was also a time to pay tribute to one of Recs' great stalwarts when Batley came to City Road for Tommy Dingsdale's benefit match, on 11 April 1932. A fantastic player, who had the misfortune to be around at the same time as Jim Sullivan and Jim Brough, Tommy held no less than six records for the club, largely as a result of his goal-kicking prowess, but his sidestepping runs in broken field endeared himself to the fans. At his best a combination of dazzling brilliance and grim determination, Tommy joined York in August 1932 and became the landlord of the White Horse Hotel in the city. He was tragically killed in June 1940, when the car he was driving plunged down an embankment and crashed onto the railway line between York and Tadcaster. Dingsdale was killed instantly. Although the two passengers travelling with him managed to escape, the car was hit by the King's Cross to

Aberdeen express train and was carried along the track for a quarter of a mile. Dingsdale was in the car as the train struck, but was thrown clear by the impact. Eight of his former team-mates at City Road acted as pall bearers at his funeral: Joe Bates, Bill Mulvanney, Joe McComas, Albert Fildes, Oliver Dolan, Frank Bowen and brothers Johnny and Billy Greenall.

Those players who had been the backbone of the Recs side for many years were growing old and proved extremely difficult to replace. Yet the Recreation club could still provide four players for the county in the 1932–33 season – Oliver Dolan, Bill Liptrot, Billy Bowen and Pat Martin. That same season the club needed two replays to progress against Oldham in the Lancashire Cup, but trophy hopes disappeared at the hands of Warrington, who beat the Saints in the Final. The Recs finished in 16th position after a disappointing campaign, with Saints 11th. It was to be a time when both sides were to feel the pinch financially and as the great depression began to bite an ongoing battle for survival ensued. There would only be one winner.

Billy Greenall – keeping it in the family

Billy Greenall and his elder brother Johnny occupied the scrum-half berth for the majority of St Helens Recs' 20 year existence as a professional club. In an interview in 1987, his memories of his playing days were as sharp as ever: "I began playing at school and I had the honour of captaining Lancashire in the first ever schoolboy county match against Yorkshire at Hunslet. I signed for the Recs when I was 18 and mustn't have been more than 8 stones wet through. My brother John was in the first team then and I played in the 'A' Team until he retired. The club tried Jimmy Pyke in his position at first, then Jimmy Innes. After that they gave me a game. My first match was against Swinton. They had a top-notch team and Bryn Evans was their scrum-half.

Before the match the trainer Ted Forber just told us to do our best – he wasn't expecting miracles. Anyway, they beat us 11–8 and were such a good side that they ran away with the league that season. Our skipper Bill Mulvanney came up to me afterwards and said: 'You did very well. I think you're better than Bryn Evans!' My second match was against Leeds at City Road. They had four 'aeroplanes' in their threequarter line – real flyers – and beat us comfortably. My third match was at Wakefield. The great Jonty Parkin was their scrum-half and they beat us 2–0. Mulvanney said to me: 'I said you're better than Bryn Evans, didn't I? Well, I think you're better than Jonty Parkin.' I thought he must have been pulling my leg, but it gave me a tremendous boost – a great piece of psychology. What amazed me in those days was that there were about seven in the first team who had played together for so long that they sort of froze out any stranger who came into the team. Yet they took to me from the very first match. Nearly all of them were local lads, except Albert Fildes from Runcorn and Tot Wallace from Barrow. It was marvellous to play with them.

I was 21 and working at Ravenhead glassworks when I played my first derby match against Saints. One of my workmates told me that his wife was going to buy him a new cap for Christmas. 'Every time Saints score I'm going to throw the cap into the air,' he said. I didn't think the Saints would lose him many caps, especially on Christmas Day against us – because I just couldn't see them scoring! The Saints were in good form at the time, mind you, and there was no score at the interval. We played down the slope after half-time and

'Durdock' Wilson was marking Alf Ellaby on the left wing. There was a scrum on half-way and we got the ball. I broke away and headed for Ellaby's wing. I got Ellaby between Durdock and me, which confused him – he didn't know which one of us to go for and I spotted the line in the corner of my eye and put Durdock in for the only try of the match.

"There are two Saints players who stood out for me in the derby clashes. Alf Ellaby was one of the nicest fellows who ever played the game – a perfect gentleman. Give him the ball and one man was no use – Ellaby would just run past him. He would overrun his opponents with pure speed. He was over six feet tall, though not too bulky – a perfect build for a winger. Give him the ball on his own line and it was a try. On our line or the visitors line there was always an extra man there to make things a little more difficult. On his own line he only had his opposite number to beat. He went the full length of the field many times. Walter Groves was the scrum-half, who had a reputation as a bit of a hard knock. He was my opposite number in my first derby match. From the first scrum he came over to me, put his arm round my shoulder and asked if anyone was knocking me about. 'Tell me if they do,' he said. 'I don't care who it is...if they bother you, they'll be sorry!' This happened every match I played against Walter. At the end of the game he used to wait for me and put his arm over my shoulder.

"We used to get £2/10 for a home win, with £2 for a loss. We signed on every season, of course, and I once asked the committee to change the wage structure by taking something off losing pay and increasing winning money as a bit of an incentive. They took five shillings off losing pay, making it £2/15 for a win; 35 shillings for a loss. You got an extra pound away from home, plus two shillings extra, or 'tea money' as they called it. When we played in Yorkshire we had two meals on the train there and back. They took us to Wembley in 1929 to watch Wigan and Dewsbury, even though we had lost in the semi-final and let us take our wives. Apparently they had booked the train in case we managed to get there.

Alf Frodsham used to play on the other wing at Saints to the great Alf Ellaby and came to join us at Recs. We played Salford in a Challenge Cup tie and Frodsham was marking 'Barney' Hudson. Before we went out, I said to Alf 'When we're packing on your touch go round on the inside and take the ball.' Hudson kept following him. We were drawing at half-time and Alf said that he'd had enough. I told him to do it just once more and if it didn't work, leave it. 'As you go round this time, shout "inside" to make sure Barney follows you.' Alf says: 'He's following me without shouting – he's knocking bloody spots off me.' So I said 'just try it one more time... scream your head off for the ball and make him follow you.' We kicked off in the second half and the full-back caught the ball and found touch on half-way. We were playing towards City Road and as the pack got down I said to Frodsham: 'This time Alf!' The Recs forwards swivelled round a little bit as they got the ball out and Alf shouted at the top of his voice 'Inside Bill!' Hudson was so determined to nail Alf that he got tangled up with his own back row forwards. Meanwhile, all I had to do was run up the touchline on the blind side and put the ball down – there was no-one within miles of me. Frodsham was the first to run over. He put his arm round my neck. 'I wouldn't have thought about that,' he said. 'I know it's worked,' I said. 'Now forget it. It won't again.' Barney Hudson was a bit of a hard knock, who always seemed to hit the first opposition player he came to after the final whistle.

For some reason, I always used to give one team nightmares. Every time I played against Broughton Rangers, either in the 'A' team or the first team I always managed to score. One day we were playing them at home and we got a penalty near the Broughton line. While they were arguing as to who was going to stand on the mark, I asked the referee if everything was in order. He told me to carry on, so I simply kicked the ball past the fellows on the mark, picked it up and strolled over for a try. I thought it was funny, because all the Broughton players continued to argue amongst themselves. Jimmy Pyke, the assistant secretary, was paying us after the match and he explained that some of the Broughton committee had phoned up and did not ask for the result – just to find out if that little so-and-so Greenall had scored again. Apparently they had two players' meetings to try and work out how to stop me from scoring. Billy Dingsdale, brother of the former Recs' full-back Tommy played for Broughton that day and told me all about it.

In the mid–1930s I went to Oldham and stayed there for a few seasons and captained the side. I trained with the Recs on a Tuesday night and travelled to Oldham on a Thursday. I was a real heavyweight then, approaching 10 stones. Believe it or not, my first match for Oldham was the day after Good Friday at Watersheddings against the Recs. For the first time in my career I scored three tries and we won the match. Ted Forber picked me up as I left the field, pointed me towards the Recs' committeemen in the stand and shouted: 'Here's the fellow you've given away and he's beaten us all by his blinkin' self.' I played with Oldham for about three years and then the War started. I joined the Army then – the first licensee in St Helens to be called up – and stayed in the Forces for five years. I always wondered why our John never came to watch me play, until I finished, then I realised – you lose interest. I bet I haven't seen more than three matches at St Helens since I finished. It isn't the same. I was too busy as a licensee anyway. You know... we kept pubs for 30 years – The Ring O' Bells, Horseshoe and Black Bull - and I've never tasted whisky in my life. When the Recs won the Lancashire Cup I was the only one who didn't have a drink out of the trophy – it had all sorts in it."

Great Britain 21 New Zealand 11, second test 13 November 1926.
Back: J. Bacon (reserve), H.. Smith, H. Bowman, A. Fildes, J.H. Dannatt (manager), W. Burgess, A. Thomas, J. Evans, S. Rix; front: F. Gallagher, L. Fairclough, C. Carr, J. Parkin, J. Sullivan, J. (Tot) Wallace. Albert Fildes and Tot Wallace both scored tries.

A key signing from Saints, Alf Frodsham provided much-needed experience in the Recs threequarter line in the early 1930s.

Left: This cartoon of the Recs appeared in *The Cullet* magazine. (Courtesy Pilkington Brothers)

Right: Who's playing? These posters were put up in the latter part of the week in local pubs and clubs, generating much discussion and debate.

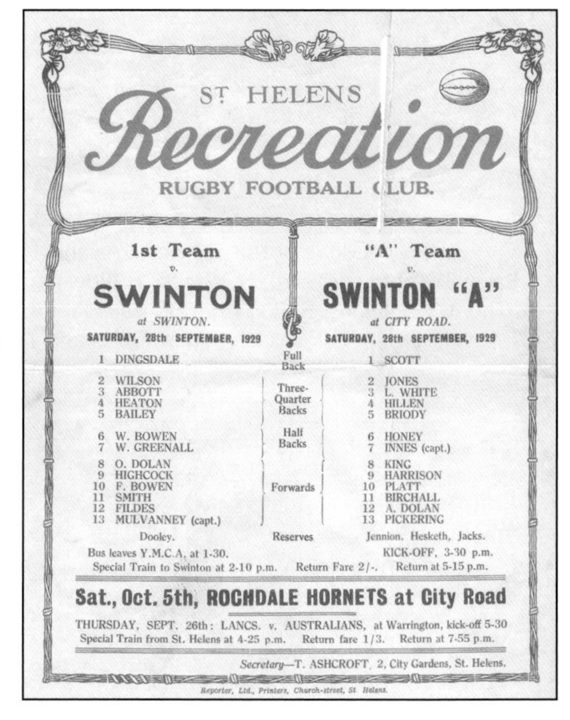

ST. HELENS

Recreation

RUGBY FOOTBALL CLUB.

1st Team v. SWINTON at SWINTON. SATURDAY, 28th SEPTEMBER, 1929		"A" Team v. SWINTON "A" at CITY ROAD. SATURDAY, 28th SEPTEMBER, 1929
1 DINGSDALE	Full Back	1 SCOTT
2 WILSON 3 ABBOTT 4 HEATON 5 BAILEY	Three-Quarter Backs	2 JONES 3 L. WHITE 4 HILLEN 5 BRIODY
6 W. BOWEN 7 W. GREENALL	Half Backs	6 HONEY 7 INNES (capt.)
8 O. DOLAN 9 HIGHCOCK 10 F. BOWEN 11 SMITH 12 FILDES 13 MULVANNEY (capt.)	Forwards	8 KING 9 HARRISON 10 PLATT 11 BIRCHALL 12 A. DOLAN 13 PICKERING
Dooley.	Reserves	Jennion, Hesketh, Jacks.

Bus leaves Y.M.C.A. at 1-30. KICK-OFF, 3-30 p.m.

Special Train to Swinton at 2-10 p.m. Return Fare 2/-. Return at 5-15 p.m.

Sat., Oct. 5th, ROCHDALE HORNETS at City Road

THURSDAY, SEPT. 26th: LANCS. v. AUSTRALIANS, at Warrington, kick-off 5-30

Special Train from St. Helens at 4-25 p.m. Return fare 1/3. Return at 7-55 p.m.

Secretary—T. ASHCROFT, 2, City Gardens, St. Helens.

Reporter, Ltd., Printers, Church-street, St Helens.

6. 1933 to 1939: The last hurrah

The Recs were now virtually unrecognisable from the side that took rugby league by storm in the 1920s. Yet under the influence of new coach Charlie Seeling, the former Wigan and New Zealand international forward, they showed that they could still mount a challenge for major honours in the early part of the 1933–34 campaign, especially in the Lancashire Cup, where they had always been traditionally strong. Although the pack was considered to be somewhat lightweight in comparison to its predecessors, Recs had two key players who could have a profound influence on a match. The game still revolved around set scrums, so a good hooker and scrum-half were essential for success. Recs had both. Skipper Oliver Dolan, now in the veteran stage, was a brilliant hooker, who could be relied upon to win a steady stream of possession, particularly when the pressure was on. The scrum was fed by Billy Greenall, who was capable of making lightning breaks from the scrum base, mesmerising defenders with one of the best dummies in the game. Most of all was the Recs' indefatigable spirit, that always seemed to characterise their teams.

The City Road club was given the honour of hosting the opening match of the Australian tour on Saturday 26 August 1933. The Australian team, travelling in a "deluxe motor coach" nearly missed their turn-off on the newly-completed East Lancashire Road. According to manager Harry Sunderland, it was the sight of the Australian flag flying from the stand at City Road that alerted the party that they had reached their destination.

Tour Match
St Helens Recs 9 Australia 13
Saturday 26 August 1933

A large crowd assembled to see Recs' Oliver Dolan and Australia's Frank McMillan lead out their respective sides onto the pitch that resembled a lush, green carpet. There was a minute's silence before kick-off, however, in memory of Ray Morris, the Australian centre who had died of meningitis in Malta en route. After the preliminaries, the visitors certainly made things difficult, with their powerful forward surges and dazzling threequarter play. Yet the Recs' defence held firm during the opening 20 minutes and from a scrum near the visitors' line, Billy Greenall went on one of his unstoppable runs and touched down without a hand being laid on him. Ten minutes later, the little wizard was at it again, unsettling defenders with a series of beguiling dummies, before putting Ronnie Prescott over with a superbly-timed reverse pass for the second unconverted try.

It was not long before the Australians struck back, when Wally Prigg sent right-winger Ridley racing over in the corner. Although the home side held a 6–3 lead at half-time, further tries from Folwell and Ridley, plus two McMillan goals gave the Australians a hard-fought 13–9 success, courtesy of their superior weight and speed, although the Recs were far from disgraced on what had been a scorching autumn afternoon. "Women attired in gossamy summer dresses and men in flannels watched the match," wrote Nemo. "While the men mopped their heated brows with handkerchiefs, they marvelled at the stamina of the players who could survive 80 minutes of football under such boiling conditions."

Oliver Dolan had played a captain's part, by beating his opposite number Folwell by 45 heels to 35 – an average of a scrum a minute. At the special dinner at the Fleece Hotel afterwards, Harry Sunderland, the Australian tour manager, was generous in his praise of Dolan and of Greenall in particular: "There is one little player I saw, and I hope, one of the players we shall have the privilege of seeing in Australia. He is the little boy Greenall. He made us feel green an' all at times." Another guest from down under was the famous *Sydney Sun* journalist Claude Corbett, who coined the term 'Bodyline' to describe the England cricket team's bowling attack in 1930. Souvenirs of the occasion were presented to the players and officials of both teams by Pilkingtons and took the form of glass ashtrays with the symbol of the kangaroo inset.

Unfortunately, just like his elder brother, Billy Greenall was never selected for an Australian tour and, although a regular county player, never represented his country, despite being one of the greatest scrum-halves in club rugby between the wars.

St Helens Recs: Peter Barnes, Albert Bailey, Billy Bowen, Pat Martin, Bill Laithwaite, Ronnie Prescott, Billy Greenall, George Highcock, Oliver Dolan (capt), Bill Liptrot, Green, Bob Grundy, Bill Grundy.
Scorers: Tries: Greenall 2, Prescott.
Australia: F. McMillan (capt), A. Ridley, D.M. Brown, C.G. Pearce, F.W.H. Newmann, F.J. Doonar, V.A. Thicknesse, R.E. Stehr, A.F. Folwell, P. Madsen, S. Pearce S, Denny, W. Prigg.
Scorers: Tries: Ridley 2, Folwell; Goals: McMillan 2.
Referee: Mr F. Peel (Bradford)
Half-time: 6–3
Attendance: 8,882; *Receipts:* £614

A proud tradition

Despite some less-than-satisfactory performances in league matches, the Lancashire Cup could always be relied upon to revive flagging spirits. Recs began the 1933–34 campaign by grinding out a 5–0 victory at home to the cup-holders Warrington, followed by a rather more impressive 19–5 success over Swinton at City Road. It was the semi-final that grabbed the headlines, however, with the Recs drawn at home to Saints, who themselves were going through a transitional phase.

The game attracted a 13,000 crowd, the biggest of the season, and the Recs hoped to benefit from several extra training sessions that had been so successful in the previous round. What the fans got was an exciting encounter, choc full of gruelling tackling and a severe test of the stamina of both teams. It was also an evening tinged with tragedy, because Recs committeeman Joseph Littler suffered a fatal heart attack during the match. Centre Bob Heaton opened the Recs' account with a penalty after seven minutes and following a fine passing movement, Billy Greenall shot through a gap and beat three would-be tacklers before touching down under the posts, making Heaton's conversion a formality. A towering penalty from Saints' giant second-rower Jack Arkwright reduced the deficit, but it was the Recs who held sway 7–2 at the interval.

In what was largely a forward battle, the lighter Recs pack dominated, with Billy Greenall winning the battle of the scrum-halves against Harry Frodsham. Midway through the second half, however, Alf Ellaby, playing in the unaccustomed position of right centre, broke through and streaked for the line, only to be brought back by referee Laughton, who ruled obstruction. A further penalty goal from Bob Heaton, together with some expert hooking from Dolan, gave the Recs a well-deserved victory. Despite the ferocity of the encounter, Saints' Albert Fildes gave his former team-mate Oliver Dolan a pat on the back after the final whistle as they walked towards the dressing room.

The weeks before the Final were, to say the least, difficult for the Recs. The powerful York outfit – including former Recs favourites Ted Forber and Tommy Dingsdale – came to City Road just two days after the semi-final and inflicted a 45–17 defeat on the exhausted home side. Just before the final whistle, a piece of foul play by former Wigan winger Lou

Brown nearly caused a riot. Brown belted young Albert Bailey flush on the chin after he had passed to Laithwaite. The normally placid Recs threequarter ran after his assailant and exacted revenge. Both players were sent off by referee Dobson and Bailey was quite lucky not to miss the Final as a result. Yet there were further problems, with injuries to Grundy, Laithwaite and Heaton, who all decided to play in the Final at Swinton on 18 November.

Lancashire Cup Final
Oldham 12 St Helens Recs 0
Saturday 18 November 1933 at Station Road, Swinton

Oldham were a mid-table outfit, yet quite capable of raising their game on their day. The Recs seemed to have a large percentage of supporters in what was a rather disappointing crowd of just over 9,000 as both sides slugged it out in a dull first half seemingly bereft of clear scoring chances. Oldham's major strength lay in the elusiveness of stand-off Tom Egan, who had his opposite number, Billy Bowen, beaten for pace on a number of occasions. A penalty goal from full-back Tom Rees opened Oldham's account after the interval, with Sam Bardsley scoring a converted try shortly afterwards. The Recs were seemingly devoid of attacking ideas by this stage and Jack Stephens completed a memorable day for the Roughyeds with the second converted try of the afternoon.

After the presentation of the trophy to the victors by Lord Derby, it was a rather reserved team that returned to St Helens for their traditional slap-up meal at the Fleece Hotel. Oliver Dolan and his team-mates knew that they had been beaten by the better side and there were no complaints.

St Helens Recs: Alf Frodsham, Bill Laithwaite, Albert Bailey, Bob Heaton, J. Turton, Billy Bowen, Billy Greenall, George Highcock, Oliver Dolan (capt), Bill Liptrot, Mason, Jim Green, Bill Grundy.
Oldham: Tommy Rees, Albert Taylor, Sam Bardsley, Jack Stephens, Les Lewis, Tom Egan, Jack Reynolds, Jack Read, Jack Scaife, Ted Hodgson, Trevor Thomas (capt), Abe Clayton, Fred Ashworth.
Scorers: Tries: Bardsley, Stephens; Goals: Rees 3.
Referee: Mr Peel (Bradford)
Half-time: 0–0
Attendance: 9,085; *Receipts:* £516.

Worse was to come in February when Oldham also knocked the Recs out of the Challenge Cup after a replay in the Second Round at the Watersheddings. Compared to previous years, there was a drop in playing standards, with the team finishing 18th in the table.

A loss of £1,259 was announced at the Recs' annual meeting, with the slump in league fortunes the major cause. League gate receipts had decreased from £3,202 in 1932–33, to £2,561 in 1933–34. Although alarm bells had started to ring at City Road, the Recs were not alone in this respect. In early May, Saints were on the verge of going out of business with falling gate receipts and declining numbers of season ticket holders. That they survived is down to voluntary subscriptions and valuable income from the Million Penny Fund – but it was close. Saints had to take drastic action and sold Alf Ellaby to Wigan, in August 1934.

Just like old times?

Before the 1934–35 season began at City Road, the names of Tommy Smith, Frank Bowen and Durdock Wilson were removed from the Recs register. County stand-off Pat Martin was

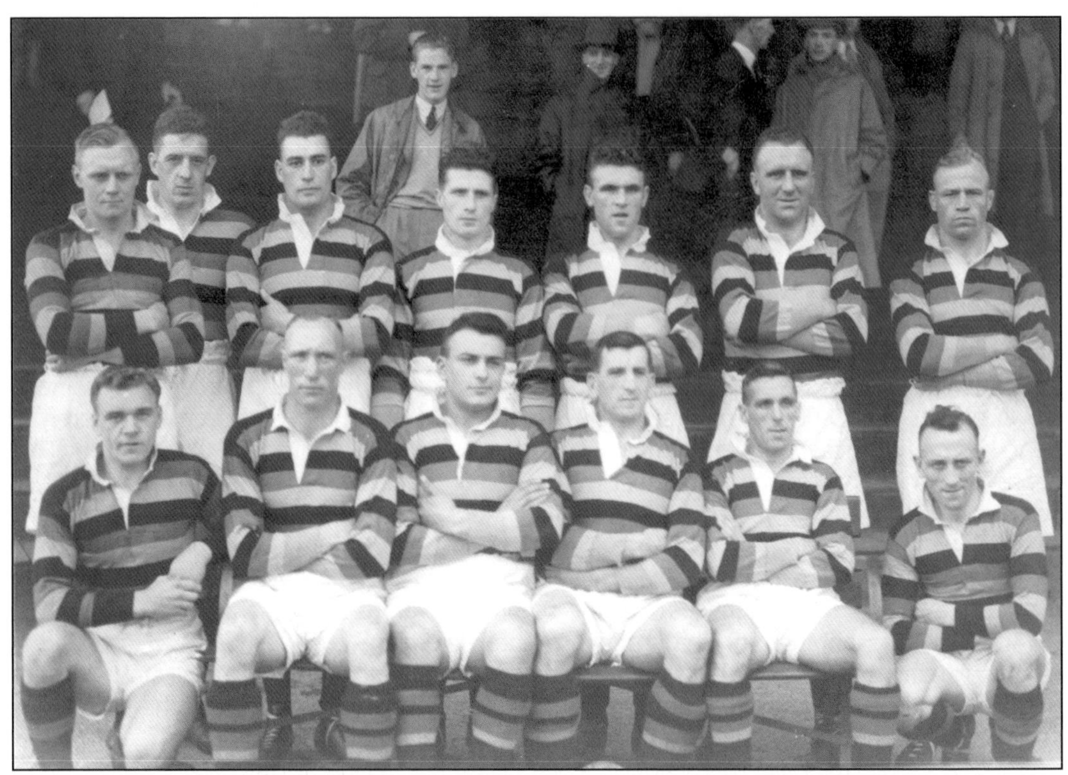

Recs line up for the match against Liverpool Stanley on 1 September 1934. Back: Bill Laithwaite, Jimmy Jennion, Albert Bailey (Capt), H. Kelly, Jack Howard, Bob Heaton, Jim Green; front: Ronnie Prescott, Jumbo Highcock, Horace Randolph, Oliver Dolan, Peter Barnes, Billy Greenall. (Courtesy George Highcock)

Recs on the attack against Warrington in the mid 1930s. Albert Bailey looks to get his winger away. (Courtesy Denis Whittle)

St Helens 2 Recs 2, Lancashire Cup Second Round, 25 September 1935. Recs' forwards Jimmy Jennion (top) and Jack Howard bring down Saints' front-rower Worsley in a mid-field skirmish. Horace Randolph is the Recs player immediately behind the action.

Liverpool Stanley versus St Helens Recs 1 September 1934. Second-rower Jimmy Jennion tackles Stanley's Maloney. Billy Greenall watches approvingly. (Courtesy Denis Whittle)

also transferred to Liverpool Stanley. It was truly the end of an era. The club relied on an increasing number of younger players to carry them through, with former centre Billy Ashall taking on the role of trainer for the first team and Joe Bates the 'A' team. Oliver Dolan captained the side, with Billy Greenall as his deputy. More than 1,500 watched the final practice match at City Road, as a spirit of optimism prevailed. To a large degree, this was realised, as the team improved markedly on the performances of the previous season to finish in 10th position – St Helens were 21st – although gates still did not improve, with an average of only 2,000 fans at City Road for the end of season matches.

The Lancashire Cup first round tie brought mighty Wigan to City Road on 8 September, with 15,656 fans packing into the ground. There was an unusually large contingent of Saints fans at the game, who had come to see Alf Ellaby and it took just a few minutes before their former hero opened the try scoring for Wigan, to add to Jim Sullivan's opening penalty goal. The Recs defence held firm until half-time, helped by Dolan's scrum-dominance, although the ball rarely found its way to the wing.

Wigan centre Gwynne Davies scored just after the restart, but the best moment of the match centred around the Recs opening score shortly afterwards. Alf Frodsham, playing at stand-off, shot away from the pack on the open side and wrong footed the Wigan threequarters. He handed on to centre Bill Laithwaite, who promptly gave a return pass. Alf drew a couple of Wigan defenders before giving the ball back to Laithwaite, who scored wide out – a marvellous piece of inventive football that brought the crowd to its feet. Another Sullivan penalty, followed by tries from Innes and Ellaby, sealed the game for the visitors, although Frodsham scored his second, virtually on the final whistle, following Greenall's tantalising grubber, making the score 20–8 to Wigan.

The beginning of the end

Defeat at Wakefield in the Challenge Cup was met with the tragic news of the death of the club President, Colonel Norman Pilkington at the age of 57 on 8 February 1935, after a long illness. Born in 1877 at Rainford Hall and a member of the famous glass-making family, Col. Norman was chairman of the company from July to December 1931 during the re-organisation of the board and took a strong interest in the Recreation Club. He was educated at Clifton College, Bristol and played for the Recs in their pre-northern Union days. His sporting ability always came to the fore and he became a double rugby and cricket blue in 1898, his first year at Cambridge, captaining the First XV. He was one of three St Helens men to have represented England at rugby union before the Second World War, playing on the wing against Scotland. The Recs' Jim Pyke was the first. Jack Heaton, whose brother played for the Recs in the 1930s, was the other.

A man deeply involved in local affairs, he represented South Eccleston on the Town Council and came back from the First World War with a DSO after serving in the 5th South Lancs regiment. Very much a hands-on director, he was popular with the workforce because of his involvement in the Recreation section. His funeral was akin to a royal occasion in St Helens, with thousands lining the route to pay their respects as the gun carriage wound its way to the Hardshaw cemetery. Colonel Norman was a fierce champion of the Recs cause and an important link with the firm itself. The club's position was severely weakened as a result and never recovered.

By the end of the 1934–35 campaign, gates were a great cause for concern at City Road. "Is a 2,000 gate sufficient for a team holding 8th place in the league?" wrote 'Citizen', after the game against Hull, in April. Full-back Peter Barnes and winger Turton were sold to

Streatham & Mitcham before the new season began. Halfway through the campaign came the decision to sell Billy Greenall to Oldham – another body blow from which the club never really recovered. The Recs nearly lost another stalwart by accident. Front-rower Jumbo Highcock had a narrow escape against Hull at the Boulevard, when a six feet section of goalpost cracked off and fell to the ground, grazing his head in the process, as he stood beneath the cross-bar. Apparently Jumbo gave the woodwork a wide berth after that.

Despite the election of Tom Ashcroft as chairman of the Northern Rugby League in 1935–36, both St Helens clubs were struggling against falling gates and a general apathy towards rugby in the town – something unthinkable compared to the heady days of the 1920s. Saints embarked upon an advertising campaign in the local press to try and drum up dwindling support. The Recs, as a works team, did not, although, in retrospect, it would not have made much difference. They finished 26th in the table in 1935–36, below newcomers Streatham & Mitcham and Acton & Willesden. Saints finished 23rd.

Ernie, Horace and Ted – A Recs trio

Despite being the era of the great depression nationally, 1926 to 1933 were boom years for rugby league in St Helens, both at City Road and Knowsley Road.

But from then until the Second World War in 1939 Recs and Saints suffered a dramatic decline in fortunes with gates numbered in hundreds rather than thousands, with the consequent economic constraints meaning tightening of belts at the clubs. However, the flow of local talent continued via hopeful starlets from the schoolboy game, along with those who sampled their oval ball baptism of fire in the daunting St Helens Amateur League. Such a tried and tested trio of teenagers were winger Ernie Large, forward Horace Randolph and centre Ted Kerwick, each of whom had been lured to Recs by the persuasive tongue of legendary trainer Ted Forber.

Ernie Large

Raised in Clyde Street and a pupil of Lowe House school, lightning-legged Large cut his rugby league teeth on waste land near Beechams known as 'the Bruk', a fertile breeding ground that also yielded Saints stars like George Parr, Tommy Leyland, Josh Gaskell and Roy Robinson plus Warrington and Great Britain star Eric Fraser. A glasscutter at Pilkingtons, Large became Recs' youngest signing at the age of 16 in 1932, and adorned the left wing berth for the next six seasons, scoring many superb tries in the process. Among Ernie's high spots was being included in the Recs-Saints team defeated 15–7 by Australia at Knowsley Road in 1937. Other City Road heroes in the local line-up were Albert Bailey, Eli Dixon, Bill Parr, Tommy Dunn and Jack Atherton. During that season Large also enjoyed the rare distinction of marking Alf Ellaby at Central Park – and Ernie kept Alf try-less. "Luck played a big part in that," recalled the Recs winger, "because Alf saw little of the ball."

Recs' resignation from the Rugby Football League following their 1919 to 1939 stint meant that redundant players were seeking pastures new, but that had to be put on a six-year hold due to storm clouds of war hovering overhead. After Army service in India Ernie joined Oldham – he rode pillion with another former Rec, Bill Parr from North Road – where his regular centre was Norman Harris, grandfather of latter-day legend Iestyn. "I was very happy at Watersheddings," reflected Large, "from where I was selected for Lancashire, and was in the frame for a place on the 1946 [Lions] tour, but Jimmy Lewthwaite got the casting vote. However all that changed one day when I was delivering milk for the Co-op in

Haydock when a car stopped and out stepped Workington manager Gus Risman, who persuaded me to join the new side that he was building at Borough Park. I stayed there for one season before travelling to Cumbria in winter proved too much, so I was transferred to Saints in 1949 where I appeared in a handful of games prior to ending my career with Liverpool City, for whom I played against Saints when Knotty Ash Stadium was opened."

A schools crossing man in his later years, gentleman Ernie Large loved to relive his rugby league days, particularly with Recs, at his Mill Street home just half a mile from City Road. He died in 2006 at the age of 89.

Horace's heyday at City Road

A blockbusting forward who grew up in the town centre, Horace Randolph was a couple of years older than Ernie Large when he also trod the well-worn path to St Helens' other professional club in 1934. "Saints were interested," said 6 feet 15 stone Horace Randolph when interviewed in 1992, "But I chose Recs because they were a team of mainly local lads who worked at Pilks and I knew most of them from schooldays."

He waxed lyrical about his signing-on fee of £50 (a fortune then) with the going-rate on Recs match days being £3/15 for a win, £2/15 for a draw and £1/15 for a defeat. The huge sum of £10 was offered for victory in the games against Wigan – but not Saints...

Of Italian descent, the Randolph family, with 13 children, lived in Waterloo Street. "Dad was a boxing fanatic," remembered Horace, "to such an extent that the rear of our house was converted into a miniature stadium with a full-size ring in the back yard. My brother Dominic regularly traded punches with me or anyone else who fancied their chances with the gloves on, and there was many a bloodied nose or 'shiner' to be repaired in the Randolph home in those distant days."

Horace played in the Holy Cross school rugby league side that won the Waring Cup in 1927, and also represented Lancashire at this level. He then transferred to Cowley and with it rugby union, where he lined up alongside brothers Jack and Bob Heaton, Bill Gornall and Bill Laithwaite. Bob and Laithwaite also finished up at City Road. "However, dad did not like me dabbling with rugby union and sent me back to Holy Cross," said Horace. "He then formed his own rugby league team of early teenagers, and I think this was the launching pad for me signing for St Helens Recreation."

Horace recalled the game in the depression days of the 1930s, and goings-on at City Road in particular. "Characters? Any number of them," declared Randolph. "Who could forget brothers Johnny and Billy Greenall, with their mother Hannah vowing touchline retribution to opponents daring to rough them up? George Jumbo Highcock, Albert Bailey, Oliver Dolan, Peter Lythgoe, Albert Pimblett, Ted Kerwick – the list was endless. But they paled into insignificance compared to larger than life trainer Ted Forber. What he didn't know about rugby league wasn't worth knowing and he was not averse to rule-bending and gamesmanship – all in the cause of his beloved Recs of course."

One had to look further than the vagaries of the weather to understand why goalkicking legend Jim Sullivan had scant success at City Road. Examination of the ball often provided a clue. Street-wise Forber was aware of Sullivan's liking for a fully inflated ball – they were the leather case-type – and Ted ensured that a slight reduction in pressure did not go amiss on match days.

Turning to famous occasions in the red, amber and black jersey, Randolph recalled a Recs trip to Rochdale when singing star and Lancashire lass Gracie Fields kicked off, packed down in the first scrum and rounded off her party piece by cartwheeling along the touchline.

Rightly proud of his disciplinary record of a single dismissal Horace was nonetheless rather coy over this. He contented himself by revealing that he plunged into his early bath at Barrow, with the media describing the rampaging Randolph as being fed on tiger's meat and lion's blood. His saddest day, along with that of his Recs team-mates, was the club's swansong at Hull KR in 1939 when, ironically, Horace received rave notices for a power-packed performance in a defeated and understandably demoralised side.

At the start of the War, he managed to squeeze in a game for Dewsbury against New Zealand at Crown Flatt before Adolf Hitler's untimely intervention, whereupon Randolph donned khaki with the Royal Army Service Corps, and was involved in the evacuation from Dunkirk. He played the odd game for Wigan while on leave. Demobbed in 1946, Horace and his wife Bertha opened an ice cream and sweet shop and eventually settled in the Green Leach area, where they celebrated their diamond wedding in 1992. Horace Randolph died before his better half in 1995, but his niche in the pantheon of immortals who graced the Recs in the 1930s is assured.

Recs' youngest signing

Many rugby league greybeards think only of Ted Kerwick in relation to Leigh because, arguably, it was with the Hilton Park club that he enjoyed his best playing days. However, that should not cloud the fact that he is St Helens born-and-bred, and began his rugby league at grassroots level with St Teresa's and Sacred Heart schools teams. The nephew of former Recs stars Joe Bates and Bob Birchall, Ted figured at loose-forward and centre in those pre-war days, a time when he represented both St Helens and Lancashire Schoolboys. Kerwick vividly remembered two games against Yorkshire, first at Wakefield when the gate was 5,000, followed by a bumper 12,000 at Knowsley Road.

Schooldays over, Ted worked in the building trade and signed amateur forms for St. Helens Recs at the age of 16 in 1938, He was at stand-off when the club played its last game at Hull KR the following year. The side went their separate ways on Manchester Victoria railway station without formality and became free agents. Ted believed rugby league would have kept its grip better in St Helens if Recs had survived until the post-war boom. He treasured the ball he took from that emotional last game before donating it to the City Road Hall of Fame.

Oldham quickly snapped up Kerwick, but he guested for Wigan for two years early in the war prior to enlisting in the Royal Artillery. With military service over Ted found traipsing to Watersheddings a chore, and the Roughyeds agreed to his transfer request. Warrington official Chris Brockbank soon had Kerwick photographed in a Wires' primrose-and-blue jersey, only for Leigh's chairman Jack Harding to beat him to Kerwick's signature.

This led to that momentous 1952 Lancashire Cup Final between Leigh and Saints at Swinton, St Helens's first big occasion for 20 years. Operating at centre and marking Duggie Greenall, Ted had probably his finest game in a Leigh shirt and made three of his team's four tries in a 22–5 victory.

During his time at Leigh's Kirkhall Lane, Kerwick gained county and international honours before being coaxed up to Workington by Gus Risman in 1953. However, his parents' sudden deaths persuaded Ted to hang up his boots and take over their public house, the Golden Lion, in St Helens.

At least he thought he had retired from rugby league, only for Widnes to persuade him to give the game one more season prior to calling it a day. Ted later became the landlord of the Seven Stars in Eccleston. At the time of writing, the last of the revered City Road players, Ted Kerwick and Audrey, his wife of over 60 years, live at Windle, St. Helens.

(The photo shows Ted Kerwick recalling his playing days with the ball used in Recs' last-ever professional match at Hull KR.)

St Helens United

During the halcyon days of St Helens rugby League between 1927 and 1933, rugby followers in the town boasted that a team from the Recs and the Saints could have beaten any team in the country. The production of local talent was at a peak and, in addition to providing two teams, there were enough St Helens born players travelling to other clubs in Lancashire and Yorkshire to have furnished a third St Helens side.

By the late 1930s, however, rugby league was no longer flourishing in the town and both the Saints and Recs were in decline. A measure of their fall from prominence could be seen when the fixtures for the visiting Australian tourists for 1937–38 were announced. In previous years both the local sides had matches against the Kangaroos. Times had changed. The Saints and Recs were no longer considered strong enough to face the tourists individually and a combined team was selected for the first and only time.

St Helens XIII 7 Australia 15
Thursday 2 December 1937 at Knowsley Road, St Helens

The match was played on a gloomy Thursday afternoon in December in front of less than 2,000 spectators at Knowsley Road. Left-centre Jack Beaton opened Australia's account with a penalty and second-rower Eric Lewis powered through for a try to give the Green and Golds an ominously early 5–0 lead. The St Helens lads were made of sterner stuff, however, and from a scrum near the Kangaroos' line, Saints' Jackie Bradbury picked up and plunged through the dissolving scrum for a fine try. His club-mate Stan Powell's conversion hit the post and bounced over to put the St Helens XIII on level terms at 5–5.

It was only in the second half that the greater power of the Australians was seen to good effect, more so when the Recs pair of Eli Dixon and Ernie Large were forced to leave the field with injuries. Beaton and Williams added further tries for the Tourists and they eventually won a thrilling contest 15–7.

St Helens: Albert Butler (S), Albert Bailey (R), Eli Dixon (R), Jack Fearnley (S) Ernie Large (R), Stan Powell (S), Jackie Bradbury (S), Bill Parr (R), George Roberts (S), Tommy Dunn (R), Emlyn Hughes (S),
Jack Atherton (R), R. Hutchinson (S).
Scorers: Try: Bradbury; Goals: Powell 2.
Australia: G. Whittle, L. Dawson, B. Williams, J. Beaton, D. McLean, E. Norman, R. Thompson, H. Pierce, P. Fairall, F. Griffiths, G. MacLennan, E. Lewis, W. Prigg (capt).
Scorers: Tries: Williams, Beaton, Lewis; Goals: Beaton 2, Thompson.
Referee: Mr Armstrong (Huddersfield)

Attendance: 2,000

Walking on the original City Road pitch is an extremely spiritual experience for any true rugby league fan. Some of the greatest players in the British game played there at various times between the wars – names such as Harold Wagstaff, Jim Sullivan, Gus Risman and Jonty Parkin. Yet the famous old ground played host to numerous overseas stars and personalities from Australia and New Zealand. Famous Kangaroos include hooker Sandy Pearce, who played in the 1922 clash with the Recs at the age of 48; mighty loose-forward Wally Prigg, a star of the 1933–34 squad, along with centre Dave Brown, and tour manager Harry Sunderland. A powerful Recs side recorded its only victory over a touring side in 1926, when New Zealand, including centre or winger Len Mason, who later joined Wigan, and nuggety scrum-half Wilson Hall, who played for Castleford, were beaten 28–14. Tour match results make interesting reading:

Date	Result	Attendance	Receipts
21 Jan 1922	Recs 5 Australia 16	5,000	£450
30 Oct 1926	Recs 28 New Zealand 14	6,000	£347
14 Dec 1929	Recs 8 Australia 22	9,000	£640
26 Aug 1933	Recs 9 Australia 13	8,882	£614
2 Dec 1937	Recs/Saints XIII 7 Australia 15	2,000	£118

The combination of two teams from one place, in the manner of the St Helens XIII occurred four more times, all against the Australians: Hull and Hull KR combined in 1956, 1959 and 1963, and Workington and Whitehaven in 1959. The Humberside and Cumbrian teams were also unsuccessful against the Kangaroos.

Formidable talent at City Road to celebrate the career of hooker Oliver Dolan (last player on far right of back row) a Recs stalwart. Alf Ellaby was in a Recs' jersey (third left, front row), between Jimmy Jennion (left) and Horace Randolph. Other notables include Albert Pimblett (back, extreme left), with Oldham's Alex Givvons next to him. On the far right of the back row is 'Butcher' Prescott, former Saints forward and a keen Recs committeeman during their time as professionals. (Courtesy Curtis Johnstone)

Recs' very own boy wonder

St Helens Recs completed one of their most important local signings when they secured the services of I7-year-old sprint champion Albert Pimblett in August I936. Previously there was an informal agreement between the talented athlete and the Recs committee implying if, and when, he decided to make rugby league a career it would be at City Road. His understanding with Recs officials however, did not deter representatives of several other clubs from outside the area who were all eager to secure his signature. The representative of one persistent rival club stayed half the night at Pimblett's home in Sutton Heath Road in a desperate attempt to sign him. Albert however, proved to be a man of his word and would not go back on his agreement with Recs. While he was at St Austin's school in Thatto Heath, he represented St Helens schools at rugby league for three consecutive seasons from 1930, as well as Lancashire schools in the 14 to 16 age group against Cumberland and Yorkshire. He later represented England schools against France.

The ability of Ellaby as a scoring machine for Saints was equalled by Pimblett in junior rugby. Previously Pimblett had created a unique record in schoolboy rugby by crossing his opponents' line eight times in just four representative games. In the first round of the Lancashire Cup he scored twice against Wigan Schools, a further three tries against Swinton and with Jimmy Stott, who later became a household name with Saints, as his centre partner he notched nine of the 11 tries scored by St Helens Boys in their 41–8 Lancashire Cup Final win, before a 10,000 crowd at Knowsley Road.

At I5 years of age the St Austin's junior was rated by many judges as the finest schoolboy winger of his time and when he took to the running track under the guidance of coach Dick Marsh from Peasley Cross, he was just as successful as he had been on the rugby field. The phenomenal running of the youngster, coupled with his earlier performances led many people to believe that St Helens may have produced a future world-beating athlete. Pimblett's outstanding performance was winning the Lancashire youths 100 yards sprint at the Bury Athletic club meeting in the amazing time of 10.2 seconds – just 0.2 seconds slower than Alf Ellaby's best time for the 100 yards. At 16 years old he had gained every rugby league honour possible for a boy of his age.

It was 1933, however, when Pimblett made his first big break in sport. He represented St Helens and Lancashire schools, won both the boys and youths 100 yards finals at Pilkington Recreation Sports and was also county sprint champion on two occasions. An unfortunate clash of track events at Pilkingtons Recreation and Bury on 6 July 1935 denied him the opportunity of completing a unique record in junior athletics. The youths 100 yards championship at Bury clashed with the Recs sports and prevented him from completing a trio of successes as Recs 100 yards youths winner for 1933, 1934 and 1935. This would have given him a three race championship twice over, because he had already won the boys 100 yards three times and the youths 100 yards twice. Due to a scarcity of events at youth level in 1936, he went on to compete in senior events with remarkable success.

There was little doubt that Pimblett would be a tremendous asset to the City Road club once he had decided on a career in rugby league. His appearances in training at City Road certainly stimulated the emotions of many Recs followers who saw him in action prior to the start of his professional career. It had been some considerable time since a youngster with so much potential had been seen at the ground. Tall and beautifully built he tipped the scales at 12 stones, but what impressed the Recs followers most of all was his natural football ability – he could give and take a pass at speed, swerve or sidestep round opponents with considerable ease.

Spectators expected to see a ready-made Ellaby, but the step-up from junior to senior rugby league was a very big one indeed. Nevertheless, many of the 4,000-plus crowd at City Road for his debut against Salford on 29 August 1937 craned their necks for a better view every time the ball travelled in his direction, for there was nothing the Recs fans loved more than a meteoric rise to fame. They had been virtually starved of this in previous seasons and gave Pimblett a fine reception when he cleverly outwitted several opponents to give Bailey a simple touchdown. They rose as one and went wild with delight however, when he outpaced several defenders including the speedy Osbaldestin to score a spectacular try himself. He had some 50 or 60 yards to run when he took possession of the ball with the Salford defence, headed by full-back Osbaldestin, in full cry after him. Pimblett drew clear of the opposition in effortless fashion. In that moment a star was born.

Despite his tender years, Recs followers were convinced their new idol had everything that a possible future international wingman required. He went on to score a try in each of the first three games and equalled the club try-scoring record with 33 tries in his first full season in rugby league – including five hat-tricks. Pimblett also ended the season as leading English try-scorer in the Northern Rugby League charts, just seven tries behind the leader Eric Harris of Leeds. Albert also marked Alf Ellaby at Central Park after Alf had joined Wigan. Despite these achievements, his club could only finish in 10th place in the table. He was chosen for Lancashire the following season and crowned his county debut with a try in Lancashire's 23–17 win over Cumberland at Workington on 18 September. He was also a member of the Lancashire team that defeated Australia 7–5 at Warrington 11 days later.

When St Helens Recs finished in I939, Pimblett was persuaded to join Huddersfield, but his service with the Yorkshire club was curtailed by the outbreak of the Second World War. Pimblett joined the Guards and saw service in the Middle East, North Africa and Italy. He also saw plenty of rugby during his army days and captained a Mediterranean Forces side which gained prominence in the services. It was during this period of his career that he developed his powers as a centre, but later, he was severely wounded at Anzio in Western Italy. So badly mutilated were his shoulders, back muscles and leg that he was informed his career as a sportsman was over. But Albert refused to accept the decision and proved the experts wrong. After many operations and a long spell in hospital, he gradually

Yorkshire 10 Lancashire 10 – Albert Pimblett playing for Lancashire on 26 October 1938
Back: O. Peake, J. Croston, A. Pimblett (St Helens Recs), D. Cotton, R. Roberts, H. Millington, N. Silcock, J. Arkwright (capt); front: A. Higgins, J. Robinson, W. Belshaw, T. McCue, T. Shannon.

regained the strength in his limbs and made a splendid recovery. He was later transferred to the Physical Training Corps as a Sergeant Instructor. Following his discharge from the army, he returned to Huddersfield and in 1946 was transferred to Halifax, where he became a successful centre and club captain. Travelling and training difficulties later unsettled the player and it was Warrington's good fortune that the Yorkshire club agreed to release him. He quickly developed a devastating wing partnership with Brian Bevan, who became the world record try scorer, a partnership that regularly notched as many as 90 tries a season.

Pimblett's selection to represent England against Wales, at Wigan in September I947 and France in Bordeaux the following season was seen in many places as apt reward for the painstaking effort, courage and determination he revealed following his wartime injuries. Yet the honour which precipitated the high point of Pimblett's oval-ball odyssey was his selection for all three tests against the Australians in 1948, when he scored four tries as Great Britain retained the Ashes.

Championship, Lancashire Cup and League medals followed for Albert with Warrington when other St Helens products in Jock Johnson and Ike Fishwick were also in the Wire line-up. Pimblett's greatest regret was that injury robbed him of a Wembley winner's medal against Widnes in 1950. The curtain fell on a remarkable sporting career for Albert John Pimblett when he played his last game as captain of Salford in 1951, who, ironically, were his first opponents in 1936.

Return of the wanderer

As was the custom in the years between the wars, it was not unusual for a celebrity to perform the kick-off at matches. The Recs' opening game against Leigh at City Road, on 13 September 1938 was started by flying winger Jimmy Owen, one of their most popular players, who had left the game somewhat prematurely in the mid-1920s.

Jimmy, who was more than aware of the fickle nature of sporting stardom, wandered through Canada, Fiji and Australia, before settling down in New Zealand and working for a glass merchants in Auckland. He had formerly been a backwoods farmer in Canada and had also coached a top-class rugby union team in Auckland. The New Zealand scenery clearly appealed to Owen, a devotee of outdoor pursuits such as yachting, fishing and hiking – with tennis and bowls thrown in for good measure. He had married Marjorie Smith, the daughter of a sheep farmer at Southlands and was bringing up two children. Jimmy had come back to England to see his mother and, true to the nature of this remarkable man, had hiked from London to Birmingham, before catching a train north to St Helens.

He recalled how he had met several of his former team-mates during the 1928 Australasian tour: "When St Helens sent out its seven stars, I saw Les Fairclough play the most brilliant football I have ever seen. It was the team in which Frodsham, Dolan, Frankie Bowen, Frodsham and Fildes played. I met them all at several of the matches. It was like meeting a bit of old St Helens to see them again."

Although the City Road crowd had a new hero – Albert Pimblett – on the flanks, the team was a shadow of what it had been when the seven stars had left for Australia. Saints were also facing hard times before the 1938–39 season got under way, with chairman Alderman Dodd admitting that the Knowsley Road club was still in serious financial trouble, needing to bring in gate money of £200 per match to survive, instead of the £131 average of the previous campaign. They were uncertain times overall, however, with the threat of war in Europe, and the City Road works used to assemble the town's 101,000 gas masks.

Recs beat Leigh on the opening day, but the side struggled to make an impact in the league, despite a 5–4 Boxing Day victory over fellow strugglers Saints at Knowsley Road. The fates were starting to conspire against the Recs' long-term future. Alarm bells started to ring at the end of January, when it was announced in the *St Helens Reporter* that the club had no option but to cash in on its prize assets: "The employment of local talent in the old days paid off. It couldn't last forever and during the past few seasons, the Recs, while still continuing their policy of playing local lads, have not repeated the success of the boom years. The economic depression and a few other factors caused the gates to dwindle and the present season has been marked by disaster in regard to injuries to players. Every member of the team has been injured this season and the compensation bill has been a hefty one. With a team constantly chopped and changed by injuries many defeats have been sustained that otherwise would have been victories and the gates have gone lower and lower. With three months to go, Recs are already faced with a deficit of over £1,000. Something had to be done about it and last weekend the Recs committee decided to place three of their star players on offer – Pimblett, Tracey and Lythgoe."

Stand-off Frank Tracey was the one to leave City Road. Born virtually next door to the ground, he had been a schoolboy star and one of the best ball distributors in the league. Recs supporters were naturally dismayed that he was snapped up by Saints, who were gradually showing signs of recovering from their financial problems. Both Recs and Saints could only cast envious glances at Wigan, who had a £12,000 reserve fund to cover any impending crisis if needed.

Challenge Cup Second Round
St Helens Recs 3 Wigan 8
Saturday 18 February 1939 at City Road, St Helens

The Wigan rugby millionaires were Recs' opponents at City Road on 18 February 1939 in the Second Round of the Challenge Cup, and more than 14,000 packed into the ground. "It was just like old times all over again," said the *St Helens Reporter* as Recs fans waited to see if their team could revive a disappointing campaign with the ultimate giant-killing act.

Heavy drizzle fell, making handling difficult, but the game got off to a real flyer, with a try to the home side from the very first scrum. Hooker Bunny Lewington won the ball and the brotherly partnership of Harold and Eli Dixon at half-back sprung into action. Eli broke through from his brother's pass and after piercing the Wigan defence sent the perfect ball wide to Albert Pimblett, who left full-back Jim Sullivan scrambling in his wake for a magnificent touchdown in the corner. This early success was short-lived, as Wigan winger Morley held off Ernie Large's challenge to score an unconverted try in the opposite corner.

In a riveting spectacle, Recs were unfortunate to go five points down half-way through the first half when former Saints stand-off Jack Garvey kicked over the head of Recs full-back and captain Peter Lythgoe. A large posse of players chased after the ball. In the last few yards, Wigan centre Denis Williamson got the advantage and dived to touch down, before falling headlong into the railings at the back of the ground.

Despite the deficit, Recs fought desperately to pull the game around. Twice, near the end, Jack Howard, hardly the biggest of men, dodged through several defenders and hurled himself at the line, only to be pulled down on each occasion inches short. Although the home side had displayed their famous indomitable spirit in the face of adversity, their forwards were too light to make a decisive impression on the Wigan pack despite a large percentage of the ball coming from hooker Lewington. "It was a courageous battle," wrote the 'Colonel' in the *Reporter*. "The lads of the village – a team costing only an old song – fought against Wigan, whose team has cost a fortune to build." City Road would never see the like again.

St Helens Recs: Peter Lythgoe; Albert Pimblett, Albert Bailey (capt), Charlie Reynolds, Ernie Large; Eli Dixon, Harry Dixon; Bill Parr, Bunny Lewington, Bill Rankin, Horace Randolph, Bob Grundy, Jack Howard.
Scorers: Try: Pimblett
Wigan: Jim Sullivan (capt), Jack Morley, Ossie Jones, Denis Williamson, Eddie Holder, Jack Garvey, Hector Gee, George Banks, Davies, Percy Moxey, Gwyn Williams, Ike Jones, Jack Bowen.
Scorers: Tries: Morley, Williamson; Goal: Sullivan.
Referee: Mr Taylor (Wakefield)
Half-time: 3-8
Attendance: 14,000
Receipts: £770

The end is nigh

Eight straight losses in March and April 1939 emphasised the club's uncertain future. There was only a sparse crowd at City Road to see an injury-wracked Recs take on Liverpool Stanley, with a reserve threequarter line and the debut of young Teddy Kerwick at stand-off. Some of the missing supporters had probably travelled to Peasley Cross to swell the 6,000 crowd who watched St Helens Schoolboys take on Manchester in the English Schools Shield football competition. The round-ball game had once again come to haunt the Recs in their hour of need.

By mid-April, things were looking bleak for the Recs, with rumours of Albert Pimblett's proposed move to Huddersfield making the headlines in the local press. On Wednesday 26 April, however, the die was cast. In an official statement issued by the club, it was revealed that during the Recs' 20-year existence, a financial loss had been incurred every season except the first two and that loss had been borne by Pilkington Brothers Ltd. The total loss for the last four seasons had not been less than £4,000, of which at least £1,200 was the loss for the current season. Statistics showed that the attendance at home matches had progressively decreased to an average of 2,000, of which about 15 per cent was represented by members of the Recreation Club and 50 per cent by unemployed people and by boys, youths and ladies, all of whom paid a reduced admission charge. The loss per home match was not less than £70.

The statement went on: "Bearing in mind the object of the Recreation Club is fundamentally to provide recreation and entertainment for its members, so very few of whom support the rugby league section of the club, the executive committee of the Recreation Club, after full consideration of the facts, was reluctantly forced to the conclusion that there was no alternative but to recommend to the directors of Pilkington Brothers Ltd that the Recs RFC should cease to exist. With the concurrence, therefore of the directors and committee of Recs RFC formal notice of the club's resignation from the Rugby League, to take effect from 30 April 1939 has been sent to the Secretary of the Rugby Football League and henceforth there will be no form of professional football associated with the Recreation Club."

John Wilson, the secretary of the RFL later sent a letter to the Recs secretary, Tom Ashcroft, acknowledging the Recs' resignation from the RFL as from 31 July. The letter added: "The effect of this is that your club is entitled to transfer such players as you can up to that date, after which the players not transferred will be free agents."

Wigan 26 St Helens Recs 11, 26 April 1939 at Central Park, the Recs' last game in Lancashire. The all locally born line-up is: back: Billy Ashall (assistant trainer), Horace Randolph, Ted Kerwick, Bill Rowson, Harry Simm, Jack Howard, Bob Grundy, Bill Rankin, Ted Forber (trainer). Front: Ronnie Prescott, Peter Lythgoe, Jack Atherton, Albert Bailey (capt), Eli Dixon, Albert Pimblett.

The final farewell
Hull Kingston Rovers 25 St Helens Recs 12
Saturday 29 April 1939 at Craven Park, Hull

The famous red, amber and blacks travelled to Hull Kingston Rovers for their last match on Saturday 29 April 1939. 'Recs Fall at Final Hurdle' was the headline in the following Monday's *Liverpool Echo*, as the visitors could win. "There was no ostentation about the last appearance of St Helens Recs at Craven Park, Hull, on Saturday," wrote 'Tacklow'. "The proceedings went through without ceremonial and, not unnaturally, the visitors lacked inspiration and were beaten 25–12. Although there was little at stake as far as the Recs were concerned, they did score in the last minute, when Bailey's interception try was converted by Dixon. "The team trooped off somewhat disconsolately", added Tacklow, "but I thought the Recs claimed one of the game's outstanding performers in 16-year-old Kerwick, a half-back who is going to be in Recs' best tradition, even though he will soon be moving elsewhere. He is a typical example of the younger school of City Road stars who would have rebuilt the reputation of the club had not the death knell already sounded."
Hull Kingston Rovers: White, Spamer, Eastwood, Whitworth, Milner, Morgan, Naylor, Beaumont, Ramsden, Blanchard, Clarke, Bedford, Cayzer.
Scorers: Tries: Bedford, Beaumont, Eastwood, Cayzer, Milner; Goals: Milner 5.
St Helens Recs: Eli Dixon, Albert Pimblett, Albert Bailey (capt), Jack Atherton, Ernie Large; Ron Prescott, Ted Kerwick; Bill Rowson, Bunny Lewington, Bill Rankin, Horace Randolph, Harry Simm, Jack Howard.
Scorers: Tries: Bailey, Prescott; Goals: Dixon 2, Bailey.
Referee: Mr A. Harding (Broughton)

Spectators quickly gathered around the players' exit and gave a sustained round of applause as the Recs left the pitch for the last time, without fuss and ceremony. Later, in the Pavilion, Rovers directors were seen discussing terms with both Pimblett and Kerwick, but the negotiations came to nought. At a special dinner at the Station Hotel later in the evening, Recs chairman James Stewart made a brief farewell speech to the players and hoped that they would soon be fixed up with new clubs in the future. One of the first to leave was secretary Tom Ashcroft, in May 1939, who joined Liverpool Stanley in a similar capacity. He had served on the Lancashire committee for 20 years and was also a member of the Rugby League Council for 16 years. The bulk of the players became free agents and were scattered among several clubs when rugby league got off to a new start after the Second World War. Albert Pimblett joined Warrington; Charlie Reynolds went back to his native Widnes; Ted Kerwick made a name for himself at Leigh and Ernie Large popped up at Knowsley Road for a spell. Unfortunately, former full-back Peter Lythgoe was to pay the ultimate price for his country, losing his life after the Normandy landings of 1944.

The demise of the Recs came as no surprise, given the obvious financial circumstances of the last few years and it became clear that Pilkingtons would not keep on subsidising the club. "It was no surprise when the Recs packed up," said former Saints assistant secretary Len Kilshaw. "A works team never has the same grip as the town team. No one at the Recs could have done what Councillor Frank McCormick did to save the Saints. During the crisis at City Road, there was a feeling of complacency that Pilkington Brothers would once again pull them out of the soup, but it never happened."

Yet there were other reasons for the club's demise apart from sheer finance. The First World War had a profound effect upon St Helens, with many of the 13,000 men who went to war in Europe failing to return. The result was a lowering of the birth-rate during the War, so 20 years later, recruiting local talent, which was the Recs' life blood, was difficult.

It is also recorded that the Recs committee did not treat junior clubs in the town equally, tending to favour those clubs who were part of the local Pilkington Works competition over other established teams in the town. By a combination of luck and judgment, the committee had built up a superb first team by the early 1920s and did not ensure that ready replacements were available. As a result a great team got old together causing irreversible problems by the middle of the next decade. Replacing players was not a straightforward task. The committee could not simply put in a bid for a player. They first had to get the finance committee's agreement and then the board of directors. As economic depression deepened in the 1930s, it was also not always possible to provide work within the firm for any new players – something that had been a major enticement in the past.

Every worker at Pilkingtons paid a penny each week (later tuppence) for the privilege of having a rugby league team. The Recreation club administration was unwieldy and the football club committee had representatives from all works, including collieries, within the firm. Inevitably, judgments were clouded by favouritism and vested interests, hindering progress. In retrospect, the football committee would have operated more efficiently with fewer, better-qualified members – something that would have been nearly impossible to implement. If the aim of the Recreation section was to "provide recreation and amusement for the workforce", it was apparent that the rugby league section no longer fulfilled those requirements by the early months of 1939. St Helens Recs RFC was thus consigned to sporting history – one of 33 clubs to disband since the start of the Northern Union in 1895.

Recs players training at City Road: back: Albert Pimblett, Ronnie Prescott, Hamson, Ernie Large, Billy Bowen, Horace Randolph, Ted Forber (trainer); front: Jumbo Highcock, Jack Howard, Peter Lythgoe, Jimmy Jennion, Albert Bailey. (Courtesy Denis Whittle)

Recs' winger Turton is held by a Leigh defender at City Road in the late 1930s. Note the dearth of spectators on the terraces. (Courtesy Denis Whittle)

Memories of the last season

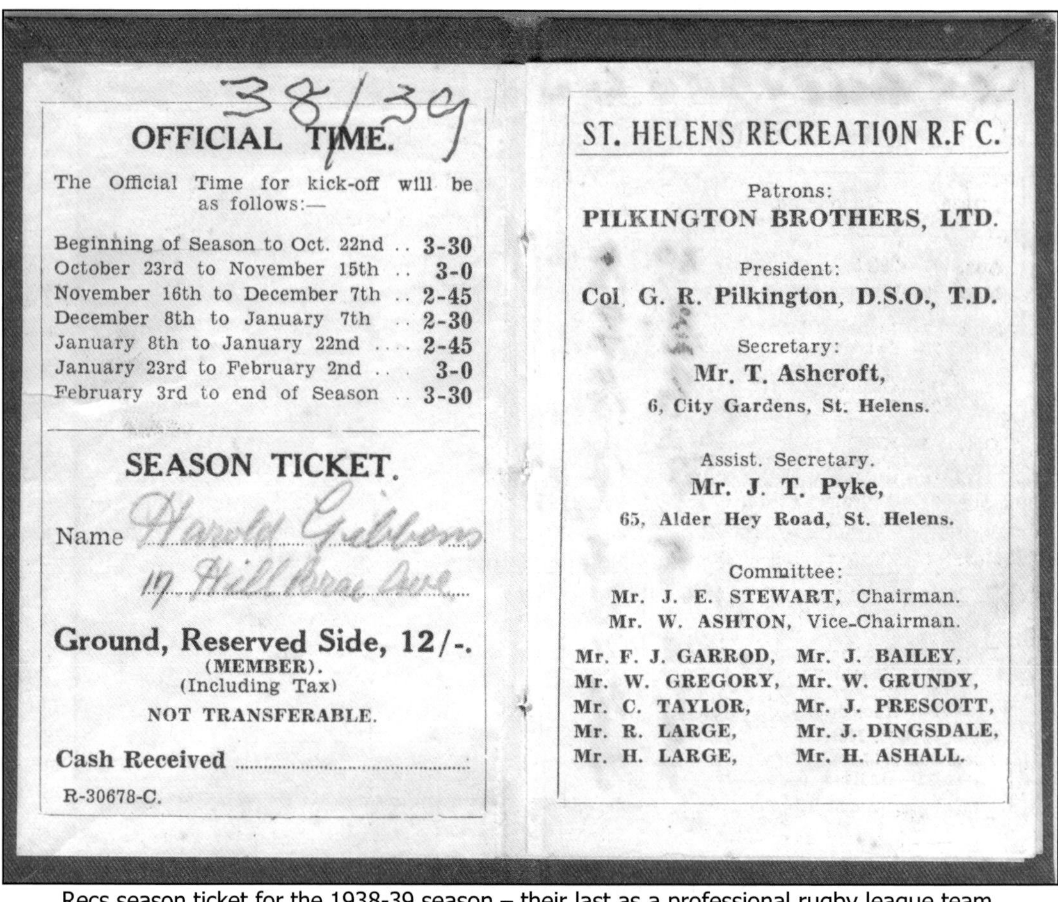

38/39

OFFICIAL TIME.

The Official Time for kick-off will be as follows:—

Beginning of Season to Oct. 22nd	3-30
October 23rd to November 15th	3-0
November 16th to December 7th	2-45
December 8th to January 7th	2-30
January 8th to January 22nd	2-45
January 23rd to February 2nd	3-0
February 3rd to end of Season	3-30

SEASON TICKET.

Name Harold Gibbons

17 Hill Brae Ave

Ground, Reserved Side, 12/-.
(MEMBER).
(Including Tax)
NOT TRANSFERABLE.

Cash Received ....

R-30678-C.

ST. HELENS RECREATION R.F C.

Patrons:
PILKINGTON BROTHERS, LTD.

President:
Col. G. R. Pilkington, D.S.O., T.D.

Secretary:
Mr. T. Ashcroft,
6, City Gardens, St. Helens.

Assist. Secretary.
Mr. J. T. Pyke,
65, Alder Hey Road, St. Helens.

Committee:
Mr. J. E. STEWART, Chairman.
Mr. W. ASHTON, Vice-Chairman.

Mr. F. J. GARROD, Mr. J. BAILEY,
Mr. W. GREGORY, Mr. W. GRUNDY,
Mr. C. TAYLOR, Mr. J. PRESCOTT,
Mr. R. LARGE, Mr. J. DINGSDALE,
Mr. H. LARGE, Mr. H. ASHALL.

Recs season ticket for the 1938-39 season – their last as a professional rugby league team. (Courtesy Harold Gibbins)

St. Helens Recreation Football Club

Patrons - Pilkington Bros. Ltd.
President - Col. G. R. Pilkington, D.S.O., T.D.

THE
OFFICIAL PROGRAMME
Season 1938-39
PRICE - ONE PENNY

Good Friday, April 7th, 1939

RECS
versus
Huddersfield

At City Road Kick-off 3-30 p.m.

Programme for the Recs versus Huddersfield match at City Road, which the home side lost 17–10. The team won only one of their last 10 league matches – a 17–10 success against York in the final professional match at the famous old ground.

7. 1949 to 1963: Phoenix from the Ashes

The demise of the original St Helens Recreation Rugby League Club was followed by the Second World War, when sport took a back seat. There were many sacrifices made during the conflict by members of the Pilkington organisation and the rugby section in particular was saddened to hear of the death of former centre Peter Lythgoe, who had been killed in Northern France on 12 August 1944. A member of the Royal Armoured Corps, he was 29 years old. In the days of post-war austerity, however, sport provided a much-needed release for the youth of St Helens and the local junior rugby league began to flourish, with the resumption of fixtures during the 1945–46 season.

Over the next few years there was talk of the Recs being reborn into the professional code, but nothing transpired. One old Recs enthusiast argued that with rugby league currently experiencing boom years, there would be a ready-made crowd of 15,000 from the Saints camp to watch the rival team at City Road, but clearly such an idea was rather far-fetched. In the spring of 1949, however, things began to stir with a group of enthusiasts who wanted to revive the club as an amateur organisation. The group – Bill James, Tom and James Metcalfe, Peter Lee and Bill Denson – submitted an application to the Pilkington Recreation Committee at its Grove Street headquarters. The new rugby section, if given the green light, would play in the St Helens amateur Junior Rugby League in the 1949–50 season. Just as importantly, the club would be able to use the facilities at the City Road ground once more, thus reviving the soul of the pre-war Recs side.

The application was granted by the committee, with one significant amendment: the original rule of March 1886 that only Pilkington employees, past or present could play for the Recreation Club, was rescinded. The first meeting of the new Rugby League section took place on 25 July 1949 at Ruskin Drive. The City Road ground was in a state of some dilapidation by this time, having only been used for the occasional inter-town amateur game or schoolboys match. The only thing left standing was the grandstand itself, a wooden structure built during the association football years at City Road in the early part of the century. This did have the necessary changing rooms, although the structure was initially deemed unsafe for spectators. The perimeter fence was broken down and most of the old spectator banking had gone, but it was not long before basic repairs took place to get the ground up to standard for the Recs' return.

According to former secretary Jim Clitheroe, speaking in *The Cullet* magazine in 1964, the committee brought wireless poles for posts, cleared dressing rooms of debris, transferred seats from the stand to the rooms below, cleaned up the two sunken baths, installed modern gas-fired water heaters and even marked out the playing area. The newly formed Pilkington Recreation ARLFC was up and running – at least in terms of facilities. There was now the task of recruiting a side capable of competing in the thriving open age section of the St Helens and District Amateur League.

Under trainer Vinty Matthews, a Pilkington employee and former Forces Physical Training Instructor and former Recs professional half-back Ronnie Prescott as coach, the team gradually took shape, recruitment coming initially from the inter-departmental works teams at the Pilkington factories – a similar process to that which served the original Recs when they started up again just before the First World War. Sadly, during the early days of the new club another link with the past was severed with the death of Hannah Greenall, the mother of Johnny and Billy Greenall, aged 79. She gave birth to seven sons and two daughters during her lifetime and was a Recs die-hard. Only serious illness or some other vital reason ever prevented her from watching the Recs at City Road and she frequently travelled with the team when they played away from home.

Those times seemed a long way off in the early 1950s as the Recs began their rebirth in a league of 14 clubs. Recs would face the following teams in combat during the season: British Sidac, Brook Street Legion, Clock Face Miners, Fosters Recreation, Liverpool Rangers, Liverpool Stanley, New Church Tavern, NCB, Rainhill Ex-Services, Ring o' Bells, Unos Dabs, UGB and the mighty Vine Tavern.

A tough baptism

The first fixture for the new club was a tough nut to crack – at the legendary Vine Tavern in Thatto Heath – a formidable outfit who had qualified for the First Round of the Challenge Cup on two occasions since the war and in both matches nearly beat their semi-professional opponents. Their captain and loose forward was Eli Dixon, a former City Road star before the War and the public house they took their name from in Thatto Heath was owned by another Recs legend, Frankie Bowen.

The Recs wore their new kit for the first match – red and blue hooped jerseys and white shorts – the change kit was green and white hoops – as they trudged from the changing rooms at Main Avenue to the Vine Tavern pitch at Brown Edge nearly half a mile away. The walk could be an intimidating experience and this was no different, as on the way Vine Tavern supporters told them in detail what would happen to them once the game begun. In front of such a partisan crowd, numbering almost 2,000, it was no surprise that the Recs were beaten 32–3, with their lone try coming from front-rower Albert Grice. In the Recs side that afternoon was second-rower Les Corns, the son of Peter Corns, who had scored the first try when Recs had previously returned to rugby, against Pemberton Rovers, on 6 October 1914.

The first match at City Road was a league encounter against famous old club Uno's Dabs, in front of a large crowd. The visitors took a six point lead, which was later reduced by another try from Albert Grice, although the visitors defence held firm. The two sides clashed at City Road later in the season, in the Challenge Cup first qualifying round. Once again, the visitors won. It was a learning curve for the team in its first year, which the club had expected. The Recs were satisfied with their fourth place, however, despite losing to UGB in the championship play-offs at the end of the campaign. Vine won the championship, after a replay against UGB at City Road, with more than 4,000 watching the match.

As the 1950–51 campaign got under way, there were other distractions in the town apart from rugby league. Local-born motor cycle ace Geoff Duke was breaking all records on his way towards world champion status and former Nazi Herman Goering's bullet-proof car was on show near St Helens Town Hall. The Recs also had an aura of impregnability, by topping the league table for most of the campaign and finishing as league leaders – a proud day for everyone connected with the club. However, success was always a double-edged sword for an amateur club in those days, with professional league clubs eager to recruit their best players.

Wilf Roach had come out of the Army and joined the Recs for the 1950–51 campaign. "Vinty Matthews was the coach at City Road and Vine Tavern were definitely the side to beat," he remembers. "We went to Brown Edge and beat them 15–0. I scored a hat-trick that day and they didn't like it one bit – especially Archie Hill, who gave me a load of stick. We played Pemberton Rovers in the qualifying rounds of the Challenge Cup and won 5–0. There was a Leeds scout watching me and I was invited to go and talk to them. That same week I went in a chip shop in Westfield Street and found my name on a team sheet for the Saints 'A' team. I didn't know about it and I should have been listed as 'AN Other' but it didn't matter. It had always been my dream to sign for my home town club and that's where I went. I was a member of a good side at City Road and we were unbeaten before I signed for Saints near the end of the season."

The Recs came top of the table, but lost in the Championship play-offs at the end of the campaign, a bitter disappointment for coach Ronnie Prescott and his men.

Time to remember

Progress continued at City Road, with continuing success in the local junior competition, despite the demands of National Service, and occasionally losing players to the professional game. On the evening of 20 November 1951, it was also a time for reminiscences, as the Recs held their first reunion of players since the old club had disbanded in 1939. Colonel Guy Pilkington, President of the club in its heyday, was chairman for the evening. He proposed the toast 'St Helens Recreation Rugby League Football Club' and remembered the time when the club had seven internationals and 13 players who had played for the county. "Certain matches stand out," he recalled. "I remember Recs playing Huddersfield when they were at their best. I did not see the match at Huddersfield, but I did see the replay at Recs ground. It was a keen match, but Ashall and Owen got hurt or we should have won. Then we had that series of matches when we nearly went to Wembley. Unfortunately we drew with Wigan and in the replay lost by one point."

The Colonel remembered a bet he had placed with Saints' committeeman Frank McCormick before one particular derby clash and was delighted when the Recs won 33–0. He spoke of the great South African forward Attie van Rooyen, who played for Wigan and Widnes. In the Recs team during one encounter was Jimmy Honey, who defied the odds with some superb tackles on the big fellow, taking him by the legs and up-ending him. "We've had some very grand times and games and I wish those times would come again," he sighed. "But I am afraid St Helens cannot afford two professional rugby league teams. However, we are now getting some quite good amateur rugby played and the old Recs ground can still produce some good players."

Former captain Oliver Dolan replied to the Colonel's speech by referring to the warmth of the Recs' spirit of days gone by and the club's proud record. That spirit permeated the whole of the team, from committee men to players and was in evidence in the hurly burly of the scrum, the quiet of the dressing room and the boardroom.

There were to be several more reunions over the next decade, although the number of people associated with the old Recs gradually diminished. Apart from legendary supporters like Mrs Greenall, several prominent players had died over the past couple of years. Former stand-off William 'Wee' Pierce perished in a road accident; second-rower Jimmy Jennion died as a result of heart problems; Joe McComas, licensee of the Queen's Arms Hotel in Fingerpost, passed away after a long illness; hooker Albert Simm died aged 61 and, most tragically of all, Harry Grundy took his own life, in October 1951. He was 56 years old.

The Recs were league leaders at the end of the 1951–52 campaign, but lost to the Vine Tavern in the top four play-off final at Knowsley Road. They also were successful in the West Lancashire League. Hughie Leyland, a bustling, pacy winger, was a member of the side: "I signed for the Recs in 1951 after playing for the Warrington 'B' team and in my first season I played three times for the St Helens open age [Town] team. We played Wigan at

City Road and I scored three tries," he remembers. "Ronnie Prescott was the coach. He was a member of the pre-war Recs team and even played sometimes when we were short, but he must have been getting on a bit by then. In my second season I played for Lancashire and the Recs won the St Helens League and the West Lancashire League. In the St Helens League there were not as many teams - UGB, Pilkington Recs, Vine Tavern, and Clock Face. We played the Vine Tavern twice at Knowsley Road and got beaten on both occasions. I broke my collar bone in the first match and we lost 12–8. Bert Walsh and Ronnie Barton, who went to Liverpool City, were great wingers at City Road. 'Chidder' Chisnall was stand-off and later joined Rochdale Hornets. I used to come inside off the wing on the burst and he used to give me the ball. I scored quite a few tries doing that. Norman 'Nodger' Unsworth was a brilliant loose-forward – a real star. Jake Round was also a belting goalkicker. Trainer Vinty Matthews would give us some of the old goalposts to carry when we were training. I'll always remember one of his sayings: 'You're playing for the big apple today lads!' We won quite a few matches, but we never saw any of that fabled fruit."

Hughie's three tries against the Wigan Town team alerted senior clubs and he was offered £300 and a job by Leeds to turn professional. "They wanted me to play six matches before they signed you on, but I wasn't interested," he recalls. "I did join Wigan, who had also come in for me and I had three trial matches before breaking my collar-bone. Ronnie Prescott said 'I'm glad you are going to Wigan – I was going to take you down anyhow.' In my first match I was marking Saints winger Steve Llewellyn – nicest bloke in the world he was – and I tried to stop him as he was diving over and he burst my nose. There was blood everywhere. I never really settled at Wigan and I retired in 1954 when I got married. When I was in the Army, I was stationed in Mogadishu and we toured Nairobi playing rugby [union]. I played for the East African Army. Quite a distinction – Recs, Wigan and Mogadishu. Years later I told my lad I was a helicopter pilot, shades of Black Hawk Down."

Four cups and all that

The next season, 1953–54, was a pivotal one for the club. Indeed, the fifth year following their rise from the ashes was to prove their most successful to date. The team topped the St Helens and District Junior League and won the top four play-offs by defeating the old enemy Vine Tavern 34–8 at the UGB sports ground in Eccleston. The side went one better by lifting the West Lancashire League Cup in a hard-fought 13–5 victory over UGB at Clock Face. The semi-final against a powerful Wigan Road WMC outfit at their ground in Leigh had been a tempestuous affair, however. Five minutes before the end, when Recs were winning 17–8, the tie disintegrated into a free-for-all and the referee effectively abandoned the match, after two players from each side had received their marching orders. It took a meeting of the League management committee to sort out the mess. They eventually allowed the result to stand.

The final trophy was the Bootle Charity Cup, an end-of-season affair, when the Recs played Liverpool City (formerly Stanley) in a special challenge match. The Recs won, but at a considerable cost. Several members of the side signed for the professional club shortly afterwards. Coach Ronnie Prescott left for a similar position with the Liverpool outfit, while players Gordon Crosby, Jake Round, Bert Walsh, Ronnie Barton, Frank Briers, Billy Rigby, Alan Davies and Jack Owen followed suit. There were further departures, with Bobby Chisnall signing for Wigan and Norman Unsworth joining Rochdale Hornets – little wonder that the first era of amateur football at City Road was to end in some turmoil, a situation frequently faced by the top amateur clubs, even today.

Pride of City Road: Pilkington Recs and the four Cups – 1953–54. Back: Ronnie Prescott (coach), Norman Unsworth, Bernard Coleman, Eric Leach, Johnny Owen, George Hutton, Gordon Crosby, Geoff Halsall, Jake Round, Jim Parr (committee), Eddie Prescott (assistant coach); middle: B. Denson (committee), Vernon Greenough, Billy Rigby, Joe Robinson (chairman), J. Laycock (president), Harry Ody, Frank Briers, Alan Davies, Jackie Owen; kneeling: Charlie Tierney, Bobby Chisnall, Ronnie Barton, Bert Walsh, Billy James (secretary). (Courtesy Brian Peers)

A 'where are they now?' glance at the assembled group makes for a fascinating study but understandably, by 2006, several had died. These include Norman Unsworth, Eric Leach, Johnny Owen, George Hutton, Frank Briers, Charlie Tierney and Bert Walsh. Crosby, Barton and Walsh also signed for Liverpool City; Unsworth did likewise for Rochdale Hornets; Leach later became a referee and was a linesman at a Wembley Challenge Cup Final. He then became Saints' kitman in the 1980s. Alan Davies emigrated to Australia. However, arguably the most celebrated star on the photograph to turn professional was flying winger Bobby Chisnall who, after representing the Army in rugby union at Twickenham in 1957, then joined Wigan and then Widnes with whom he won a Challenge Cup medal in 1964.

Harry Ody and the rebirth of the Recs

Among those who attended the first meeting to discuss reforming the club was teenage scrum-half Harry Ody, a local lad who cut his rugby league teeth at schoolboy level, and was simply itching to resume his love affair with the game in the famous red-amber-and-black jersey. He took up the story of the Recs' rebirth (albeit as Pilkington): "I was just 17 at the time and following talks with Pilkington's directors they handed us the keys to City Road and effectively told us to get on with it. We joined the St. Helens Amateur League. In addition several of our players 'moonlighted' in the Pilkington Works League."

"I can vividly remember opening the gate at the back of the stand, and it was almost surreal to enter the disused dressing rooms and think of the giants of the past who had stripped there, in particular on finding a Number 11 shirt that could have been worn by Tommy Smith or Albert Fildes. The Metcalfe family were the driving forces at City Road in those distant days and later we unearthed another back-room boy in secretary Billy James who, quite simply, Pilkington Recs revolved around."

Pilkington Recreation - Lancashire Cup Winners 1956-57
Back: Jim Burkhill (chairman), Ronnie Leyland, George Hutton, Frank Hudson, Ronnie Appleton, Bernard Dwyer, Bernard Coleman, Arthur Sherwood, Teddy Johnson, Jackie Owen, Alan Foster, Jim Parr (committee); middle: Les Hand, Vinty Matthews (Trainer), Archie Hill (Capt), Billy James (committee), Eric Tierney; front row: Alan Fisher, Harry Taylor, Bernard Jeffries, Charlie Tierney.

Pilkington Recs circa 1959. Back: Billy James (committee), Eddie Morley, John Carrigg, Peter Marr, Chris Willett, George Hutton, Ron Leyland, Henry Green, Geoff Irwin, Joe Robinson (secretary), Vinty Matthews (trainer); front row: Les Hand, Harry Taylor, Archie Hill (capt), Bernard Jeffries, Eric Tierney, Bernard Dwyer. (Courtesy Mrs Irwin)

Charlie Seddon scores against Sutton Manor at Houghton Road. Peter Metcalfe is next to him on the right. (Courtesy Hughie Leyland)

Hughie Leyland flies over for a Recs' try against Sutton Manor – in front of family and friends. (Courtesy Hughie Leyland)

Pilkington Recreation 1961-62
Players only back: Peter Metcalfe (coach), Ernie Forber, Glyn Friar, Alan Platt, Keith Webster, George Hutton, Keith Polding, Peter Marr, Peter Eckersley, Billy Webster (committee); front: Eric Tierney, Geoff Fletcher, Tommy Metcalfe (Secretary), Jimmy Bailey, David Pilkington (president), Kevin Casey, Jim Clitheroe (chairman), Colin Whittaker Bobby Jones; kneeling: Champ Johnson, Geoff Lea (Courtesy Ernie Forber)

"As for myself I remained loyal to the club apart from brief flirtations with Saints and Liverpool City, as did a number of my City Road team-mates, while my most treasured of countless unforgettable memories was captaining 'Pilks' in the four-cups season of 1953–54. These trophies were the St. Helens League, Championship, West Lancashire League and Bootle Charity Cups."

Resurgent Recs

Despite producing their post-war peak in 1953–54, it proved impossible to sustain such success because of the departure of so many of the club's playing personnel to professional rugby at the end of the campaign. Indeed, there was a crisis in St Helens Junior rugby itself. "It is a punishing struggle to keep youth and open-age amateur rugby functioning at all," wrote Peter Smith in the *St Helens Reporter* in August 1954. "Can the organisations hold on for better times? The effect of the war-time holding-up of football has still not been overcome. No-one wants to do anything to apply the last rites, but clubs like Clock Face and UGB, with many years of un-beaten playing record need – as well as want – many matches. In anticipation of such lean times, the idea was borne to spread the organisation and compete with other clubs in other towns experiencing similar troubles – Wigan, Leigh, Widnes and Warrington. While in the youth section, this West Lancashire Youth League functions successfully, and help is given to clubs financially, not all open-age sections agreed and those who did agree failed to fulfil the full spirit of the arrangement. Meanwhile, every effort is needed to allow such keen clubs as Clock Face, UGB and Pilkington Recs to play as many competition matches as they can."

Another obstacle faced by the local amateur rugby league was the continuing development of rugby union teams in the town. A St Helens Recreation Rugby Union Football Club was formed in the summer of 1954, with the full support of Pilkington Brothers. Company chairman Sir Harry Pilkington kicked off in their inaugural match against a Wigan union side at Alder Hey Road. This clearly exacerbated the problems for the XIII-a-side code. The late 1950s saw three union clubs in the town – West Park, St Helens RUFC and Pilkington Recreation running a minimum of three senior teams every week, plus a Colts XV, with regular fixtures. Matches received comprehensive coverage in the local press, unlike their league counterparts, which could be rather sketchy at best.

By 7 September 1954, there were just six teams in the St Helens Amateur Rugby League: Clock Face, Pilkington Recs, UGB, Vine Tavern, Liverpool Hornets and Bowling Green (Sutton). By early October, the St Helens and Wigan leagues had met to form a joint open-age league, but times were still hard, with games watched by a handful of spectators. "I heard a rumour that at the end of the season would see a wholesale resignation of junior rugby league officials and the end of the league itself," wrote local journalist Peter Smith in March, 1955.

Such premonitions of doom were, thankfully, premature, but it remained a difficult task to maintain appropriate competition, with the small number of clubs. In January 1957, after a meeting of the open age districts of St Helens, Leigh and Wigan, a new league was formed from teams from those areas who were considered to be the strongest:
Wigan: Triangle Valve, Highfield, St. Patricks;
Leigh: Wigan Road YMCA, Robin Hood, Astley and Tyldesley Collieries, Golborne;
St Helens: Thatto Heath British Legion, Pilkington Recs, UGB.

Mr Hayton, the secretary of the new league remarked: "We have come to the conclusion that local district matches are a thing of the past. The only way to put the game back on top is to have inter-town matches over an area as wide as possible."

The new league structure certainly suited Pilkington Recs, who capped a magnificent season in 1956–57 by securing the St Helens League Leader's trophy and the West Lancashire Junior League. In an epic clash at City Road, the Recs faced a powerful Oldham St. Anne's side at City Road in the semi-final of the Lancashire Junior Cup. Recs' full-back Bernard Jeffries kicked his side ahead with a penalty after just three minutes, but Oldham replied with a goal from Jones.

The Recs' heavier pack soon got a firm hold on the game and the backing up of Sherwood, Fisher and Hutton paid dividends. Then – the try of the match as Archie Hill received, handed on to Leyland and the ball travelled along the threequarter line until it came to left-centre Glover who went over for a great try near the corner. Jeffries converted and kicked two more goals before the interval to give the Recs a solid lead they never relinquished, finishing winners by 18–8.

In the Final at Weaste (Salford) on 29 April, the Recs swamped Salford Juniors 20–9 to lift the coveted trophy for the first time – a proud moment for stand-off and captain Archie Hill, a true Recs 'Great.' "He was a nippy little bugger and had all the tricks in the book," remembers Harry Ody. "He could inspire those around him and he was always talking on the field – a real cheeky chappie. Despite his size he also had a crunching crash-tackle and didn't seem to be afraid of anyone."

Over the passage of time, details have become somewhat sketchy of that famous afternoon at Salford, but the Recs Lancashire Cup Final team lined-up as follows:
Jeffries, Hand, Davies, Dwyer, Tierney, Taylor, Hill (capt), Johnson, Sherwood, Fisher, Hutton, Owen, Leyland.

Another milestone occurred when Recs back-rower Ron Leyland was selected for the England amateur side that lost 32-23 to France in Tonneins. Indeed Recs' first-ever amateur international scored one of England's five tries on a rock-hard pitch in front of more than 8,000 spectators.

Bernard 'Archie' Hill

Will-o'-the-wisp. Chaplin-esque. Steptoe-esque. These appendages and more besides might describe Bernard Hill, who ghosted across the City Road turf more than a generation ago. More fitting perhaps might be the 'artful dodger' or 'mighty atom,' for a player known throughout amateur rugby league circles as Archie, a nom-de-plume inherited from his elder brother Billy.

No-one knows why, including Bernard, one of six sons and three daughters raised in Banner Street, Greenbank, from where he attended the nearby Sacred Heart School. The Hill family moved later to the Grange Park and Thatto Heath area, where widower Archie lives at the time of writing and from where he is guided through his occasional memory lapses by caring partner Margaret Crooks.

Once settled in 'Donkey Common' he switched to the oval-ball hotbed of St. Austin's school, under the watchful eye of legendary headmaster Gerry Landers, and at a time when other starlets like Bernard Dwyer senior, Tommy Finn and Arthur Pimblett were making their rugby league names.

School days over, Archie went to work at Pilkingtons and became a popular figure in the mixing room at Ravenhead, and it was a natural progression with rugby in his red-amber-and-black blood that he would graduate to City Road.

While there he played an integral part in Recs' success in the late 1950s and early 1960s, where his speed off the mark, telling pass and eye for an opening saw him prove to be the benchmark for other Thatto Heath-bred maestros such as Johnny McCabe and Billy Simmons.

There are many tales about the 5 feet 6 inches 10 stone pocket battleship, but he was definitely destroyer-class tackling-wise, as a certain dreadnought American dubbed Hank discovered when Archie torpedoed him while guesting for Vine Tavern against Liverpool City at Knotty Ash. Another tale is that, because his late wife Betty did not approve of him playing rugby, Archie used to hide his boots in the back-yard bin and then make good his escape when his better half's back was turned. One of Hill's abiding memories of City Road was when Recs stalwart Eddie Morley emptied the trainer's bucket over a referee who had given the opposition the benefit of several questionable decisions. Whether the culprit also received the early bath treatment has never been revealed.

A larger-than-life character who enjoys a 'swift half' and a game of snooker at Thatto Heath Royal British Legion, Bernard Hill no doubt now reflects on a life lived to the full with friendship and laughter every inch of the way.

Building for success

The face of St Helens was changing radically by the start of the 1960s. A new railway station was planned for Shaw Street; there were three new secondary schools built to accommodate the post-war baby boom and a new technical college began to take shape in the town centre. Pilkingtons also announced the construction of a £2 million head office complex between the Ravenhead works and Prescot Road for themselves and their subsidiary Fibreglass. This reflected the company's position then as the world's largest manufacturer and exporter of glass and is still a distinctive landmark in the town today.

The Pilkington Recreation Club's annual report for 1960–61 included reference to a wide range of clubs and activities for the benefit of the workforce, ranging from sporting pursuits such as archery, bowls and hockey, to more diverse pastimes as 'Fur and Feather,' contract bridge and dance and drama. Subscriptions from members amounted to £5,428, with the maintenance of grounds and buildings, plus general administration £15,419. There were several difficulties facing the rugby league section, however, with a shortage of committee men and the inconvenience of sharing the City Road ground with the football section, resulting too frequently in fixture clashes. Despite the problems, coach Peter Metcalfe had assembled a strong squad who took them into the first round proper of the Challenge Cup in 1960–61 – a chance to play professional-quality opposition for the first time since 1939 and gain the code some much-needed publicity in the local sports pages dominated by rugby union, football and even snooker.

The Recs were well equipped for a good cup run. Although the pack was rather lightweight, it was extremely mobile, including a formidable front-row partnership of Geoff Irwin and England international Kevin 'Buck' Casey. Chris Willett was a capable hooker, with Ken Parr, Peter Eckersley, George Hutton, Jimmy Rigby and Bernard Dwyer vying for places in the back row. "Bernard was one of the best loose-forwards," recalls Peter Metcalfe. "He wasn't just a tough lad. He could run and carry the ball in front of him with two hands. As defenders came up he would either pass or give them the dummy." In the halves, Archie

Hill was a real handful, partnered by Brian 'Champ' Johnson. The threequarter line had pace in the form of flying wingers Les Hand and Eric Tierney, with Harry Taylor and Ernie Forber providing steel in the centres. Forber's precision goalkicking was another crucial weapon in the Recs' armoury. During the 1960–61 campaign he notched an incredible 45 points in the 95–0 slaughter of Haydock Rangers. Finally, at full-back Tommy Vose was a sturdy last line of defence.

There was disappointment in the Challenge Cup first qualifying round for the Recs, when United Glass failed to raise a team – something that happened from time to time with amateur teams. The Recs Challenge Cup odyssey was soon to gather momentum. Astley and Tyldesley Collieries were defeated 56–5, giving Recs a welcome bye in the third qualifying round. The Recs managed to scramble a draw away to a strong Cadishead and Oldham side in the fourth qualifying round – but only just, as Ernie Forber recalls: "They were beating us 13–11 on a pitch knee-deep in slutch. We got a free kick straight on the touchline. Archie [Hill] says to me 'Are you having a go, whistle's about to go?' Anyhow, that big heavy leather ball sailed between the sticks and it went to a replay. We hammered them back at City Road by over 30 points."

Rochdale's Mayfield fell 23–9 in the next round, giving the Recs a match against Walney Central in the final qualifying round at City Road. Former Barrow and Great Britain stand-off Willie Horne was the Cumbrians' player-coach, but didn't turn out on the day. Walney had four other former professionals in their ranks in what promised to be a mouth-watering clash, under the gaze of over 600 enthusiastic supporters at City Road and RFL secretary Bill Fallowfield, no less.

Despite Recs being renowned for their ability to score tries, it was goals that counted against the Cumbrians. A hat-trick of penalties by Ernie Forber, plus an opportunist drop-goal from Harry Taylor was enough to see the Recs through with an 8–0 scoreline. It was the first time during the season that the Recs had failed to cross their opponents' line, but they were not bothered and looked forward to the televised draw in seven days time. Meanwhile, both teams sat down to a hot-pot supper, during which the St Helens Junior Rugby League chairman Billy James produced a bottle to celebrate Recs' triumph. Walney Central's chairman thanked the St Helens club for their hospitality, both on and off the field.

Peter the prophet

The wheel had turned full circle. During their time as a professional outfit between the wars, St Helens Recs had themselves played amateur opposition three times in the Challenge Cup, winning two of the ties comfortably, although Castleford provided stern resistance at Wheldon Road in 1925–26, losing 18–12. Now it was Pilkington Recs who were the underdogs and before the draw, coach Peter Metcalfe told his squad that their opponents would be number 13 out of the bag. His players scoffed at this prediction, but, sure enough that is what happened. Recs would play Hull Kingston Rovers, with the match taking place at Craven Park in Hull.

The *St Helens Reporter* devoted a whole page to a preview of the big match, with photographs of the Recs players in training for the big day. Hopes were high for success. Interestingly, the draw could even have produced a St Helens 'derby,' with Saints coming out next after Hull KR.

It was many years since an amateur team had beaten a professional outfit and the Humbersiders were certainly no mugs, eventually finishing fifth in the Yorkshire League and 12th in the championship table. Possessing a fearsome pack, they were on average more than a stone heavier than the Recs and had in their ranks free-scoring winger Graham Paul, and full-back Cyril Kellett. The gulf was potentially very wide indeed, yet one thing was certain – the Recs, with their famous indefatigable spirit would fight to the very end.

Challenge Cup First Round
Hull KR 56 Pilkington Recs 8

Saturday 31 January 1961 at Craven Park, Hull

The rain bounced down overnight in Hull prompting more than 200 phone calls to Craven Park asking if the game was still on. At kick off there were still deep pools of water dotted around the pitch, which resembled a muddy morass. Such conditions clearly suited the larger Hull KR forwards, who tore into their opponents in a deliberate softening-up ploy in the first quarter. In a magnificent exhibition of backs-to-the-wall tackling, the Recs held their more illustrious opponents to 14–3 at the end of the first half, winning the applause and admiration of a normally parochial crowd.

The constant down-the-middle pounding by the Hull KR forwards took its toll, regularly drawing in three or four opponents and some slick passing created the overlap on several occasions. Les Hand, in particular, was left to cope with three or more attackers. He could do little more than try for an interception, something he attempted on three occasions, unsuccessfully, as opposite number Graham Paul notched a hat-trick in the first 20 minutes. Five minutes later, his luck changed as he plucked a pass out of the air in his own '25' and shot towards the try line. Paul, a noted sprinter, gave chase but couldn't stop him touching down midway between the posts and touchline to a great roar from the Recs supporters who had made the trip to Humberside.

Rovers continued their onslaught in a one-sided second half with a further 10 tries and seven goals. Yet they couldn't break the Recs' spirit, which was typified by skipper Archie Hill who, according to Alwyn Thomas in the *St Helens Newspaper* "tackled men five or six stones heavier than himself without a second thought and marshalled his men magnificently." Although Peter Eckersley scored a second try for the Recs, injuries had started to mount. Ernie Forber was knocked out after launching a flying tackle on his opposite number. He collapsed on the touchline and took no further part in the match.

Coach Peter Metcalfe, now a retired hotelier living in Filey had nothing but praise for his battered team: "I told them that even though they were playing professionals, they should throw the ball about and enjoy it. After half-time the Rovers pack really gave it to our lads. They were outclassed, but they did a fine job and didn't let anyone down in the slightest." Indeed, the Recs dressing room resembled a casualty clearing station after the final whistle – a measure of their never-say-die attitude.

This is a game still recalled by City Road diehards of a certain vintage, rekindling the famous Recs fighting spirit that was shown against Leeds in the Headingley cup tie of 1928.

Hull KR: Kellett, Paul, Major, Riley, Harris, Matthews, Elliott, Coverdale, Flanagan, Ackerley, Jenkin, Taylor, Trowell

Scorers: Tries: Paul 3, Riley 3, Harris 3, Taylor 2, Major, Flanagan, Elliott; Goals: Kellett 7.

Pilkington Recs: Tommy Vose, Eric Tierney, Harry Taylor, Ernie Forber, Les Hand, Bernard Hill (capt), Brian Johnson, Geoff Irwin, Chris Willett, Kevin Casey, Ken Parr, Peter Eckersley (1T), Bernard Dwyer.

Scorers: Tries: Hand, Eckersley; Goal: Forber.

Referee: Mr Welsby (Warrington)

Half-time: 14–3

Attendance: 3,025; *Receipts:* £364

The 1960–61 Challenge Cup run

Left: Tea at City Road after training before the Hull KR cup-tie. Left to right: Harry Taylor, Ernie Forber, Ken Parr, Peter Metcalfe (coach), Chris Willett and Peter Eckersley. (Courtesy Ernie Forber)
Right: Bringing on the heavy roller! Recs' forwards Peter Marr, Jeff Irwin and Peter Eckersley put in some hard training before the Challenge Cup tie against Hull KR. (Courtesy Mrs Irwin)

Recs versus Mayfield in the qualifying round. Back: Ken Parr; Bernard Dwyer; Kevin Casey; Chris Willett; Peter Eckersley; Jeff Irwin; front: Harry Taylor; Eric Tierney; Bernard Hill; Ernie Forber; Champ Johnson; Les Hand; Tommy Vose. (Courtesy Mrs Irwin)

Marching on

Although the Recs were disappointed not to make further progress in the Challenge Cup, like previous St Helens amateurs Unos Dabs, UGB and Vine Tavern who had reached the first round proper, the team made significant progress in two other competitions. On 26 April 1961, the Recs took on Rylands Recs in the final of the Lancashire Junior Rugby League Challenge Cup, a match played at Wilderspool, Warrington. Tom Watkinson of Manchester officiated, who was later to be the man in the middle for the Challenge Cup Final between Saints and Wigan at Wembley.

The Pilkington side were penalised for offside from the first scrum and Rylands' winger Affleck gave them a lead that was never relinquished. Nervous and impetuous, the St Helens side failed to control the ball in key attacking situations and were severely hit by the loss of Buck Casey just before the interval. He needed nine stitches in an eye injury at Warrington Infirmary, thus missing an amateur international appearance for England against France.

Tries by Rylands' McGann and Cullen increased the lead to 10 points by the interval and the game was finally put out of reach with a further three-pointer by Dennett just after the restart. It was only in the last quarter that Pilkingtons showed some cohesion, with Pilkington's man-of-the-match Ken Parr scoring a consolation try in front of the posts.

The 17–7 victory was Rylands' fourth in the competition and the disconsolate Recs were forced to turn their attentions to the St Helens Cup and a final clash with old rivals UGB to gain some consolation. This was a game full of open, expansive rugby. Yet it was the Recs pack who took command, with tries from Ken Parr, Geoff Irwin, Peter Eckersley and the majestic Bernard Dwyer. Forceful centre Ernie Forber added a further three-pointer, together with three goals. Eric Tierney chipped in with a drop-goal in Recs' eventual 23–4 triumph. Skipper George Hutton proudly received the trophy from Mr Seeley, a Rochdale Hornets director and the celebrations began in earnest, bringing to an end one of the most memorable seasons in the Recs' long history, as they won 31 out of 35 matches and scored 882 points in the process. The report of the Pilkington Recreation Club was fulsome in its praise, especially given the lean periods of the past decade: "They always manage to keep going despite their difficulties. We feel sure that their success last season will have the effect of stimulating interest and obtaining support in the future," it said.

Les Hand – flying down the wing

Ask this old-time fleet-footed winger to choose the most memorable try he scored for Pilkington Recs and he wouldn't have to think cap for long. For it came at Craven Park on Saturday 28 January 1961, when Recs faced Hull Kingston Rovers side in the Challenge Cup. Despite the defeat, Les Hand nevertheless enjoyed his moment of glory just before half-time as Recs trailed 14–0. For 5 feet 9 inches, 12 stone Les snapped up an interception deep in home territory and raced 75 yards to touch down, despite a desperate chase by Hull KR's Graham Paul. Hand had also scored against Mayfield (Rochdale) in one of the qualifying rounds.

A former Lowe House pupil born in Napier Street, Les worked at Pilkingtons and Sutton Manor colliery. Interviewed in 2007, he was a 76-year-old grandfather, living at Clock Face with wife Renee and was understandably a trifle hazy regarding a rugby league career that kicked off more than 50 years ago. A 'Bruk lad' in that he cut his oval ball teeth on that erstwhile stretch of barren land between Westfield and Talbot Streets, and was often joined in battle by brothers Charlie 'Chuck' and Eric 'Spike' Tierney, George and Ray Hutton, Brian 'Champ' Johnson, John Carrigg and Sid Glover.

Hand also turned out for St Anne's and Clock Face and was offered trials by Warrington, who were obviously impressed when Les breasted the tape just inches behind Brian Bevan during an impromptu sprint after a training session at Wilderspool. Les liked singing in local pubs and clubs, where his impersonations of crooner Frankie Laine had the punters rocking in the aisles. Les Hand also shared the mic with Ken Dodd on many occasions at 'Chessies' watering hole, Cooper Street, and has photographs to prove it.

A French frolic

Unfortunately, the Recs could not repeat their Challenge Cup heroics during the 1961–62 campaign, after a defeat at Cadishead in the fourth qualifying round. The team was still a relatively strong one, however, and remained unbeaten for almost two years in the League before going down 11–5 to Wigan St Patricks at City Road in March 1962. The Recs were still the best side in local rugby league, winning the St Helens and District League and Cup. The club was also able to launch an under–19 squad, who participated in the local Continuation League.

"I started the season after the Recs played Hull KR," remembers John Forster, a powerful front-rower later dubbed 'The Warhorse.' "It was in the under–19s and we had the likes of Geoff Fletcher, Alex Smith, Geoff Lea and Eddie Fuller in the side. Tommy Metcalfe trained us, but we were struggling for players at times. The club then decided to enter two teams in the open age competition to keep the lads who had come through the under-19s. When I went there the new social club hadn't been built. There was the old main stand and if you were early you would get the keys from the lodge and open up the dressing rooms. They were belting baths in there. The stand was roped off and not in use. Kids used to try and climb up the back of it."

There was definitely something to look forward to when Recs players and officials embarked on an end-of-season jaunt to France, where they played two games in Paris, one of which was won against a Select XIII at the Olympic Stadium – a truly trailblazing event. John Forster was one of the 33-strong party: "Scrum-half Archie Hill was always getting into scrapes and ended up losing his passport," he recalls. "They asked for any identification and he got back into the country using his labour club card. But there was worse to come afterwards. The sponsors refused to pay. All the lads at the Recs got billed for £20. But later on we were all getting injections to go to South Africa six months after, but Pilks called it off. I was an apprentice on £2 14s a week in those days, working at AECs. There was only a few of us who didn't work at Pilks then."

The problems at Pilkington Recreation mirrored depressing times both at home and abroad. Even the normally parochial local press talked about deteriorating relations between West and East and the possibility of nuclear conflict; 'Teenagers fed up and bored with life in St Helens' was a typical feature in the early 1960s and in early 1963 came the worst blizzards to hit the country since 1947. Pilkingtons faced a severe shortage of local sand for their glass-making process, as the top soil was frozen solid for many weeks and Tom Ashcroft in the *St Helens Newspaper* reported that the rugby league club was in trouble: "The St Helens rugby league club, Pilkington Recs has been barred from taking part in amateur rugby league for the time being. The decision has been made at Rugby League Headquarters as a result of incidents after a recent cup tie at City Road between Recs and Rylands Recs, a Warrington club. A senior rugby league referee, Mr J. Howker of Rochdale, who was in charge of the cup-tie, had a bucket of water thrown over him as he was leaving the field and a reserve player for Rylands had to receive hospital treatment for a head wound. I understand that the League's decision has been taken on the grounds that they have not received the full report called for. After the game, a Recs official said he saw the two teams enter the dressing room without incident. He had no knowledge of the incidents which had taken place. Although Pilks Recs lost, he said it was quite a clean game."

Although the matter was later sorted out, the club's reputation received an unwanted dent as a result – an unfortunate end to a season which was often disrupted by the adverse weather conditions. A new committee was formed, with Tom Metcalfe taking over as chairman and Jim Clitheroe transferring from chairman to secretary. On the positive side, the open age team retained the local League Championship and the players could look forward to superb new changing rooms and social facilities at the newly-built Windle City Club – another major milestone in the continuing development of the 'Resurgent Recs,' but in what was perhaps a sign of the times, things would not go smoothly.

Picture: Match poster for the Pilkington Recs versus Ile de France Select XIII Challenge match. The Recs are billed as St Helens FC. (Courtesy Ernie Forber)

Recs' former players and officials at a reunion in the late 1950s. Front-row notables include (right to left): Billy Greenall, Jumbo Highcock, Durdock Wilson and Albert Fildes. (Courtesy Denis Whittle)

Recs coach Peter Metcalfe, pictured in his Lancashire County amateur shirt.

OFFICIAL PROGRAMME — TWOPENCE

Daily Dispatch

SCHOOLS' RUGBY LEAGUE SHIELD COMPETITION

FINAL

ST. AUSTIN'S

ST. HELENS

versus

ALL SAINTS'

WIGAN

Wednesday, 21st May, 1952

on Messrs. Pilkington's Ground, City Road

(*by kind permission*)

KICK-OFF - 7 p.m.

Admission: ADULTS 6d. - SCHOLARS 3d.

City Road – the schoolboys' Wembley. Major finals and representative matches were played at Recs' headquarters after the Second World War, attracting huge crowds.

Blackbrook versus Recs at McDonald Avenue.
Harry Taylor, Chris Willett and Les Hand get ready to repulse a home attack.

8. 1963 to 1975: Triumph, turmoil and tragedy

Bingo, beat groups – especially the Beatles – and comedian Ken Dodd were all the rage in St Helens around 1963. Pilkingtons announced profits of £5,824,000 for 1963 and their 'secret' float glass process at Cowley Hill had been seen by Princess Margaret and Lord Snowdon in November of that year. There were protests at plans to axe the Liverpool-Wigan railway line as part of the Beeching proposals and older supporters of the St Helens Recs were saddened by the death of their former Great Britain second-rower Frank Bowen, at the age of 67. The Pilkington Recs team remained members of the St Helens and District Amateur Rugby League and enjoyed a mixed season in 1963–64. Knocked out of the Challenge Cup at home by Latchford Albion, the red, amber and blacks were also beaten by local rivals Blackbrook in the semi-final of the Lancashire Amateur Cup.

There was a chance to make amends, however, when both Recs and Blackbrook contested the open age final of the St Helens and District Amateur Rugby League at Bobby's Lane, Eccleston, home of the United Glass side. Both teams were at full strength, although that was not always the case during the season, with work commitments occasionally leading to a weakened team. For example, at Rainhill Ex-Services club, the Recs side was supplemented by several Rainhill players to make up the numbers.

Recs' strength lay in the power of their forwards, whereas Blackbrook's threequarter line had more pace. John Forster gave the Recs an early lead with a well-taken try, to which Peter Twist added a penalty goal after 10 minutes. This was followed immediately by a second Forster try and just before half-time Peter Marr scored a try that was converted by Twist. At 13–0, the game was effectively beyond Blackbrook's reach. Despite dominating the scrums after the break, Blackbrook could not penetrate the Recs defensive line. A further goal from Twist extended the lead, with Derek Hornby completing the scoring with a well-taken 30-yard try. It was sweet revenge for the Recs after their Lancashire Cup demise and the fifth time in a row that they had lifted the trophy, which was presented by Bill Chester, chairman of Blackbrook Sports Club.

Members of the St Helens and District Open Age League in 1963–64 included the following: Astley and Tyldesley, Blackbrook, Bootle Borough, Hill House Recs (Thornton), Kirkby Rangers, Liverpool Fire Service, Lower Ince, Pilkington Recreation, Rainhill Ex-Services and United Glass.

Recs' own 'Billy Fish'

Billy Simmons joined Pilkington Recs in 1964 and went on to become one of the greatest amateur scrum-halves of his generation, with town, county and international honours aplenty. Billy remembers encountering one of the more prominent members of the Recs team before he signed on at City Road: "I worked at Pilkingtons timber yard as did Ernie Forber and he was a really respected player and goalkicker. Every Wednesday the *Daily Herald* had an amateur rugby league review. Because it was a timber yard, you had to go down to a smoke room if you wanted to smoke or have your break. We used to go into this room and it used to have benches round. Often the headline in the paper was: 'Forber scores three tries and kicks seven goals,' or whatever. While Ernie was reading his paper, it always seemed like the headline was facing us. He was proud of his achievements. In the timber yard I used to look upon Ernie as a bit of a hero. He later joined the pro ranks at Liverpool City and Huyton.

Local Heroes – St Helens Cup winners 1963-64
Pilkington Recs line up before the Final against Blackbrook at Bobby's Lane
Back: Jim Clitheroe (secretary), Stan Birtles (chairman), Denis Brown, Derek Hornby, John Forster, Denis Carrigg, Eric Frodsham, Peter Marr, Peter Metcalfe (coach), Bob Cunliffe (kit man); seated: Jimmy Bailey, Les Kay, Eric Tierney, Peter Twist; front: Colin Whittaker, Archie Hill. (Courtesy Les Kay)

Rejuvenated Recs 1965-66
Back: Eric Frodsham, John Ledger, Peter Metcalfe (coach), Bob Cunliffe (kit), Kenny Jones, John Forster, Les Kay, Kevin O'Connor, Dave Conway, John Bracken, Colin Whittaker (trainer); front: Dave Ashton, Trevor Chesworth, Billy Simmons, George Parsons (Chairman), Terry Farrell, Dicky Evans, Alan Baldwin. (Courtesy Pilkington Brothers)

I remember my first game at Recs. When I went in the dressing room, Peter Metcalfe, the coach, asked me where I played. I was a scrum-half so that day, Nudger Bailey went to full-back and Archie Hill moved to stand-off. To be honest, despite the likes of Eric Frodsham and John Forster, it was still what I would class as a mediocre outfit. But then the team at Rainhill Ex-Servicemans packed in. We got a nucleus of players from there who came to join us at City Road – Alan Baldwin, Les Chisnall, Eric Chisnall, Joe Spooner, Terry Cross, Dennis Colbon – and we became a reasonable team. I thought that was the making of what went on in the future and we became well-respected. Talking of Eric Chisnall, I actually played my first game at Recs with Eric. He went to Rainhill Ex-Servicemens the first year I played. He broke his arm playing against us and he stopped playing until the arm was right and then he came to us with the rest of them.

The team spirit at the Recs was absolutely brilliant later on. The lads always met in Eric's [Frodsham] mam's house. She used to make her own pies and everyone got one. She was like a mother to everyone in the team. That really brought that team spirit out. At Christmas time you used to have a present on the tree – some toffee or your kids got some toffee. A lot of what the team went on to achieve was down to Eric's mum. I used to walk through the door and she used to say 'By the bloody hell... it's Billy Fish'. I used to go fishing pre-season when some of the lads used to go training, hence the nickname she gave me."

Billy, who bossed the scrum-base in the Recs team for many years was renowned for his great pace and opportunism. In a match against H. Faircloughs in November 1966, he scored a try that was applauded by team-mates and opponents alike. The *St Helens Newspaper* correspondent reported that: "Simmons scored the best try of the game. He ran from his own 25-yard line and lost the ball while running. He kicked the ball before it touched the ground, caught it again and outpaced the defence for a try." That was Recs' own 'Billy Fish', always capable of the unexpected.

Change once more

Before the start of the 1965–66 campaign, at a joint meeting of the St Helens, Warrington and Widnes Amateur Rugby League, it was announced that a new organisation, the South West Lancashire Amateur League would be formed. This also included teams from Wigan and Leigh and would, according to the press release, "make for complete fixture lists". The chairman was Bill Chester, whose team, Blackbrook were involved in a real blood-and-thunder epic with the Recs early in December, in atrocious weather conditions at City Road. The last quarter of the match saw three Recs players sent off in quick succession, as behaviour deteriorated.

By early February 1966, it was clear that there were some problems at the Recs club. The *St Helens Newspaper* stated that: "Pilkington's open-age team seem to be having difficulty in getting a team together these days. They were short for their game with Parkside but eventually both clubs managed to have a run out. Once again, Recs met with a heavy defeat. It is hoped that the players will rally round and bring some spirit back to a club that was the backbone of the league for so long."

At one stage, it seemed as though the rugby league section would fold, with chairman Stan Birtles leaving for a job with the firm in Glasgow. Former Saints second-rower George Parsons worked in the personnel department at Pilkingtons. Some 40 years later, he recalled the gravity of the situation: "There was a telephone call from Ken Griffiths, who was the recreation secretary at Pilkingtons. Ken had worked with me in job evaluation and he says 'there's been a Recreation meeting – they're talking about packing in the rugby league section.' Apparently there had been some, shall we say, areas of mismanagement and someone had thrown a bucket of water over a referee after a match. He said they were thinking of packing it in, but my name was mentioned [as a potential saviour]. 'We're not asking you to do it for life,' he said. 'But can you get down and get it organised?' So I said OK. Anyhow, I took over as chairman. I got in Jack Atherton to help us [a pre-war Recs player; former Warrington and Liverpool City forward, senior foreman in the electrical department at Ravenhead] and Todder Dickinson and Colin Whittaker were the coaches. Part of my job was simply PR. They didn't need to be told how to use a rugby ball – even as an ex-player I wouldn't do that. They needed other kinds of help, which, as a committee, we were proud to provide. Anyhow, they didn't pack the section up and we got them back on the road again and I eventually disappeared from the set-up.

One particularly pleasing aspect was seeing Eric Chisnall become a big name at Saints – he's in their Hall of Fame now – but I remember getting a telling off when he was attracting attention at the Recs. There was this fellow on the touchline and I asked him who he was. Apparently he was a Wigan scout, who said he was looking to see who the best players were to recommend to the Central Park club. I said 'What if a player, who might be the best prospect, has an off-day? I'll tell you who I think the best player is if you ask me.' Anyhow, he took our second-rower, Eric Chisnall, for trials. Meanwhile, I got a telephone call from someone at Saints who sounded quite upset. 'Have you lost your loyalty to Saints? You've got a good player there and you let him go to Wigan.' I said that I didn't tell Eric where to go, but Wigan had made him an offer and if the St Helens club improved it, he would probably end up at Knowsley Road which, of course, he did in the end. Eric was a good player for us, as was his brother Les, who played in the centre."

There was a real surprise for Recs' players when Alex Murphy started to train at City Road, during the summer of 1966. He was in dispute with St Helens at the time and volunteered to help with the training. "He was unbelievable," remembers Eric Frodsham. "He could run faster backwards than a lot of us could run forwards." Murphy was later photographed in an Australian jersey with City Road as a backdrop for the front cover of his autobiography *Saints Hit Double Top*, published in 1967.

The crisis at City Road had eased by the autumn of 1967 and the rugby league section was able to continue. Eric Frodsham, the Recs long-serving front-rower believes George was sent 'from above' [in the company] to sort out the problems, otherwise closure was a real possibility. He liked the lads and eventually the threat of closure was averted. The club never looked back after that. "It is true that there were some discipline problems," recalls Eric. "One of our players was accused of butting a referee, but it was a case of mistaken identity and the wrong lad carried the can. George brought in Jack Atherton and Eric Cunliffe as secretary, who was a local snooker referee. Mind you, George was brilliant for us at the club. We played in seven-a-side competitions and after one he took us to Wakefield Variety Club to see the star turn, Marion Montgomery, who was a top-class jazz singer – great times."

Indeed, the Recs had to begin to re-establish themselves among the local rugby league elite after Blackbrook had contested the First Round of the Challenge Cup against York in 1967 and newcomers Moss Bank, with a youngster named John Walsh in their ranks, won the Lancashire Cup in their first season. Recs coach in the late 1960s was former Saints half-back John 'Todder' Dickinson: "I knew a lot of the lads who played down there [at City Road] and, of course, I had played with Peter Metcalfe at Saints, who was coaching the first team at Pilks at the time. I was a glass-cutter at Pilkingtons. He was moving on – I think he

Recs under-19s circa 1970 with several players who later turned professional, including Phil Hurst (Salford, back row third from right), Dave Hull (St Helens, holding ball), Bob Bolan (Widnes, front row second left) and John Tabern (Huyton, front row fourth from right). John Lyon (fourth left on the back row) a capable wicket-keeper, later joined Lancashire CCC. (Courtesy Denis Whittle)

Recs players at the George and Dragon celebrating winger Dave Ashton's 21st birthday.
Back: Eric Tierney, John Evans, Les Chisnall, Jim Mustard; third row: Geoff Lea, Charlie Tierney (hidden), Ronnie Halliwell, Alan Baldwin, John Forster, John Dickinson (coach), Bill Sheils (coach), Mr Ashton; second row: Unknown, Colin Whittaker, Dave Ashton, Terry Cross, Fred Kenyon front: Billy Simmons, Jeff Gormley, Eric Frodsham. (Courtesy Eric Frodsham)

was going to Scarborough and he asked me if I wanted to have a go, so I thought 'why not?' I was still interested in the game. At the beginning of the season, I would tell the squad 'I can't run this team on 15 players. So some weeks you might well be the star man, but you will have to make way to let someone else have a game.' This was accepted and I had a panel of about 20 or more and no matter how good they were they always had to have a miss out. If you just had 15, with one injured and another working, you were struggling.

I remember some of the teams we played against, such as Rylands Recs and Crosfields from Warrington, Blackbrook, Mayfield and St Anne's from Oldham. Recs were in the Warrington League, but we still had the local St Helens Amateur League and St Helens Challenge Cup. We had many players who signed for professional clubs, such as Bob Bolan, who signed for Widnes, Johnny Wills [for Saints] and Les Chisnall [for Leigh]. They weren't there when I started, but we gradually got a good side together. We got one or two lads coming down to the Recs who played with other teams, such as Kenny Gill. Then there was Eddie Cunningham. He was only 17 and was regularly in the open age side. Eddie should have gone to Saints straight away, but they never came down to see him. Basil Lowe was the secretary at Knowsley Road and he used to ask me who was promising. I said, 'listen... come down and have a look at this lad Cunningham.' Six weeks later, Wigan signed him, for practically peanuts. Saints seemed to be very slow at coming forward in those days.

I finished in the early 1970s, when it became too much because I was working shifts, but I knew that the team would go to further success. They always listened to advice and realised that I was there to try and improve them. Some of the stalwarts were Jimmy Mustard, Kenny Cross, Sid Wright – he was one heck of a forward – Kevin Whittle, John Forster, Dave Hull and, of course, Jackie Pimblett, who captained the side for a spell."

A town in turmoil

The Recs finished on top of the Warrington and District League in 1968–69 and were beaten finalists in the Lancashire Cup against St Thomas's of Wigan 12 months later. "On paper, there was no way they should have beaten us," recalls Billy Simmons. "It was a wake-up call for us and a real turning point for the club. From then on nobody could ever question our attitude in a major final." Recs' captain was stand-off Kenny Gill, who later took the professional ticket with Salford. Billy Simmons remembers when Australian Tim Pickup came down to play with Pilkingtons. He had initially turned out for Blackpool Borough and played in the Ken Gee Cup as an amateur for the City Road club. Tim went back home and was eventually selected for Australia at stand-off. When they played against Great Britain in the third test in 1974, his opposite number was Kenny Gill – both former Pilkington players.

The Recs' run to the Lancashire Cup Final in 1970 was overshadowed by a strike at Pilkingtons, from March to May. This was the first time since the 1926 General Strike that the company had any problems with its workforce. At its peak, 6,000 production workers downed tools, demanding basic pay of £25 a week. They currently earned £15 for a 40-hour week. Ironically, a strike meeting was called at Knowsley Road and a photograph of the occasion, in the local press, was captioned thus:
Fixture – Pilkingtons Strike (Return meeting)
Venue – Knowsley Road rugby ground
Teams – Workers v The Company
Result – (after 65 minutes) No score

At its height, the dispute was plagued by violence and at one stage, 300 police were stationed outside the company's Grove Street works. Although matters were resolved by the end of May, the glass industry would bear permanent scars and emotions still run high nearly 40 years later. The strike resulted in a short-lived split from the GMWU trade union, with around 600 workers joining the newly formed Glass and General Workers Union. Management bought matters to a head with the new union, which took token strike action over recognition, resulting in the dismissal of the 600 members, half of whom did not get their jobs back. Pilkington Recs continued, despite the troubles. Yet within the next 12 months, the club would itself be embroiled by a tragedy, the effects of which are still felt to this day.

Recs' darkest day

Saturday 9 October 1971, dawned as a balmy autumnal morning at City Road, but the time honoured pitch was transformed into a scene of devastating tragedy that very afternoon, for the club was plunged into deep sorrow when skipper Jackie Pimblett sustained severe spinal injuries against UGB and died later in hospital.

Shorthanded up front, Recs switched 6 feet 14 stone Jackie – normally a back – to prop, and fate reared its ugly head when a scrum collapsed to leave him prostrate as the other forwards regained their feet. Coach John Dickinson raced to 26-year-old Pimblett's assistance. However it was immediately obvious to both Todder and the teams that this was an emergency situation. It is almost superfluous to state that the game was abandoned. Dickinson's findings were endorsed by St John's ambulance men Harry Middlehurst and Dennis Doyle who, having examined Jackie, ordered his removal to Providence Hospital from where he was transferred to a special unit at Southport's Promenade Hospital.

Meanwhile his devoted parents Harry – himself a former rugby league star – and mother Betty had been informed of their son's plight. Pimblett senior was rushed to his bedside by Billy Dingsdale, the former Warrington centre. Jackie was conscious on their arrival, but the full extent of his injuries had not been determined. He was subsequently diagnosed as having fractured the third vertebrae of the spinal column: essentially a broken neck. Despite emergency surgery, he died four days later, on Wednesday, 13 October. Team-mate Ken Cross later told the South West Lancashire coroner, Ronald Lloyd, exactly what had happened: "Jack was injured in the first 10 minutes of the game. He cut both knees and went off the field, but came back on soon after. After another 10 minutes, we packed down for a scrum. Jack was prop-forward. The ball was hooked out of the scrum, but three or four players collapsed on to the floor. Jackie shouted to us not to move him. We found that he was completely paralysed and he had to be carried off the field." Later a verdict of death by misadventure was recorded.

A glass-cutter at Pilkingtons, the popular Pimblett was survived by his wife Carol and sons Michael, aged seven, and Clifford, aged five, while the usual atmosphere of bonhomie at City Road gave way to one of encircling gloom for months to come. Testimonial matches in aid of Jackie's family were staged at Recs' ground and The Willows, Salford, while the Recs donated a player-of-the-year trophy which perpetuates the name of the never to be forgotten Jackie to this day.

All-round sportsman Jackie began his rugby league career at Rivington Road School, and was captain of the team that won the Ellison Cup and *Evening Chronicle* Trophy in 1958 in a line-up which included Saints' latter-day Hall of Fame member Jeff Heaton. Jackie also

Jackie Pimblett

Schoolboy star Jackie playing at Knowsley Road.
(Courtesy Pimblett family)

RL Veterans team at Salford, Sunday 16 November 1972 in aid of Jackie Pimblett memorial fund. Back: Roy Britch (Recs' secretary), Alan Prescott, Bob Dagnall, John Stopford, Vince Karalius, Ray French, Kevin Whittle (capt), Bill Chester (Recs' chairman) Mick Martyn; front: Frank Myler, Brian McGinn, Wilf Smith, John Dickinson, Glyn Moses, Brian Bevan. (Courtesy Eric Frodsham)

Both teams and officials line-up for a special match for the Jackie Pimblett Memorial Fund: Pilkington Recs versus St Helens League at City Road. (Courtesy Billy Simmons)

Recs 11 St Helens 'B' 8, Sunday 4 August 1974
Pilkington skipper Billy Simmons receives the Jackie Pimblett trophy from Harry Pimblett
(Courtesy Billy Simmons)

captained the town side and represented Lancashire versus Yorkshire. Given such a burgeoning talent, professional scouts beat a path to his door on him reaching 16, before he signed for Saints and made an 'A' team debut at that age.

Despite putting on weight, but blessed with a fair turn of speed, erstwhile loose-forward Jackie found himself on the wing for the Knowsley Road team, for whom he scored many spectacular tries for the 'A' team and was a competent deputy for the great Tom van Vollenhoven. But with a young family to feed, he realised that greater financial rewards could be earned by working rather than playing rugby, so he drifted away from Knowsley Road. However the lure of the oval ball was in his blood and legend had it that he flirted with rugby union at Moss Lane.

After a further dalliance with football, as a goalkeeper with the local NALGO team, he was back where he belonged with the XIII-a-side code, albeit at amateur level with Pilkington Recs, where his engaging personality, strength of character and leadership qualities quickly saw him appointed as skipper at City Road.

He was carried by members of the Recs' pack at his funeral and the team he led walked behind the coffin on the journey from his home in St Teresa's Road to St Thomas's Church. They all wore red, amber and black ribbons. On 18 October, the Saints players donated all their wages from the home victory against Oldham to the fund for Jackie's family.

It is indeed a tragic irony that Jackie Pimblett's untimely passing early in the 1970s occurred as his club stood at the threshold of the most successful period in its sometimes chequered history, particularly in the field of senior level Challenge Cup ties. Former chairman Bill Chester recalled that the Recs revival had really gathered momentum when Jackie was elected captain and committee member at the start of what became a tragic season for the City Road club.

Harry Pimblett – Jackie's dad

Arguably the oldest living Saint at the time of writing – he was 88 in 2007 – and residing in the Newtown district of St Helens, gentleman Harry Pimblett reflected on the vicissitudes of life that have seen him lose his only child, his beloved wife and his right leg through contact with the MRSA superbug – but he has certainly maintained his dignity.

Born in Cooper Street and a pupil at Windle School, Queen Street, he worked at Pilkingtons and for St Helens transport department, and played football for the YMCA before signing for Saints in 1938 for £30. But he had to play six first team games before picking up the money and a cash-strapped board kept him on five appearances for a long time. Six-footer Pimblett senior answered the call of King and Country by enlisting in the Welsh Guards in 1940 – the same regiment as Steve Llewellyn – and he served in North Africa and Italy, and was taken prisoner at Perugia during the bloody battle of Monte Cassino.

After being discharged from the Army, Harry cuddled Jackie for the first time when the toddler was just 18 months old. He then picked up the threads of a rugby league career left in tatters by the War, and marked his return to Saints with a 60-yard try when Wigan were defeated at Central Park. However, Saints lost against Warrington and Belle Vue Rangers over Easter 1947, so the players received two pay packets each containing £3 and another with £6 in it. Pimblett was deducted £4/18 in income tax and also forfeited three half-days holiday pay. Full-back-cum-winger Harry tackled the club about this in pointing out that, taking everything into account, playing in all three fixtures had put less than a fiver in his pocket. Secretary Bert Murray's reply was that Harry must have thought it worth it otherwise he would not have turned out.

Pilkington Recs circa 1971–72 line up at City Road. Back: Brian Collins, Joe Gleave, Todder Dickinson (coach), Geoff Phillips, Eric Peel, Joey Hull, Duggie Greenwood, Rufus Hill, Jimmy Mustard, John Forster, Eric Frodsham, Kevin Whittle, Terry Cross, Bob Dagnall, George Morrison, Tony Fairclough, Harvey Bolan; Front row: Andy Casey, Ken Cross, Ian Jones, Johnny McCabe, Bob Bolan, Billy Simmons, Colin Whittaker (trainer), Roy Britch (chairman). (Courtesy Billy Simmons)

On the verge of greatness: Recs line-up in front of the Windle City Club in their new red jerseys in 1971–72. Back: Jimmy Mustard, Joe Spooner, John Forster, Dave Hull, Geoff Phillips, Joey Hull, Eric Frodsham, Bob Dagnall, Terry Cross; front: Andy Casey, Geoff Gormley, Kenny Cross, Kevin Whittle (capt), John Finney, Ian Jones, Tony Fairclough;
front: John McCabe, Billy Simmons.
(Courtesy Billy Simmons)

Money, or rather the lack of it, was the root cause of Harry leaving Saints for Belle Vue Rangers following a career at Knowsley Road which, despite the demands of military duty, nonetheless saw him make 104 appearances and score 22 tries and kick three goals. While at Belle Vue Harry played alongside other players with a Saintly ring such as Stan McCormick, Eric Ayles, Jack Fearnley and Ray Price. Pimblett remained loyal to the Manchester-based club until its demise in 1954 when he hung up his boots at the age of 34.

His abiding memory with Rangers? Dropping a 45-yard goal in a 12–10 victory at Knowsley Road in 1947. His last word on his sorely-missed son who would now be 63 years old? "He was a real good lad and liked nothing better than bringing his Recs team-mates round to our house in Havelock Street for a meal cooked by me," recalled Harry Pimblett.

'A real purpose to succeed'

The death of Jackie Pimblett hit everyone associated with the Recs very hard indeed. Yet there was more tragedy to follow. "We lost three lads in 18 months," remembers Eric Frodsham. "Apart from Jackie, Eric Tierney died of a heart attack aged 39 playing for Prescot RUFC at Runcorn and the following Easter, Jimmy Mustard died of cancer. I was heartbroken."

"Jimmy was a really funny fellow to be out with," recalls Billy Simmons. "He had this saying. He would put up an 'up-and-under' and shout 'Catch the pigeon' and we used to fall about laughing. When we played tick in training, he would let you run to within two yards of the line and he'd tick you. They were sad times at the club, but what happened really galvanised the team and gave us a real purpose to succeed."

It was Jackie Pimblett's dream that the side could get into the first round proper of the Challenge Cup and the Recs duly beat Millom 26–11 in the final qualifying round at City Road, with tries from Rufus Hill, Tony Fairclough, John McCabe, Billy Simmons, Eric Frodsham and skipper Kevin Whittle. Ian Jones kicked four goals. The Recs had a new figure in the number nine jersey who guaranteed them a steady stream of possession from the scrums. Former Saints and Great Britain hooker Bob Dagnall, aged 39, had come down, initially, to train for the Jackie Pimblett commemorative match and with regular hooker Jeff Gormley out for the season, was persuaded to sign on for the club by Todder Dickinson.

Challenge Cup First Round
Bramley 19 Pilkington Recreation 5
Saturday 29 January 1972 at McLaren Field

The Recs drew Bramley at McLaren Field in the first round proper of the Challenge Cup and were given a civil send-off from the Town Hall Square by Mayor Charles Martin – a Saints director – and Lord Pilkington. Many telegrams were sent to encourage the team, among them, a personal one for Bob Dagnall, who celebrated his 40th birthday the following day. In freezing temperatures, the Recs tackled like demons early on and went in at half-time just 6–5 down. Bramley were so shattered that their chairman Bill Norfolk was forced to offer his team an increase in winning pay in the dressing rooms during the break. Yet the Yorkshiremen effectively won the tie on the hour, when, in sheer desperation, full-

The Challenge Cup tie at Bramley

Recs in new blazers and slacks are seen off by the Mayor, Councillor Charles Martin, the Mayoress and Lord Pilkington. The team played in new kit.

Back: Geoff Phillips, Bill Chester (chairman), Peter Burnett, Eric Frodsham, Brian Collins (committee), John Forster, Jimmy Mustard, Bob Dagnall, Kenny Cross, Tony Fairclough, Sid Wright, Roy Britch (secretary), Harry Middlehurst (first aid), Eric Tierney, George Morrison (PRO). Front row: Ian Jones, Rufus Hill, David Hull, Billy Simmons, Bob Bolan, Kevin Whittle (captain), Joey Hull, John McCabe.

Heartbreaker. The try that shattered Recs' hopes. Home scrum-half Astbury kicks through for Dewhirst (out of picture) to follow up and score. Referee Wood dismissed Recs' claims for offside.
(All photos and match programme courtesy Billy Simmons)

back Dewhurst followed a kick though and touched down, despite Recs' pleas that he was offside. The professionals took over from that point, eventually winning 19–5. But the Recs had earned the respect of the crowd for their gallant performance and were able to enjoy a beer or two afterwards, courtesy of a £10 donation from the St Helens Amateur League.
Bramley: Dewhurst, Goodchild, D. Sampson, Smith, Austin, Briggs, Astbury, M. Sampson, Price, McCurley, Cheshire, Idle, Wolford. Subs: Keegan, Craker
Scorers: Tries: Goodchild 2, Dewhurst, Austin, Astbury; Goals: Dewhurst 2.
Pilkington Recs: Bob Bolan, Joey Hull, Ian Jones, Dave Hull, Andy Fairclough; John McCabe, Billy Simmons; Eric Frodsham, Bob Dagnall, John Forster, Ken Cross, Sid Wright, Kevin Whittle (capt). Subs: Jimmy Mustard, Geoff Phillips
Scorers: Try: Hull; Goal: Jones.
Half-time: 6–5
Referee: Mr R. Wood (Barrow)
Attendance: 600

It is an indication of the good-humoured banter and team spirit that prevailed in the City Road dressing room in those times that no fewer than seven of the squad on duty at McLaren Field rejoiced in nicknames. These aliases apply to this day and are as follows: Phillips (Jethro), Forster (Doctor Spock), Dagnall (Uncle Bob), Wright (The quiet man), Jones (Jasper Carrot), Cross (Evel Knievel), and Frodsham (Big E), the last of whom readily supplied this light-hearted information.

Furthermore the roll-call of appendages doesn't end there, for centre Billy Hill was dubbed 'Rufus' due to his red thatch; handsome winger Eric Tierney 'James Bond'; full-back Peter Glover '101' because he was always on time when clocking off at Pilkingtons; scrum-half Brian Johnson 'Champ' because he always wanted to be a winner, and finally press correspondent George Morrison 'Denis Hartley', which resulted from his likeness to the Castleford prop forward. Later on, Denis Litherland became 'Nellie Pledge' because he worked in a pickle factory. No doubt there are many more that have been lost in the mists of time, or remain concealed in the long grass at City Road.

A Roses battle royal

The Recs were guaranteed a place in the First Round of the professional Players No.6 trophy in 1972–73, chairman Bill Chester proposed a 'mini-trophy' also be contested by the two amateur teams who had qualified for the Challenge Cup. Thus the Recs played home and away against a powerful Dewsbury Celtic outfit. The first match at Dewsbury RFC's Crown Flatt for the newly-instigated *Rugby Leaguer* Cup was refereed by top RFL official Eric 'Sergeant Major' Clay and ended in a 7–7 draw. In the second leg at Knowsley Road, in a match also refereed by a top official, Mick Naughton, the match ended in a 13–13 stalemate after extra time.

A toss of the coin meant that the third and deciding game in the competition took place at Dewsbury Celtic's Crow's Nest Park at the start of the 1972–73 season. In what was their first competitive match of the new campaign, Recs led 11–9 at half-time courtesy of tries from Andy Casey, Sid Wright and Jim Walker. However, former Hunslet half-back Johnny Halpin, the Celtic captain, scored four tries to seal an 18–12 victory for the Yorkshiremen and was presented with the trophy by David Hodgkinson, the *Rugby Leaguer's* editor. "We threw it away," sighed dejected skipper Kevin Whittle after the match, a reference to his team's occasionally slipshod handling. However, the Recs were now justifiably ranked among the top amateur teams on both sides of the Pennines.

Players No.6 Trophy First Round
Bramley 26 Pilkington Recs 5
Saturday 23 September 1972 at McLaren Field

Recs' Yorkshire hoodoo was to continue later in the campaign, when Bramley once again triumphed 26–5 at McLaren Field in the first round of the Players No.6 Trophy. The Recs showed their terrific fighting spirit for large parts of the encounter, although the larger Bramley pack gradually gained the ascendancy after the interval. In a closely-fought first half, the Recs trailed 10–5 and caused the home defence some major headaches. Indeed their only try, when Kevin Whittle and Billy Simmons combined to send Geoff 'Jethro' Phillips crashing over, was an absolute beauty, which Ray Shuker converted.

Phillips is still in awe of Kevin Whittle's ability and influence on the team. "He was outstanding," he remembers. "When I scored that try at Bramley, it was him going through. All I did was take the pass. Anywhere across the field he knew exactly what he was going to do – a fantastic player."

Bramley: A. Keegan, P. Clegg, A. Smith, M. Thornton, J. Austin, J. Hughes, P. Astbury, P. Jarvis, R. Price, A. McCurley, A. Cheshire, G. Idle, J. Wolford. Subs: Cain (for McCurley), ANOTHER.
Scorers: Tries: Smith 2, Clegg, Thornton, Hughes, Astbury; Goals; Keegan 4.
Pilkington Recs: Dennis Colbon, Jimmy Walker, Rufus Hill, Ian Jones, Ray Shuker, John McCabe, Billy Simmons; Eric Frodsham, Bob Dagnall, Geoff Phillips, Kevin Whittle (capt), Kenny Cross, Jeff Gormley. Subs: Andy Casey (for Jones), John Forster (for Gormley)
Scorers: Try; Phillips; Goal: Shuker.
Half-time: 6–5
Referee: Mr A. Fryer (Warrington)
Attendance: 750; *Receipts:* £133

Jeff Gormley, a BARLA international hooker was playing loose-forward that day, with Bob Dagnall in the hooking role. "Unfortunately, I got a knock on the head and had to come off," he remembers. "Afterwards in the bar, Bob was showing this young lad how he beat him in the scrums. I said 'Why are you telling this lad all your secrets, Bob? You've never told me anything.'

'Christ Jeff', he says, 'I thought you knew all about it. I'll show you in training on Tuesday.'

Bob was a big bloke, with short legs. He told me to pack down and try to get the ball, which I did. He says 'now try and get it again.' He came over and put his arm over me with all his weight pressing down so that my legs were effectively locked. I couldn't move – there was no chance I could strike for the ball. He says 'I don't need to show thee any more!' Those were the tactics I used for the rest of my career."

City Road colossus – that was big 'E'

Pilkington Recs legendary front-rower Eric Frodsham lives in Lingholme Road, opposite Recs' original 19th century playing pitch. Eric, all 5 feet 10 inches and 19 stone of him, bestrode the hallowed City Road turf for a record 25 years and now, at a sprightly 65, reflected on that remarkable saga in the red, amber and black jersey.

His childhood was in town centre Randon Street, near the Bruk. He has many memories he shares with brothers Jack, Stan and Les. They were watched over by devoted mum Mary, who hailed from nearby Napier Street. Elder sibling Stan also wore the Recs shirt as did his son Eric, who went on to coach the City Road squad. Completing the family oval ball circle, Eric junior's boy Gareth is currently keeping up the family's rugby league tradition with a place in Saints' Super League squad.

'Big E' waxed lyrical on both match days and training nights after which the players descended on the Frodsham abode, where good-natured mum served up chips, fish, 'tater' pies and endless cans of lager. Top management at the glass giants' factories also followed the fortunes of their team with great enthusiasm, none more so than club president David Pilkington who, when Eric was injured in Scotland, laid on transport home and the offer of treatment at Fairfield Hospital.

Another great occasion was when Sir (later Lord) Harry Pilkington invited the Recs squad and committee to a reception at his Windle Hall mansion to celebrate his 70th birthday. His step-daughter actress April Wilding and her actor husband John Stride were also present. "It was a visit we will never forget," recalled Eric. "The sheer grandeur of the house included paintings by Constable, Turner and Rembrandt, while the gardens were simply magnificent, and the lavish refreshments found us doing an Oliver Twist in asking for more. Furthermore our vice-president, Lady Mavis Pilkington proposed the toast to the Recs at a dinner in the team's honour which was held at the Lakeside Restaurant in Prescot Road in 1980. She amused and astounded the guests with her knowledge of rugby league," added 'Big E.'

Having played in the front row meant that Eric was in a good position to say who were the hookers he rated best in his time at City Road: "Lightning striker Bob Dagnall, Chris Willett and Jeff Gormley in any order you like," came the immediate reply. Eric also remembered some of the players and officials who have died. He fondly recalled Jackie Pimblett, Peter Marr, Derek Hornby, Jimmy Bailey, Jimmy Mustard, Colin Whittaker, Denis Carrigg, and 'Daggie,' plus back-room boys Bill Chester, George Morrison, Roy Britch and Vinty Matthews. Half-back Whittaker crossed the Rubicon to head for City Road from rugby union and, once there, promptly named his pet dog 'Rex!'

BARLA – A brave new world

On 3 May 1973, the formation of the British Amateur Rugby League Association (BARLA) revolutionised the amateur game, giving it autonomy from the Rugby Football League. Although considered as a rebel body when first formed, the organisation became an outstanding success, co-ordinating and developing the amateur game, especially at youth level. Another phenomenal achievement was the historic tour to Papua New Guinea, Australia and New Zealand in 1978, which included Recs players John McCabe, Joey Hull and Peter Glover. By breaking away from the RFL, BARLA became eligible for funding from the government's Sports Council, itself set up in 1972, which had provided as much as to £1 million to rugby union. There was also the need to establish a free gangway between the amateur rugby league and rugby union, and after 15 years of negotiation, this came to pass in 1987. BARLA controlled regional league and cup competitions and instigated the National Cup – something that Pilkington Recs would dominate for the next decade. Indeed, the growth of BARLA coincided with the rise of the Recs into one of the greatest amateur clubs the game has ever seen.

The Recs continued in the First Division of the North West Counties League, a structure born out of the government's county boundary changes at the start of the 1970s. Although by joining BARLA in those early days, the Recs were barred from taking part in the Challenge Cup, it was their reputation as cup fighters that gained them widespread acclaim in rugby league. The team gave due notice of their top-class credentials in the first

Lancashire Cup Winners 1974 versus Folly Lane at Knowsley Road
Back: Jimmy Harmer, Tommy Garvey, Eric Frodsham, Tony Fairclough, Rufus Hill, Billy Simmons (capt), Steve Smith, Jeff Gormley, John Forster, Geoff Phillips, Bob Bolan; front: Colin Whittaker (trainer), Andy Casey, John McCabe, Steven Simmons (mascot), Stuart Hill, Brian Edgerton
(Courtesy Billy Simmons)

Lancashire and Cumbria Cup Final under the aegis of BARLA, at Knowsley Road on 17 March 1974. Their opponents were Swinton's Folly Lane, no mean cup fighters themselves.

It was a tough encounter, typified by some terrific passages of open rugby and desperate defending. Rufus Hill opened the scoring for the Recs with a drop-goal, which was cancelled out by a penalty from McAtee. After Folly Lane registered the first try of the match, it was time for the Recs to show their mettle, with Sid Wright, Steve Smith and John Forster opening up the Folly Lane defence for the backs. A Hill penalty was followed by a magnificent try from Tony Fairclough, the result of brilliant approach work from Hill, Gormley and Simmons. Second-rower Steve Smith forced his way over with a terrific blind-side surge for a further three-pointer, which Fairclough improved. Folly Lane bounced back with a penalty try, awarded by referee Dennett after obstruction on Folly Lane's winger. McAtee's goal put his side level, at 10–10. Pilkington again swarmed forward and it was scrum-half Simmons who took up the attack, feeding Hill, who slipped a great pass to Fairclough who scored in the corner.

Folly Lane reduced the deficit to 15–13 after the break, but the Recs rose to the occasion once more when Sid Wright set the backline in motion. McCabe, Hill and Simmons handled superbly to put Fairclough in for his second try. A further penalty from Fairclough was followed by more crisp handling for Stewart Hill to complete the scoring and a memorable 23–13 victory for the Recs. It was the start of a dynasty of success in cup rugby for the club over the next decade, which was to earn them an awesome reputation in amateur circles – and beyond.

Going national

One disappointing aspect of the 1973–74 campaign was the side's 4–3 reversal at the hands of the Cumbrian team Hensingham, courtesy of a last-minute drop-goal in the third round of the newly established BARLA National Cup. It was clear that individually and collectively the team was good enough to lift the prestigious trophy at the second attempt in 1974–75. The Recs began with a convincing victory against local rivals St Helens B, before traditionally tough opponents Latchford Albion fell at City Road in the second round. Next, Reckitts (Hull) were defeated 13–7. Then followed a real test – a titanic Roses clash away to competition favourites Dewsbury Celtic, who were unbeaten for 26 matches. Despite fielding several former professionals, the Yorkshiremen were outplayed in every department by a Recs team hitting form at just the right time. The final score of 21–6 did not flatter the visitors.

Stand-off John McCabe and captain Sid Wright were the stars as Langworthy were dispatched 26–0 with relative ease in the quarter-final, leaving Cumbrian outfit Egremont between the Recs and their first National Cup Final. A totally comprehensive 27–7 victory, including a hat-trick from winger Andy Casey ensured a final place against Lancashire rivals Mayfield of Rochdale, the side who had knocked the Recs out of the Lancashire Cup 17–11 earlier in the campaign. The Final was originally scheduled for early April at Knowsley Road, but a waterlogged pitch saw the date rearranged for the following month – something that was to Recs' advantage, because Mayfield's big pack were more suited to boggy conditions.

Frank Martin's report, which follows, in the *St Helens Star* captured the essence of a superb advert for the amateur game and the greatest night for the Recs since their reformation in 1949:

Two sent off as Recs win Cup
Pilkington Recs 22 Mayfield 4

"Pilkington Recs brought the National Amateur trophy to St Helens when they won the BARLA Cup Final at Knowsley Road on Friday. Although the score suggests an easy victory it was only at threequarter time that Recs stamped their authority on the game and scored 13 points. Up to this stage Mayfield had always look capable of snatching victory despite the fact that Recs. had so much of the play. Before a crowd of almost 2,000 Rochdale kicked off', in ideal conditions and the early stages saw both sets of forwards testing each others strength. Recs full back Bolan came up in support and was only held inches short of the line. This was the signal for an all out attack but Mayfield defence held. From a penalty 45 yards out Colbon put Recs ahead and after 10 minutes this lead was increased when Simmons made a half break and put McCabe over by the post. Colbon kicked his second goal. Mayfield immediately came back strongly and tackling was keen to keep them from scoring. Their captain Miller was prominent at this stage directing the attack and was well supported by the mobile hooker McGuigan. Mayfield prop forward Kettleton was sent off the field when he felled Edgerton. To the surprise of the crowd Edgerton was also despatched to the dressing room after being revived.

Miller reduced the deficit when he converted a penalty awarded for obstruction near the posts and the half ended with the score at 9–2 points. So far Recs had matched the strength of the Mayfield pack and Simmons and McCabe had been able to dominate at half back. From the restart Bolan again supported an attack to race clear at half way. In a brave attempt to stop a score stand off Edwards was injured and was carried off. Although weakened by this loss Mayfield repeatedly attacked with good passing and were rewarded when substitute Moore kicked a penalty goal to close the gap to 9–4.

With only a try and goal separating the sides now play swung from end to end and with a little steadier finishing either side could have scored. In the end Recs. prop Forster was the one to make the break when he crashed over near the posts from 10 yards out. Colbon who was the best forward on view converted the try.

Spurred on by this score Recs. began to throw the ball about and within five minutes had scored a further try when Bolan made a brilliant 40 yard run to send McCabe in for his second try which Colbon again converted. Victory was now assured for Recs and Hull rounded off the scoring when he touched down at the corner. The final whistle sounded as Colbon's attempt narrowly failed.

Man-of-the-match award went to Recs stand-off John McCabe but there must have been several close contenders from both sides for this distinction. After the match, the BARLA cup was presented to Recs' captain Wright by St Helens RLFC chairman Councillor Charles Martin." It was clearly worth the ground admission price of 20p, and 10p for children.

Second BARLA National Cup Final

16 May 1975 at Knowsley Road, St Helens
Pilkington Recs: Bob Bolan, Joey Hull, Rufus Hill, Terry O'Neill, Andy Casey, John McCabe, Billy Simmons, John Forster, Jeff Gormley, Geoff Philips, Dennis Colbon, Brian Edgerton, Sid Wright (capt). Subs: Alan Shea (for Simmons 65 minutes); Eric Frodsham.
Scorers: Tries: McCabe 2, Hull, Phillips; Goals: Colbon 5.
Mayfield: Schofield, Power, Reilly, White, Markham, Edwards, Standring, Kettleton, McGuigan, Garfield, J. Ashworth (capt), Earle, Miller. Subs: Moore (for White half-time), Mills (for Garfield 76 minutes).
Scorers: Goals: Miller, Moore.
Half-time: 9–2
Referee: J. Easter (Hull)
Attendance: 2,000 (est.)
Man of the match: John McCabe (Pilkington Recs)

A job well done

Winning the National Cup capped the best-ever season for the club to date in the amateur game, during which time the team won six out of the eight competitions entered. Apart from this jewel in the crown, the National Cup, the team won the North West Counties Division One trophy, beat Woolston Rovers to win the Jack Fleming Trophy, the Jack Pimblett Cup, the Eric Bromilow Cup and Jack Earlam Cup, the last awarded for sportsmanship and the way in which a club is run. Their success was acknowledged at a special civic reception at the Lakeside Restaurant, on Prescot Road, when the guests included Lord and Lady Pilkington. New secretary Roy Britch talked of the future and the team's participation in the first round of the John Player trophy, together with the launch of a second team, which had been in existence for the past season. "Most of the credit must go to the coach, Colin Whittaker and the trainer Austin Gillin," he added. "They worked very hard with the lads and Pilkington must be one of the fittest amateur teams in the country." The Recs had come through the most difficult time in their history by playing for the memory of their former captain and colleague Jackie Pimblett. His tragic loss had ultimately been a tremendous source of inspiration to everyone at City Road – and he will forever hold a special place in the hearts of all those associated with Pilkington Recs.

Beating Rochdale Mayfield in the National Cup

BARLA Cup winners versus Mayfield. Back: Billy Simmons (capt), Eric Frodsham, Sid Wright, Geoff Phillips, John Forster, Jeff Gormley, Terry O'Neill, Dennis Colbon; front: Brian Edgerton, Alan Shea, Andy Casey, John McCabe, Bob Bolan, Joey Hull, Rufus Hill. (Courtesy *St Helens Reporter*)

John McCabe scores one of his two tries in the match – a man-of-the-match performance. (Courtesy John McCabe)

9. 1975 to 1978: The team of the Seventies

The formation of the British Amateur Rugby League Association was a terrific boost for the amateur game, after years of relative decline. Pilkington Recs certainly prospered under the BARLA banner. In the first nine seasons of the new organisation, from 1973 to 1982, the Recs played in nine major finals, winning every one – an astonishing record. This included four BARLA National Cups, four county cups and an inter-county challenge trophy.

In 1975–76, rugby league was enjoying a golden era in St Helens, with the Recs purveying all that was best in the amateur game and at professional level, the Saints completing a marvellous Challenge Cup and Premiership double. This was the famous 'Dad's Army' team – which included former Recs stars Eddie Cunningham, Dave Hull and Eric Chisnall. The Recs had a 100 per cent record in league matches, winning the North West Counties Division One title outright. The second team also had its share of glory, being runners-up in the North West Counties Division Three. There were some disappointing moments, however, such as the club's agonising 14–13 exit in the fifth round of the BARLA National Cup – now the Tom Mitchell trophy – against eventual winners Ace Amateurs of Hull. Easy wins over Widnes B, Crosfield and Roose from Barrow were followed by an 18–9 win over Clarence Hotel from Hull before the narrow loss to Ace Amateurs. The Hull side beat Blackbrook in the semi-finals and went on to win the competition by beating Ovenden.

Player's No.6 Trophy First Round
Barrow 16 Pilkington Recs 9
Saturday 27 September 1975 at Craven Park

By winning the BARLA Cup the previous year, the Recs were included in the Player's No.6 Trophy and were drawn away to Barrow. This was going to be a tough clash, as the Shipbuilders were one of the top sides in the Second Division. However, the famous Recs spirit prevailed and at half-time, the home team were 9–2 ahead through a try and three goals from former Wigan star Colin Tyrer, to a penalty from Recs' Dennis Colbon. A chance to narrow the gap failed when Rufus Hill fired a pass to Brian Edgerton, but the ball bounced off his chest with the line virtually at his mercy. It was stand-off John McCabe who brought the Recs back into contention with a fabulous 40-metre dash to the line to score. Colbon's conversion, followed by a penalty, made it 9–9. It was still level with just 10 minutes to go, but the Recs defence was breached by a try from Tyrer under the posts, which he converted. Referee Court dismissed claims that the ball had been bounced over the line. A further Tyrer penalty sealed Recs' fate, although it had been a terrific display of courage from the amateurs. Barrow went on to finish the campaign as Second Division Champions and over the next few years would become a side noted for their cup exploits.

Barrow: C. Tyrer (capt.), P. Clegg, K. Knight, D. Jackson, K. O'Brien; R. McConnell, F. Jones, S. Hogan, H. Crewdson, J. Perry, P. Cavanagh, J. Clough, P. McLean. Subs: Leake, E. Szymala.
Scorers: Tries: Tyrer 2; Goals; Tyrer 5.
Pilkington Recs: Bob Bolan, Andy Casey, Rufus Hill, Alan Shea, Joey Hull, John McCabe, Billy Simmons, John Forster, Jeff Gormley, Steve Smith, Brian Edgerton, Dennis Colbon, Sid Wright (capt.). Subs: Terry O'Neill, Geoff Phillips.
Scorers: Try: McCabe; Goals; Colbon 3.
Half-time: 9–2
Referee: Mr T. Court (Bradford)
Attendance: 612

As North West Counties Division One champions for 1975–76, the Recs' success was reflected in the selection of scrum-half Billy Simmons (vice-captain) and winger Joey Hull for the England team to play against France at Salford on 21 March 1976. England won 16–9. It was the first cap for Hull, a powerful and direct finisher, who was to gain further honours at amateur level and would, like Simmons, cement his position as a Recs all-time great. Representative rugby was held in high esteem by the players. "In the great team of the 1970s, a lot of lads could have made pro-rugby but didn't," remembers Billy Simmons. "There was not a lot of money in the game. People were not getting paid high wages for playing and the majority had a job while they played professionally anyhow. A lot of the lads could have turned [professional] but didn't want to, especially if they were getting town, county and international honours. You could play for Great Britain and get trips to France. John McCabe, Peter Glover and Joey Hull went to Australia and they weren't going to throw that up just for the sake of a professional ticket. A lot of the lads preferred to stay as amateurs and have that recognition."

Rebuilding for glory

For the amateur players, however, there was always the burning ambition to get one over a professional team. Despite their burgeoning reputation as cup fighters in the BARLA county and National Cup competitions, Pilkington Recs were eventually beaten to a place in history by Yorkshire side Cawoods, who defeated Halifax 9–8 in a first round Player's No.6 Trophy match at Thrum Hall in 1977 – the first time that an amateur club had beaten professionals in a competitive game since 1909. Despite this, the Recs were more than capable of producing their own shock result and could pick from a strong, experienced squad of players, with their 'A' team stronger than most clubs' first teams.

For the 1976–77 campaign, Austin Rhodes was brought in as coach – a vastly experienced player at club and international level with St Helens, Leigh and Swinton. Rhodes had also coached Swinton in the First Division two years previously. Peter Glover, a rock-solid full-back and reliable goalkicker, was signed from UGB, together with centre Jim Sheffield and second-rower Les Chisnall, who had professional experience with Leigh. Recs were particularly strong in the centres, with Billy Hill, Bob Bolan and Alan Shea vying for places. The pack was formidable at BARLA level, with Ken Cross, Geoff Phillips and veteran John Forster all available for a tough-as-teak front-row, together with livewire hooker Jeff Gormley. Former Leigh forward Alan Speakman and goalkicker Dennis Colbon were also integral members of the engine room. Then came the marvellous midfield trio, featuring scrum-half Billy Simmons, stand-off John McCabe and loose-forward and captain Sid Wright, probably the best combination in the amateur game – and the equal of many in the professional ranks. The Recs had players for the occasion, especially when the going got tough. At Wigan St Patricks, in the North West Counties competition, they found themselves 14–10 down with just two minutes left. Then a wonderfully judged kick by Sid Wright got them to within five yards of their opponents' line. Jeff Gormley heeled expertly from the scrum, Wright picked up and was held just short. At the next play-the-ball, Simmons put winger Aldred in for a try in the corner. It was down to Peter Glover to send the ball floating majestically between the posts to give the Recs a 15–14 victory.

The club was in the mood to collect some silverware and on an atrocious night in late December at Knowsley Road, the Recs beat Leigh Miners Welfare to lift the Lancashire and Cumbria county cup, enabling the team to be put into the draw for the First Round of the Challenge Cup in the New Year.

Lancashire and Cumbria County Cup open age Final
Pilkington Recreation 17 Leigh Miners Welfare 0
Friday 15 December 1976 at Knowsley Road
Pilkington Recs: Peter Glover, Andy Casey, Rufus Hill, Alan Shea, Joey Hull, John McCabe, Billy Simmons, John Forster, Jeff Gormley, Ken Cross, Brian Highcock, Dennis Colbon, Sid Wright (capt). Subs: Jimmy Sheffield; Les Chisnall (for Colbon 12 mins).
Scorers: Tries: McCabe, Simmons, Wright; Goals: Glover 4.
Leigh Miners Welfare: Nixon; Corless, Warburton, Roberts, Cooke; Rowe, Riley; Evans, Harris, Dowling R, France, Gaskell, Webster. Subs: Marsh (for Corless 70 mins); Whittaker (for France 30 mins)
Half-time: 15–0
Referee: Mr R. Whitfield (Widnes)
Attendance: 500

Recs' name came out of the hat followed by those mighty cup-fighters Wigan. The tie would be played at Knowsley Road on 13 February 1977 and created enormous media interest. Indeed, some older supporters recalled the last time the two sides had met in the competition, in the Recs' last season in 1938–39, when the red-amber-and-blacks were narrowly beaten 8–3 in front of 14,000 at City Road. Things were different now, of course, although Wigan were in the process of rebuilding and hopes were high of a giant-killing.

But preparation for the cup tie was hampered by lack of match action. The last first team fixture had been against Crosfields three weeks before, although five had played county rugby and the remaining squad members had helped out the 'A' team. Another factor, according to Kenny Cross, was shift work. "Training was really difficult for those lads who were on shifts," he remembers. "The lads who worked at Triplex, like Sid [Wright], Johnny McCabe and Rufus [Hill] had to train one or two mornings at Ruskin Drive, rather than Tuesday and Thursday evenings. So the team rarely trained together, even for the big matches. Yet you knew basically what your job was when you got onto the field, so you just had to maintain your fitness as best as possible."

The Recs were also in the media spotlight, appearing on BBC's *Look North* programme, to add extra 'spice' to the pre-match build up. "The day we played Wigan, we met at the Bottom Nogs [Nag's Head] in Knowsley Road," remembers Billy Simmons, "and the landlord, Eric Halliwell gave us all a sherry." Then it was down to Knowsley Road to see a huge crowd assembling, which was to number some 11,000 as kick-off time approached.

Rugby League Challenge Cup First Round
Pilkington Recreation 4 Wigan 10
Sunday 13 February 1977 at Knowsley Road

The Recs' major ploy was to unsettle their more prestigious opponents by tackling like terriers, something that was evident throughout the 80 minutes. A good start was also essential and they got it after just seven minutes, when Wigan's international front-rower Brian Hogan was penalised for ball-stealing. Full-back Peter Glover calmly slotted the ball between the posts from more than 35 yards out to give the Recs a two-point advantage. The huge roar that greeted the goal clearly had an inspirational effect on the home side. Recs tore into their opponents with a vengeance. Experienced players like Rufus Hill, Billy Simmons and Sid Wright began to take charge. Wright raced through from a delayed pass from Simmons only to be halted inches from the line – a vital chance that went against the Recs. Les Chisnall was penalised for offside under the Recs posts, but Wigan's ace kicker George Fairbairn fluffed the simplest of chances, much to the huge crowd's delight.

Just before the half-hour mark Wigan struck back with a try from prop-forward Alan Doran, from a set-piece move and he was immediately engulfed by his delighted colleagues, almost as if they had won the trophy, rather than just taken a one-point lead against an amateur side. A nervous Fairbairn again placed his conversion wide of the mark. Recs began the second half with the same determined attitude and were duly rewarded for their constant pressure when Hogan was again penalised. Glover belted over a magnificent long-distance effort to wrestle back the advantage. "We knew Brian Hogan, who was a Blackbrook lad," remembers hooker Jeff Gormley. "He cut up a bit rough in the match and all he would say was 'It's my job – that's what I'm paid for'. There was one almighty clash of heads between him and Johnny Forster, who wasn't too pleased about it."

At 4–3 down, Wigan looked increasingly more ragged and desperate for inspiration. Fairbairn missed two more kickable chances, but as the game reached the last 10 minutes, there was disaster for the Recs, when Joey Hull was adjudged to have interfered at a play-the-ball. Fairbairn did not miss this time and with three minutes left on the clock, Melling dived over near the posts for a try that ensured victory. Fairbairn added the extras. It was desperately unlucky for the Recs, who had matched Wigan in the forwards, with Wright, Chisnall and Kenny Cross prominent. Simmons and McCabe were outstanding at half-back and the threequarters, typified by Shea and Casey, tackled relentlessly.

Although Wigan had dominated the scrums 2–1, the Central Park side were very often outplayed by their opponents. For the Pilks lads it was a mixture of frustration and sheer elation. "Fantastic, terrific, unbelievable," were the first words from chairman Roy Britch. "It was without doubt the greatest day in the club's amateur history. If I had been told before that we were going to get beaten 10–4 then I would have settled gladly for that result. But after seeing the game I was disappointed because we were better than that." Clearly the penalty decision against Joey Hull was the turning point, yet people still argue about its validity to this day. The last words were left to coach Austin Rhodes: "I asked those lads to go out and die for each other. And they were prepared to do just that."

Pilkington Recs: Peter Glover, Andy Casey, Rufus Hill, Alan Shea, Joey Hull, John McCabe, Billy Simmons, John Forster, Jeff Gormley, Ken Cross, Dennis Colbon, Les Chisnall, Sid Wright (capt). Subs: Jimmy Sheffield (for Hill 40 mins); Alan Speakman (for Colbon 72 mins).
Scorer: Goals: Glover 2.
Wigan: G. Fairbairn, J. Hornby, Keiron O'Loughlin, B. Francis, G. Vigo, B. Coyle, J. Nulty, B. Hogan, R. Martland, A. Doran, Kurt Sorenson, B. Irving, B. Melling. Subs: A. Taylor, T. Hollingsworth
Scorers: Tries: Doran, Melling; Goals: Fairbairn 2.
Half-time: 2–3
Referee: Mr Beaumont (Huddersfield)
Attendance: 11,261
Man-of-the-match: Billy Simmons (Pilkington Recs)
(Match programme illustration Courtesy Billy Simmons)

Ironically, Wigan faced their old rivals Saints at Central Park in the second round and were beaten 9–4 in front of more than 20,000 fans. What might have been. Except for the rub of the green it could have been a return to Knowsley Road for the amateur cup kings and a derby clash par excellence, recalling all the excitement of the pre-war days.

Recs in the 1970s at City Road. Back: Tony Fairclough, Eric Frodsham, Eric Peel, Bob Bolan, John Forster, Terry O'Neill, Brian Edgerton, Geoff Phillips; front: Billy Simmons, Sid Wright, Rufus Hill, Johnny McCabe, Joey Hull. (Courtesy Eric Frodsham)

A congested fixture list left Pilkington Recs struggling in the latter stages of the season and they had no option but to release their grip on the North West Counties Division One title by cancelling their four outstanding league fixtures. In the BARLA National Jubilee Cup they failed at the semi-final stage at the hands of the National Dock Labour Board outfit from Hull and three days later lost 18–15 against a powerful Leigh Miners Welfare side in the Final of the Greenall Whitley Cup – a magnificent effort, despite the absence of seven regular players. A memorable campaign was reflected in the club's presentation evening, with special guest John Lyon, the former Recs' hooker who was Lancashire County Cricket Club's wicket-keeper. The awards were as follows:

Player of the Year: Billy Simmons
Clubman of the Year: Rufus Hill (first team player and under-18 coach)
Colts' Player of the Year: Malcolm Smith
Club Loyalty Award: Brian Keating

Four players – Simmons, McCabe, Hull and Glover, plus trainer Colin Whittaker received international badges after being selected for the Great Britain squad that played France in Bastia on Corsica. The same men received county badges, together with Sid Wright and Alan Shea – an impressive achievement indeed.

(Match programme courtesy Billy Simmons)

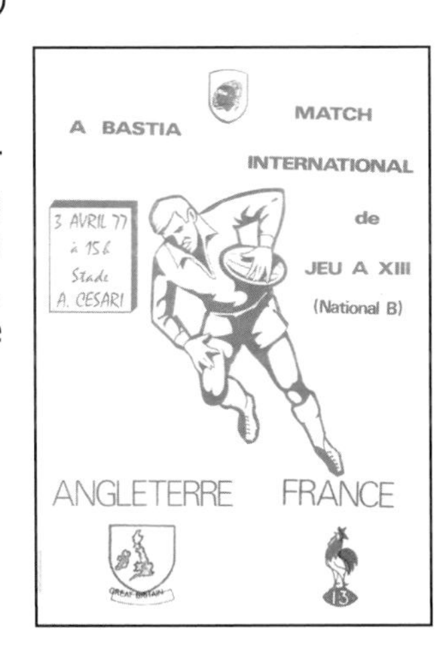

Simply the best

The Recs were now one of the most successful amateur rugby league sides ever seen in Britain. Confidence among the squad was sky high and further success was to be forthcoming. Indeed, the Recs came within an ace of glory against a virtually full-strength Saints in a special charity match at Knowsley Road in August 1977 on behalf of the Queen's Silver Jubilee Fund. The 23–17 scoreline barely reflected the visitors' dominance throughout the 80 minutes. Recs, who included former Saints front-rower Jon Stephens in their ranks, scored tries from Kenny Cross and Jeff Gormley with three goals from Glover, two from Hull and a Simmons drop-goal.

By December, the Recs had progressed to the County Cup Final – a tough proposition against Latchford Albion, a fixture played in enemy territory at Wilderspool Stadium in Warrington. Before this, however, both Recs first and 'A' team contested the Eric Bromilow Cup Final (previously known as the St Helens Cup), with the reserves giving a good account of themselves before going down 28–10. Then it was over to Warrington for the Final a week later.

Forshaw's Lancashire and Cumbria open age Cup Final Pilkington Recs 12 Latchford Albion 0

Sunday 11 December 1977 at Wilderspool Stadium, Warrington

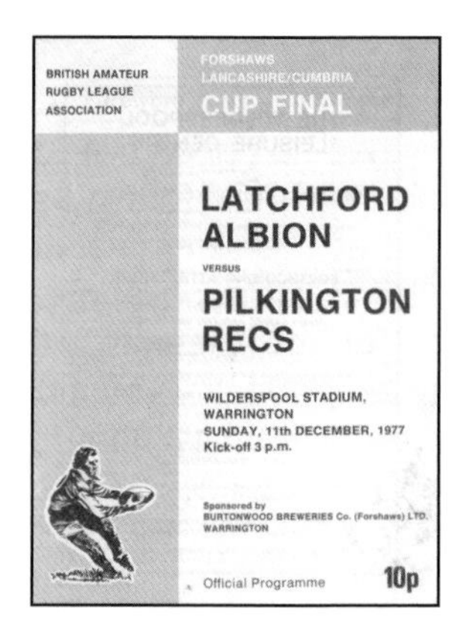

The match proved to be a one-horse race, however, as the Recs controlled the game from the start. Latchford's ill-discipline was penalised by two Peter Glover goals and after just seven minutes, a break from McCabe on half-way was taken on by Shea, who put Rufus Hill in at the corner. In the 24th minute, Billy Simmons scampered over direct from a play-the-ball. Glover's conversion gave his team an unassailable lead. "They've been calling us Dad's Army," quipped secretary Brian Woodward. "But we've won the trophy without conceding a try in any of the previous rounds." Defence was undoubtedly the key to success, against a big, powerful team. "They really towered above us, but we still beat them," remembers John Forster. It was a typically physical game of that time. "This was one of our best results," recalls Billy Simmons. "Their boss, Danny Sixsmith came over to us and said that we were the best side in amateur rugby. I'm not going to knock the modern-day game, which is a very good one, but this was in the days when if somebody ripped your head off, it was a good tackle. Latchford were tough opponents. Everybody knew when we got there that it was going to be 'hey lads hey.' They never scored."

Pilkington Recs: Peter Glover, Andy Casey, Rufus Hill, Alan Shea, Joey Hull, John McCabe, Billy Simmons, John Forster, Jeff Gormley, Steve Smith, Brian Highcock, Dennis Colbon, Sid Wright (capt). Subs: Eddie Fuller (for McCabe 70 mins); Bob Williams (for Simmons 70 mins)
Scorers: Tries: Hill, Simmons; Goals; Glover 3.
Latchford Albion: Linaker, Robinson, Williams, Shingler, Miller, Kelly, Green, Wright, Acomb (capt), Edmunds, Dykes, Williamson, Thorne. Subs: Delooze; Doherty
Half-time: 12–0

Referee: Mr Holgate (Barrow)
Attendance: 2,000 (est.)
Man-of-the-match: Steve Smith (Pilkington Recs)
(Match programme courtesy Billy Simmons)

Rugby League Challenge Cup First Round
Pilkington Recs 22 Castleford 23
Sunday 26 February 1978 at Knowsley Road

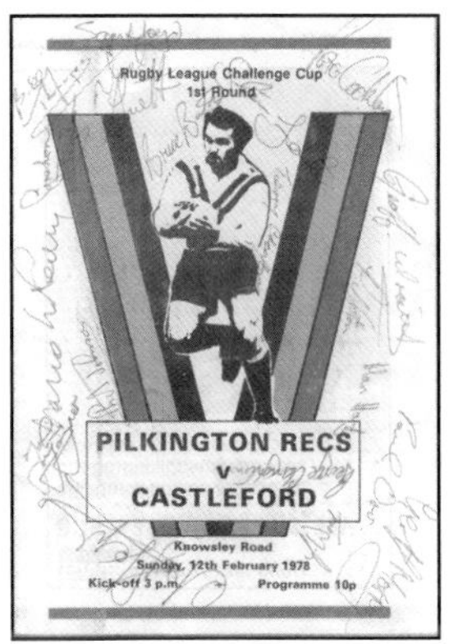

Victory against Latchford placed Recs in the Challenge Cup draw again. Their wish for a clash against a Second Division side was thwarted when they were paired with Castleford at home, which meant another fixture at Knowsley Road – and another bumper crowd.

If the Latchford game highlighted the virtues of defence, the cup-tie against Classy Cas will long be remembered for its sensational attacking rugby and sheer drama, when the Recs once again covered themselves in glory and brought great acclaim to amateur rugby league. Another good crowd at Knowsley Road saw the Recs in an uncompromising mood and willing to throw the ball about at every opportunity. Such enterprise saw the side ahead by 10 points after just 11 minutes. Joey Hull's brilliant interception try from the Castleford '25' was followed by a typically barnstorming effort from skipper Sid Wright. Both tries were converted by the immaculate boot of Glover. Inspired by Great Britain forward Mal Reilly, Cas stormed back with a try from left-centre Phil Johnson, who took advantage of a massive overlap and shortly after, Castleford front-rower Peter Cookland burst through four would-be tacklers to go in by the posts. Stand-off Bruce Burton converted the latter with ease, to peg the margin back to two points.

Somewhat surprisingly, it was Recs who upped the tempo, with two magnificent tries from man-of-the-match Jeff Gormley. His delighted grin after scoring his second is one of the abiding images of the Recs' post-war history. A further conversion from Glover looked to have the Yorkshiremen on the rack and facing a humiliating defeat. Just before half-time, however, came the slice of luck that Castleford desperately needed. A towering up-and-under from Rufus Hill was seized upon by Cas winger Steve Fenton who raced the length of the field to give his team a precious lifeline at 20–13.

The Recs continued their all-action display in the second half, but the experience of the Castleford outfit began to tell as they seized upon every half-chance and kept Recs at bay with some solid defence. Half-back pair Burton and Stephens added a try apiece. Burton's conversions gave the Yorkshiremen a three-point cushion, which was reduced by a Glover penalty, to provide the breathless crowd with a magnificent grandstand finish as the Recs battered the Castleford defence, unfortunately to no avail as referee Billy Thompson blew his whistle to end a breathtaking 80 minutes of cup tie rugby at its best.

Recs supporters gave their team a standing ovation for almost 10 minutes to celebrate what had been one of the great Knowsley Road cup ties. The players repaid the compliment with a lap of honour as a special 'thank you' for the terrific support they had received. "Deep down, the lads are disappointed," said a somewhat rueful coach Austin Rhodes. "The Fenton try just before half-time was the turning point, but the crowd was magnificent. I've never known a crowd make as much noise."

Recs versus Castleford in the Challenge Cup at Knowsley Road

Joey Hull and the fans celebrate his magnificent try. (Courtesy *St Helens Reporter*)

John Forster takes the ball into the heart of the Castleford defence.
(Courtesy *St Helens Reporter*)

Jeff Gormley looks to the referee for confirmation after his second try.
(Courtesy *St Helens Reporter*)

Jubilation in the Recs' ranks after Sid Wright's try.
(Courtesy *St Helens Reporter*)

"People still talk about the match today," remembers Jeff Gormley, who with scrum-half Billy Simmons had tormented the Castleford defence for the whole match. "They say 'why didn't you try for the drop-goal?' It was quite simply the performance of a lifetime from us without even thinking about coming back the following week."

Len Lowe watched the match from the grandstand at Knowsley Road. "I taught a lot of the Recs' lads during my time at Robins Lane in Sutton and they were desperately unlucky to lose," he recalls. "I talked to Castleford coach Mal Reilly later and he told me that his job was on the line until that length-of-the-field try by Fenton changed the complexion of the game. Something that is not generally known is that Castleford offered Sid Wright a virtual blank cheque to turn pro with them. Sid said, rather characteristically, that he couldn't be bothered and he'd sooner stay with the lads."

Pilkington Recs: Peter Glover, Andy Casey, Rufus Hill, Alan Shea, Joey Hull, John McCabe, Billy Simmons; John Forster, Jeff Gormley, Ken Cross, Steve Smith, Brian Highcock, Sid Wright (capt). Subs: Eddie Fuller; John Finney (for Smith 29 mins).
Scorers: Tries: Gormley 2, Hull, Wright; Goals: Glover 5.
Castleford: Wraith, Claughton, Smith, Johnson, Fenton, Burton, Stephens, Sampson, Hardy, Cookland, Orr, Reilly, Crampton. Subs: Morris (for Smith 60 mins); Tyreman (for Hardy 40 mins)
Scorers: Tries: Johnson, Fenton, Burton, Stephens, Cookland; Goals; Burton 4.
Half-time: 20–13
Referee: Mr W. Thompson (Huddersfield)
Attendance: 11,000
Man-of-the-match: Jeff Gormley (Pilkington Recs)
(Match programme courtesy Billy Simmons)

Apart from their Lancashire Cup Final success and near-miss with Castleford, the team were crowned Premier League Champions of the North West Counties at the end of 1977–78, another hugely successful season for the boys from City Road. There remained an incredible sense of camaraderie at City Road, with some larger-than-life characters, such as front-rower Terry Cross. "He was the king of the ad-libbers," remembers Billy Simmons. "And you took the mickey out of him at your peril. He was a real handful this particular day against Wigan St Pats. Just as I'm about to put the ball in the scrum, he pulls his opposing prop down and – bang – he lets him have one! 'You bald-headed b******, the prop yelled at Crossy. Mind you, to be fair, Terry didn't have that much hair at the time. His reply was a classic: 'Compared to you,' he says, 'I'm a hippy.'"

Thatto Heath to City Road and back

Down the decades tales of unswerving loyalty to Pilkington Recs have abounded, and few more so than that of a teak-tough middle back during the club's glory years a generation ago. Stand-off-cum-centre John McCabe spent 12 seasons donning the famous red-amber-and-black jersey, with a bulging trophy cabinet at his Elm Road home testimony to both team and personal triumphs.

He first played at Thatto Heath Council and Robins Lane schools, and on leaving played for Saints' 'B' and 'C' teams under the watchful eyes of role model coaches Bob Dagnall and Johnny Fishwick. However, despite showing great promise in switching to loose-forward over four seasons no contract was forthcoming, so disenchanted 19-year-old McCabe was lured to City Road by stalwarts Terry Cross and Eric Frodsham. It was 1970 and resourceful Recs had assembled a squad poised on the threshold of a golden age.

John McCabe in 2007 in front of his trophy cabinet,
with a memento of the Recs versus Wigan match.

A veritable pocket battleship at 13 stone and 5 feet 7 inches, McCabe regularly figured at stand-off with scrum-half Billy Simmons and occasionally Brian 'Rocky' Fairhurst, the Recs lethal midfield trio being completed by loose-forward Sid Wright who, to quote John, was known as 'the quiet man,' team kingpin and superb rugby league star. Reflecting on their stirring cup clashes with the professionals, McCabe felt the last-minute 23–22 defeat by Cas in the Challenge Cup at Knowsley Road in 1978 was sickening enough, but not as much as the 10–4 loss to Wigan in 1977, when many Recs fans believed their team was robbed.

John was in the Great Britain party that trekked to Papua New Guinea, Australia and New Zealand in 1978, a trip on which he was accompanied by fellow Recs players Peter Glover and Joey Hull. "What an experience that was," recalled McCabe, "particularly landing at PNG because I had never ventured further than Thatto Heath before." That remark obviously came tongue-in-cheek because, at international level, John had previously been on weekend rugby jaunts to Corsica and Avignon. While in the South Pacific McCabe led the appearances chart with eight games, and paid fulsome tribute to Pilkingtons for paying his wages throughout the eight-week tour.

However, there were a few sabbaticals in John's oval ball odyssey at City Road, and these were at Huyton, Runcorn and Swinton, But, as with Sid Wright, Rufus Hill and several other Recs regulars, McCabe was never really interested in taking the professional route. "Although a £50 signing-on fee would have come in handy when I was a hard-up teenager at Saints," he chuckled.

"Looking back I loved my time in amateur rugby league in mixing with decent genuine folk with no backbiting, plus first-class team spirit both on and off the field. And I will always remember the dedication of the back-room officials at City Road, notably president David Pilkington, chairman Bill Chester, secretary Roy Britch, media man George Morrison. 'Man Friday' Colin Whittaker – the list is endless," went on McCabe.

Leaving Recs in the early 1980s, John went on to win yet another National Cup Final with Thatto Heath in 1987. Superfluous to say, press secretary George Morrison inserted the amended entry into the *Guinness Book of Records*. John later took on the player-coach mantle at Thatto Heath, replacing Frankie Barrow who joined Swinton. Understandably, John was a little apprehensive at first when he was asked to assume overall control, but his early fears were soon allayed as the McCabe brand of coaching earned him numerous awards in the North West Counties League.

At the time of writing, John is in his mid-50s and a trifle more rotund than in his youth at 17 stone, he keeps in trim at the JJB gymnasium plus sessions in his garden in Elm Road where his neighbours include 90-plus John Ellaby, brother of the legendary Alf, and cousin Eddie Cunningham.

Pilkington Recs circa 1979-80 with the City Road works as a backdrop. Back: Kenny Cross, Denis Litherland, Sid Wright, Jeff Gormley, John Forster, Steve Smith, Dennis Colbon, Rufus Hill, Jeff Brown; Front: Billy Simmons, John McCabe, Steve Fuller, Les Bluck, Andy Casey, Brian Highcock, Alan Shea. Mascot: Ken Hudson

Joey Hull, John McCabe and Peter Glover in their Great Britain jerseys before the test match against Papua New Guinea at Port Moresby in 1978. Note the knee protection against the rock-hard pitch. (Courtesy Mr S. Glover)

Life at work

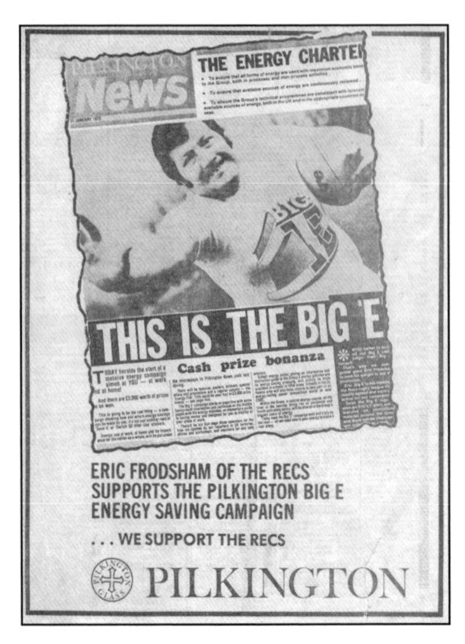

When Pilkingtons wanted someone to promote their new 'Big E' Energy Charter, Eric Frodsham was a natural choice. (Courtesy Pilkington Brothers)

Triplex, a Pilkington subsidiary company (later Pilkington Automotive) and place of work for John McCabe and several of his team-mates in the 1970s and early 1980s was demolished in 2008 to make way for housing.

10. 1979 to 1982: BARLA cup kings

After their terrific jousts with top professional opposition, it was time for the Recs to re-establish themselves as the BARLA National Cup kings. From 1979 to 1982, the team dominated the competition, with three outright victories, making four in the competition in total – a record that is still unsurpassed today. The Recs retained that vital spine of their team – John McCabe, Billy Simmons and Sid Wright, with full-back Peter Glover capable of winning matches single-handedly with his trusty right boot. There was added experience with the return of Kevin Whittle as player-coach back from the professional ranks at Swinton, adding to an awesome pack that included a fearsome front row of Kenny Cross, Jeff Gormley and the evergreen John Forster, who would keep on taking the ball up even when some of his much younger team-mates were flagging.

Both open age and youth (under-18) Finals were now held at Blackpool's Borough Park on the May bank holiday weekend and were becoming established as the highlight of the amateur season. The Recs progressed to their second National Final in 1979 against West Hull, a tough, no-nonsense side, with several former professionals in their ranks.

BARLA National Cup Final
Pilkington Recs 9 West Hull 3
26 May 1979 at Borough Park, Blackpool

In heavy, muddy conditions, Peter Glover gave Recs a 2-point lead after just five minutes with a towering 35-yard penalty. West Hull were frequently frustrated by the Recs' solid defence and suffered a crucial injury blow with the loss of winger Graham Batty. In a game with few genuine scoring chances, the Yorkshire side conceded another kickable penalty just before half-time, with Glover again making no mistake. Recs reappeared after half-time in clean jerseys and really began to turn the heat on their opponents. Sid Wright and former rugby union man 'Rocky' Fairhurst were prominent early on, with Simmons bossing the scrum base. "West Hull were a physical side and hurting our lads and we had to get rid of the prop who was doing the damage." recalls Kevin Whittle. The vital breakthrough came mid-way through the second half, when Rufus Hill drew in the defence before putting Andy Casey into the gap, who went on to score in the corner. West Hull came back briefly with a try from Windass, but with five minutes to go Peter Glover put the result beyond doubt with his third goal from near the touchline. Yet the game was to end in controversial circumstances for Kevin Whittle: "Just a few minutes remained when this lad broke down the wing and Peter Glover 'murdered' him in the corner. I was a fast-covering forward and was round there at the time and the ref sent me off... clearly a case of mistaken identity with our shirts covered in slutch."

Recs were presented with the cup by former Wigan and Great Britain star Martin Ryan, and thus became the first side to win the National Cup twice. Captain Sid Wright was rewarded after the game for his brilliant 80 minute performance when he was voted man-of-the-match and he collected the Rugby League Writers' trophy. Wright was a formidable player – a real big match player – and so important to the fortunes of the Recs team. "He was the best forward we had," remembers Billy Simmons. "He never backed down from anybody. If I was in trouble... I would want to stand shoulder to shoulder with him."

Pilkington Recs: Peter Glover, Andy Casey, Rufus Hill, John McCabe, Joey Hull, Brian Fairhurst, Billy Simmons, Ken Cross, Jeff Gormley, John Forster, Brian Highcock, Bob Williams, Sid Wright (capt). Subs: Denis Litherland, Kevin Whittle (for Cross 45 minutes - sent off 75 minutes).
Scorers: Try: Casey; Goals: Glover 3
West Hull: Geraghty, Saverton, Jordan, Bird, Batty, Fletcher, Windass, N. Dawson, Dukes, Woods, Spivey, Marshall, Shipley. Subs: Moore (for Batty); B. Dawson.
Scorer: Try: Windass
Half time: 4–0
Referee: S. Bithell (Rochdale)
Attendance: 3,200
Man-of-the-match: Sid Wright (Pilkington Recs)
(Match programme courtesy Billy Simmons)

Recs' county front-rower Kenny Cross recalled that West Hull had a huge pack, including the two Dawson brothers, who had played for Hull KR. "Three of our 'smaller' lads, Billy Simmons, Rocky Fairhurst and Jeff Gormley, were walking round Blackpool in the evening and bumped into the Dawson brothers. The Dawsons said 'How did you midgets beat us?' They couldn't believe how small they were. But it wasn't necessarily about size – it was that famous Recs spirit. When we went out on the field, we never gave up."

There was more to cheer for the St Helens amateur town team, with many of Recs players, who beat Huddersfield 15–10 to lift the BARLA Inter-Town Trophy for the first time.

Papua New Guinea tour
St Helens ARL XIII 19 Papua New Guinea 17
Wednesday 31 October 1979 at Knowsley Road

The Papua New Guinea (PNG) international team made their first ever appearance in Britain at Knowsley Road, St Helens, when they played a select St Helens ARL XIII, creating much interest among rugby league fans. Pilkington Recs players dominated the home side, with no less than nine in the final line-up. Peter Glover, Joey Hull and John McCabe had played against them during the first-ever BARLA Pacific Tour in 1978. The St Helens team won, with ace-marksman Peter Glover once again making a sizable contribution towards their success. On 4 November Recs' John McCabe and Jeff Gormley played in the first test against a PNG team in Britain. The home team won 28–12.
St Helens ARL XIII: Peter Glover (Pilkington Recs), Andy Casey (Pilkington Recs), Joey Hull (Pilks Recs), Billy Woods (Blackbrook), Alan Swift (Blackbrook), Brian Fairhurst (Pilkington Recs), Brian Harvey (Pilks Recs), Ken Cross (capt., Pilks Recs), Jimmy Dooley (Bold Miners), Joe Quinn (Blackbrook), Brendan McLoughlin (Bold Miners), Bob Williams (Pilkington Recs), Smeltzer (Bold Miners). Subs: John Forster (Pilkington Recs - for McLoughlin 70 mins); Ian Lea (Pilkington Recs – for Williams 65 mins).
Scorers: Tries: Woods, Swift, Harvey; Goals: Glover 5.
Papua New Guinea: Som (Country), Akis (Brothers), Aope (Easts), Kombinari (Brothers), Tamtu (Muruks), Limi (Country), Wartabar (Muruks), Gau (DCA), Geni (Brothers), Posu (Magani), Giheno (Rongo Tigers), Monama (Blue Kimul), Bangkoma (Rongo Tigers). Subs: Joseph (Rongo Tigers - for Giheno 52 mins); Wauiara (Muruks – for Limi 40 mins).
Scorers: Tries: Aope, Kombinari, Joseph; Goals: Kombinari 3, Som.
Half-time: 15–6
Referee: Mr T. Thornbury (Warrington)
Attendance: 2,650
Men-of-the-match: Brian Fairhurst (St Helens XIII); Wartabar (PNG)

Left: Recs' captain Sid Wright accepts the BARLA National Cup from former Wigan and Great Britain full-back Martin Ryan (left) after the 1979 win against West Hull. (Photo: Brian Peers).
Right: For Recs and Lancashire in the late 1970s – Back: Kenny Cross, Peter Glover; front: Jeff Gormley, Andy Casey, John McCabe. (Courtesy Kenny Cross).

The 1979–80 campaign was once again highly successful for the Pilkington Recs, who continued their domination of the amateur game. At the start of the season there was another chance to lock horns with a professional outfit when First Division Wigan took on Recs in the first round of the John Player Trophy at Knowsley Road. Thoughts turned to the Challenge Cup tie in 1977, when many believed that refereeing decisions favoured Wigan. Recs coach Kevin Whittle realised that recent performances by amateur clubs had increased respect from the professionals: "Wigan have Vinty Karalius at the helm and whatever his critics may think, those on the inside of the game know him to be one of the most dedicated men in rugby league. Wigan certainly won't be lacking in preparation this time."

Wigan were in a state of transition, with hardly a settled line-up. Recs relied on match practice rather than special training, largely as a result of players on shift work. The match attracted much interest in local rugby circles, with the *St Helens Star* producing a special four-page 'wraparound' souvenir supplement with its normal weekly edition – something that the amateur game in the town had long deserved.

John Player Trophy First Round
Pilkington Recs 9 Wigan 18
Sunday 16 September 1979 at Knowsley Road, St Helens

Although the crowd was down on the previous encounter against the Riversiders, the atmosphere was once more electric as both teams took to the field. The game began at a furious pace, with both sides producing some bone-crunching tackles.

Recs versus Wigan in the John Player Trophy

Team-mates celebrate Dave Manning's 35th minute try.
(Courtesy Brian Peers)

Stand-off John McCabe takes the game to Wigan as a scrum breaks up. Other Recs in the picture include Jeff Gormley, John Forster, Dave Manning, Bob Williams, Sid Wright, Billy Simmons and Peter Glover. (Courtesy Brian Peers)

Mighty loose forward Sid Wright takes on the Wigan defence. (Courtesy Brian Peers).

Beaten with heads held high: Recs' squad in the dressing room after the game.
Back: Brian Harvey, Ian Lea, Bob Williams; front: Denis Litherland, Dave Manning, John Forster, Rufus Hill, Billy Simmons, Jeff Gormley. (Courtesy Denis Litherland)

However, it was Wigan who took the lead after just four minutes, when Steve O'Neill took a pass from Billy Melling and crashed over the line. Five minutes later, it was 8–0, as Terry Hollingsworth cut through the Recs defence to send local lad Johnny Butler over for a try, which Ray Farnworth converted. Despite the deficit, there was no let up in the Recs' famous fighting spirit as they took the game to the visitors, pounding the Wigan line only to be held back by some last-ditch defending.

Then – the breakthrough after 35 minutes on the clock, when Jeff Gormley surged through a gap to send Manning over for a crucial three-pointer. Peter Glover added the extras. Three minutes later Glover hit the post with a penalty and the Recs continued to lay siege to the Wigan line, with Denis Litherland, Billy Simmons and John McCabe in outstanding form.

Unfortunately, Wigan scored once again, somewhat against the run of play, when former Saints hooker Tony Karalius and Melling combined to put prop Regan over. Although feeling the pace somewhat, two Peter Glover penalties buoyed the wilting Recs and at 11–9, the game was still in the melting pot. The Recs kept up their assault until the 77th minute, when a Farnworth penalty took the score to 13–9 and, in injury time, Wigan's Dennis Ramsdale went over for the decisive try, which was also converted.

Although the Recs could not hide their disappointment, they left the field with heads held high. They had matched a top-class professional outfit in virtually all areas again, only to be denied by that fabled rub of the green. It was almost a carbon copy of the previous meeting at Knowsley Road, when Wigan were mightily relieved to be in the draw for the second round. The prolonged applause from the fans said it all once more, as the spirit of the Recs remained undimmed.

"It was a fantastic display," gasped top BARLA official Maurice Oldroyd, "and the amateurs attracted the biggest crowd of the round – what tremendous encouragement for the game and what a tribute to the people who support it."

Pilkington Recs: Peter Glover, Andy Casey, Rufus Hill, Joey Hull, Denis Litherland, John McCabe, Billy Simmons, John Forster, Jeff Gormley, Ian Lea, Bob Williams, Dave Manning, Sid Wright (capt). Subs: Brian Harvey; Les Westhead.
Scorers: Try: Manning; Goals: Glover 3.
Wigan: Les Bolton, Dennis Ramsdale, John Butler, Trevor Stockley, Ray Farnworth, Keiron O'Loughlin, Bernard Coyle, Steve O'Neill, Tony Karalius, David Regan, Billy Melling, Denis Boyd, Terry Hollingsworth.
Scorers: Tries: Ramsdale, Butler, O'Neill, Regan; Goals: Farnworth 3.
Half-time: 5–11
Referee: Mr W. Thompson (Huddersfield)
Attendance: 7,000 (est.)

Recs at the double

Spurred on by their John Player Trophy exploits, the Recs enjoyed a near 100 per cent record in winning the North West Counties Premier League and reached the semi-final stage of the Lancashire Cup in 1979–80.

However, it always seemed to be the National Cup that really sent pulses racing at City Road and Kevin Whittle's men battled through to their third final, against old foes Dewsbury Celtic at Borough Park at the end of May, and the prospect of back-to-back-glory, something never achieved in the competition to date.

1980 BARLA National Cup Final

Loose forward Sid Wright on the burst against Dewsbury Celtic at Borough Park, Blackpool. Centre Bob Bolan (right) is in support. (Courtesy Brian Peers)

Recs' second-rower Dave Manning scorches over against Dewsbury Celtic at Borough Park, in full view of referee Walker. (Courtesy Brian Peers)

The Recs players after their victory. Back: Ian Lea, Dave Manning, Jeff Gormley, Kenny Cross, Steve Fenney, Bob Williams, Kevin Whittle. Front: John McCabe, Joey Hull, Billy Simmons, Brian Fairhurst, Bob Bolan. (Courtesy Brian Peers)

BARLA National Cup Final
Pilkington Recs 16 Dewsbury Celtic 5
Sunday 24 May 1980 at Borough Park, Blackpool

Wearing a sleek all white outfit, with red, amber and black trim, plus specially made tie-ups for their socks, the Recs blasted their opponents from the kick off and raced to an 11–0 lead in the first 15 minutes. Second-rower Dave Manning opened the scoring with a try converted by the ever-dependable Glover. A Billy Simmons drop-goal extended the lead and then it was time for a piece of magic from his international team-mate Joey Hull. Having swept inside, the stocky winger kicked over the defence, regathered and scored under the posts – a magnificent piece of skill. Glover's conversion was a formality and the Recs looked as though they were going to run away with the match.

Yet Dewsbury somehow stayed in contention and as half-time approached, they pulled a try back courtesy of substitute Chris Senior. For virtually the remainder of the match, the Recs were forced to tackle like demons to keep their line intact. A penalty from Walker reduced the deficit, but the Recs struck back in the last 10 minutes to secure victory. Substitute Kenny Cross charged down the middle and slipped a gem of a pass to the supporting Bob Bolan, who crashed over between the posts for the clinching score. Glover's conversion made the result 16–5 and the game was safe. The Recs had triumphed again. "No-one will ever equal our record," declared a delighted Kevin Whittle, as the trophy was once again presented to the winning captain, Sid Wright. Both Recs and Celtic qualified for the John Player Trophy competition for 1980–81 and the chance for another go at a professional outfit. Perhaps the draw would be kinder to the City Road men this time.

Pilkington Recs: Peter Glover, Joey Hull, Brian Fairhurst, Bob Bolan, Steve Fenney, John McCabe, Billy Simmons, Ian Lea, Jeff Gormley, Kevin Whittle, Bob Williams, Dave Manning, Sid Wright (capt). Subs: Brian Harvey; Ken Cross (for Lea 68 mins).
Scorers: Tries: Hull, Bolan, Manning; Goals: Glover 3; Drop-goal: Simmons.
Dewsbury Celtic: Greenlees; Tattersfield, Tolson, Cooke, Clark; Harpin, Doyle; Gowan, Andruchov, Oxley, Dunford, Rhodes, Walker. Subs: C. Senior (for Doyle 24 mins); D. Senior (for Dunford 56 mins).
Scorers: Try: C. Senior; Goal: Walker.
Half-time: 11–3
Referee: Mr B. Walker (Barrow)
Attendance: 4,000
Man-of-the-match: Bob Walker (Dewsbury Celtic)

There was still no stopping Recs in the early 1980s. Although key players were getting older, and John Forster had called it a day, the backbone of the side remained, which was bad news for the opposition. Once again there was the prospect of another match against a professional outfit, although there were no false promises when the draw for the first round of the John Player Trophy sent the Recs over the Pennines to Castleford – a difficult proposition indeed.

John Player Trophy First Round
Castleford 30 Pilkington Recs 17
23 November 1980 at Wheldon Road, Castleford

After both sides had registered early penalty goals, Recs roared into the lead when Dave Manning scored a well-taken try, which Peter Glover converted. Castleford bounced back with two tries from future international front-rower Kevin Ward, both converted by Gary Hyde to put the Wheldon Road side 12–7 ahead. Then the Recs came back into the contest just before half-time, levelling the scores with a John McCabe try and Glover goal.

After the interval an Ian Lea try gave the Recs a 15–12 lead; Gary Hyde kicked a further penalty for Castleford and Glover replied for Recs. In the last quarter, however, Pilks looked tired. Two tries from Castleford scrum-half Bob Beardmore, plus a try and two further goals from Hyde brought up a 30–17 scoreline that did not do justice to the Recs' fighting spirit – literally. It was a tough encounter, which boiled over after 30 minutes when Kevin Whittle and Castleford front-rower Brian Hughes were dismissed for fighting.

"Castleford were a strong side, had beaten Saints at Knowsley Road the previous week and Hughes was just hitting everyone," recalls Kevin Whittle. "Being a bit of a name in the pro game, I realised I could be in for a pasting. So with me being cleverer than the average forward, I swapped shirts with 'Arthur' Manning in the dressing room... and he didn't know about it. I went out at 12 instead of 11. It took them 20 minutes to realise Arthur was not me. Anyhow, the Castleford full-back Wraith was chasing after a kick through and I just pole-axed him. The first man in was Hughes and starts punching me and it developed into a brawl. The referee pulled the two of us out and sent us off. Then later on in the second half, Mal Reilly came on. He looked like Tutankhamen, he had so many bandages on... but he got them going again with his long passes and they made the game safe. We were really close to beating them at one stage, although 'Arthur' got a bit of stick early on."

Castleford: G. Wraith, T. Richardson, J. Joyner (capt), G. Hyde, S. Fenton, I. Orum, R. Beardmore, B. Hughes, R. Spurr, B. Johnson, D. Finch, K. Ward, J. Crampton. Subs: N. James; M. Reilly
Scorers: Tries: Ward 2, Beardmore 2, Finch, Hyde; Goals: Hyde 6.
Pilkington Recs: Peter Glover, Andy Casey, Rufus Hill, Brian Fairhurst, Joey Hull; John McCabe, Billy Simmons; Ken Cross, Jeff Gormley, Ian Lea, Kevin Whittle, Dave Manning, Sid Wright (capt). Subs: Alan Shea; Mike Bowes
Scorers: Tries: McCabe, Lea, Manning; Goals: Glover 4.
Half time: 12–12
Referee: Mr H. Hunt (Cheshire)
Attendance: 3,200

Lancashire/Cumbria County Cup Final
Pilkington Recs 33 Rose Bridge (Wigan) 3
Friday 7 December 1980 at Knowsley Road

Just six days later, the Recs played Wigan's Rose Bridge in the Lancashire Cup Final at Knowsley Road, and won 33–3 for a fourth time under the BARLA banner. Stand-off John McCabe dominated the match, while prop Kenny Cross was also in outstanding form.

Pilkington Recs: Peter Glover, Andy Casey, Rufus Hill, Bob Bolan, Joey Hull, John McCabe, Billy Simmons, Ken Cross, Jeff Gormley, Ian Lea, Bob Williams, Dave Manning, Sid Wright (capt.). Subs: Brian Fairhurst (for Cross 40 mins), Alan Shea (for Simmons 62 mins)
Scorers: Tries: Fairhurst 2, Hull, Cross, Gormley, Wright; Goals: Glover 6, Fairhurst; Drop-goal: Simmons.
Rose Bridge: Packingham, McNally, Ellison, Tomlinson, Jones, Foster, Derbyshire, Park, Halsall, Parkinson, Lloyd, Malone, Cassidy. Subs: Woodward; Roden (for Halsall 27 mins)
Scorer: Try: Malone.
Half-time: 11–0
Referee: Mr J. Haythorn (Barrow)
Attendance: 500

At the end of December, Recs beat Milford 19–4 in the Bronte Challenge Trophy, to decide who would represent BARLA in the Challenge Cup first round in the New Year. There was delight at City Road when the Recs were drawn at home to Second Division York. The game would be played at Knowsley Road and players and fans were hoping for the slice of luck against professional opposition that the club deserved which had deserted them in the recent past.

Three Fives Challenge Cup First Round
Pilkington Recs 7 York 18
Sunday 15 February 1981 at Knowsley Road

Injuries robbed the Recs of four regulars for this much awaited clash – an unwanted scenario, given the lowly status of the York club compared with Wigan and Castleford. "York were in the Second Division, but it didn't matter," remembers John McCabe. "They knew what we were capable of and didn't take us lightly. It was our cup final and they really hammered us early on." Sure enough, it was the Wasps who began strongly, with eight points in just six minutes, courtesy of tries from Phillipo and Adams, with Morgan adding the conversion. Recs' first points came after 32 minutes, with a Peter Glover penalty. Yet the Yorkshiremen increased their lead when Pryce scored another valuable three-pointer, which Morgan also converted.

Despite the 13–2 deficit, the Recs showed their terrific fighting spirit and came roaring back at their opponents in the second quarter, but failed to capitalise on territory and possession. A Morgan interception try stunned the Recs, although eight minutes from time Brian 'Rocky' Fairhurst crashed over the York line for a consolation try. In the process, he split his chin open – a wound that required five stitches later on. "We played fairly well," remembers Billy Simmons. "But if we'd had Sid Wright and Ken Cross to name just two, I'm sure it would have been a different game."

For John McCabe, at least, there would be some consolation at his Triplex workplace a stone's throw from Knowsley Road: "Loose forward Paul McDermott was about to put the ball down for a try and I hit him at the last second, man and ball," he recalls. "It was no try. The ball shot up in the air and they had to walk him off dazed. At work on Monday, the lads were saying it was one of the best tackles they had seen on Saints' ground." Unfortunately it was to be the last time that the Recs would take on league opposition at Knowsley Road. Yet in their clashes against the professional ranks they had provided some unforgettable moments for the fans to remember, adding to the rich heritage of great matches at the famous old stadium over the years.

Pilkington Recs: Peter Glover, Andy Casey, Rufus Hill, Brian Fairhurst, Joey Hull, John McCabe, Billy Simmons, Ian Lea, Jeff Gormley, Kevin Whittle (capt), Dave Manning, Malcolm Smith, Bob Bolan. Subs: Jimmy Sheffield (for McCabe 55 mins); Mick Bowes (for Smith 60 mins)
Scorers: Try: Fairhurst; Goals: Glover 2.
York: G. Smith, G. Pryce, L. Sheard, A. Redford, T. Morgan, J. Crossley, K. Harkin, A. Wardell, P. Phillippo, D. Dunkerley, B. White, B. Adams, P. McDermott. Subs: T. Midgley (for Smith 49 mins); W. Kirkbride (for Wardell 55 mins)
Scorers: Tries: Pryce, Morgan, Phillippo, Adams; Goals: Morgan 2, Crossley.
Half-time: 2–13
Referee: Mr J. Holdsworth (Leeds)
Attendance: 6,000

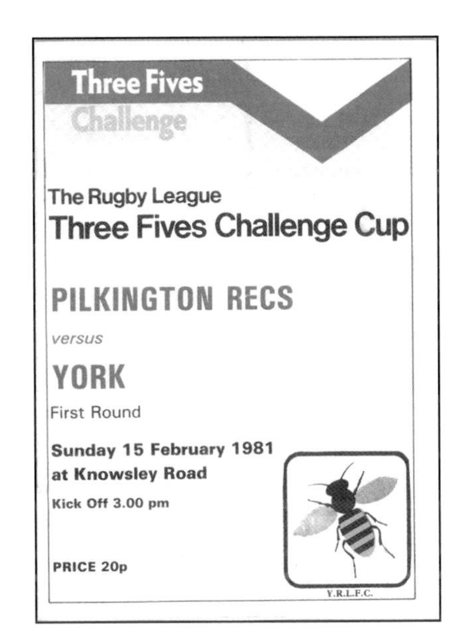

Left: John McCabe surges for the line during the Challenge Cup tie against York at Knowsley Road. (Courtesy John McCabe) Right: The match programme.

A final flourish

The 1981–82 campaign saw Recs finish as runners-up in the North West Counties Premier Division and delighted their supporters by winning the John Player Sevens competition, the final of which was played at Headingley as a curtain raiser to the John Player Cup Final between Hull and Hull KR. Recs, with Dave Manning and Steve Fenney in outstanding form, defeated Yew Tree 31–16 – the last time the competition took place. The team also progressed through to the National Cup Final once more, facing Yorkshire rivals Milford at Borough Park, Blackpool. The club also celebrated the selection of hooker Jeff Gormley for the 1982 BARLA Great Britain tour to Papua New Guinea and Australia. There were a number of fund-raising events for him at the Pilkington Recs club, including a friendly match against newly formed Thatto Heath. Unfortunately, Gormley was to miss the Final, as a result of his touring commitments, with Ian Lea taking over the number nine jersey.

BARLA National Cup Final
Pilkington Recs 19 Milford 2
29 May 1982 at Borough Park, Blackpool

It was a red-hot battle at Borough Park, as the Recs lifted the trophy for a fourth time in eight years with two spellbinding tries from winger John Winstanley and a spectacular effort from another youngster, 20-year-old Alan Greenall. Some thrilling passages of play were disrupted by two huge brawls involving virtually every player on the pitch. Somewhat surprisingly, Recs second-rower Mike Bowes was the only one to get his marching orders two minutes from time when he was picked out from a mass of players by referee Mr Randerson to be sent for an early bath.

1982 BARLA National Cup Final

John Winstanley races away for one of his two tries.
(Courtesy Brian Peers)

John Winstanley with his man-of-the-match trophy, with Recs trainer Colin Whittaker.
(Courtesy Brian Peers)

The successful Recs team and officials line-up for the camera after the win against Milford.
Back row: Eric Frodsham, John McCabe (with trophy), Ian Lea, Alan Greenall;
front: John Winstanley, Kenny Cross (cup on head), Ian Critchley,
Mick Bowes, Dennis Cook (in headlock). (Courtesy Brian Peers)

Keith Macklin (left) presents skipper John McCabe with the cup.
(Courtesy Brian Peers)

Recs owed much to the place-kicking of full-back Ian Critchley, who succeeded with five from six attempts at goal. The old firm of Sid Wright and skipper John McCabe were also much in evidence. Recs went in at half-time 7–2 ahead after Greenall had picked up a pass from his centre, Jimmy Sheffield and raced fully 65 yards to the line. Seven minutes after the interval, it was virtually all over, as 20 year-old John Winstanley took Kevin Whittle's pass, dodged inside two attempted tacklers and straightened up to leave the Milford defence stranded. In the 68th minute, there was a repeat performance, as Bolan and Manning combined to put him clear. His lightning pace did the rest.

"Milford came to Blackpool with a reputation for no-nonsense play and confirmed it," wrote Phil McNulty in the *St Helens Reporter*. "They tackled Recs with four men at a time, but showed little of the St Helens side's finesse when they got near the posts." Two-try winger Winstanley picked up a huge commemorative sword as man-of-the-match from special guest journalist Keith Macklin, donated by the Rugby League Writer's Association. As another chorus of "I do like to be beside the seaside" erupted from the victorious Recs, the occasional bouts of fisticuffs during the game had not exactly pleased watching BARLA officials and both teams knew further action would be taken.

Pilkington Recs: Ian Critchley, Alan Greenall, Jimmy Sheffield, Bob Bolan, John Winstanley, John McCabe, Brian Fairhurst; Ken Cross, Ian Lea, Kevin Whittle, Dave Manning, Mike Bowes, Sid Wright. Subs: Eric Frodsham (For Fairhurst 60 minutes); Dennis Cook (For Lea 69 minutes).
Scorers: Tries: Winstanley 2, Greenall; Goals: Critchley 5.
Milford: Turner, Peters, O'Donnell, Loveday, Harris, Bowe, Tate, Gates, Hargreaves, Kelly, Rea, Walker, Wilkinson. Subs: Phipps (For O'Donnell 50 minutes); Barker (For Walker 70 minutes)
Scorer: Goal: Turner.
Half-time: 7–2
Referee: Mr A.C. Randerson (Hull)
Man-of-the-match: John Winstanley (Pilkington Recs)

The outcome of what had been a feisty affair was that second-rower Mike Bowes was suspended for three matches by the disciplinary committee. Worse still, on Monday 21 June, both Recs and Milford were banned from the National Cup for one year. "I'm sure it will have an effect on the younger players, especially the two lads who scored the tries," commented Recs' chairman Brian Woodward. "John Winstanley and Alan Greenall are both only 20 and it did them good to enjoy success. But to have this happen will be a blow to them."

Kevin Whittle – Recs' Man Friday

A granite-hard forward whose uncompromising approach whetted the appetite of City Road fans for many seasons had a varied oval-ball career. Kevin Whittle, who hailed from Borough Road, began playing rugby league at school and then crossed the great divide by captaining Prescot BI rugby union team in 1963. However double agent Whittle figured in the XIII-a-side code, albeit covertly, by playing in a local seven-a-side knockout competition with the 'Nomads,' whose ranks included other rugby league types such as John Walsh, Joe Robinson, Eric Woodyer and trainer Colin Whittaker.

Word filtered through to Prescot however, where Kevin found he was no longer welcome, so he came out of the league closet and joined Pilkington Recs, where he was to earn town, county and international recognition. These included playing Leigh Town at City Road, Yorkshire at Hull, Cumberland at Oldham, and France at Craven Park, Hull.

Second-rower Mick Bowes (left) waits while Colin Whittaker gives Kevin Whittle his pre-match rub down. (Courtesy Brian Peers)

Given such form, the 6 feet 15 stone Whittle was soon attracting the attention of professional clubs including Wigan, whose coach was Eric Ashton. Kevin played trials for the cherry-and-whites in the second-row alongside Bill Ashurst, but was not offered a contract. Undeterred, he then signed for Swinton for whom he appeared in more than 200 games in nine seasons, during some of which former Saints star Austin Rhodes was the Lions coach. Kevin was generous in praise of the Station Road management who looked after him well and offered him a testimonial which he declined because of a broken arm, an injury which occurred four times overall.

With Whittle's stint in professional rugby league over, he issued a request to Swinton to release him, which they did with their good wishes bearing in mind Kevin's long and loyal service. So battle-hardened Kevin made a sentimental return to City Road to a team on the threshold of mighty deeds, and where former Saints star and Pilkington manager George Parsons was steadying the rocky financial and administrative boats.

Pressed as to who was the best player he had lined up with at Recs, Kevin agreed with the general opinion in singling out Sid Wright, while Whittle's most memorable match was versus works team Beecroft and Whiteman in Hull. "We were the current champions when we went up there," he recalls. "Beecroft and Whiteman was the feeder club for the Hull KR 'A' team. We'd been playing 10 minutes and we were losing 10–0. The crowd were calling out 'Call yourselves champions?'

Mick Bowes came on for Arthur Manning, who had broken his ribs. Mick could run a bit, and it wasn't long before we put him through to score under the sticks. We got level with them after half-time and then proceeded to give them a good thrashing. The crowd changed their tune... we were all a bunch of professionals now.

In the last 10 minutes we were so much on top that none of their forwards wanted the ball. Anyone who got near the ball was going to get hurt. Gormley was kicking the ball through in the scrum, letting them have the ball on their line. We knocked the stuffing out of them - a fantastic performance."

Kevin Whittle with his team mates before Recs beat Blackbrook 40–8 on 8 March 1979 at City Road Back: Bill Chester (chairman), Dave Manning, Les Bluck, Brian Highcock, Kevin Whittle, Ian Lea, Joey Hull, Peter Glover, Brian Woodward (secretary); front: Bob Bolan, Steve Fenney, Brian Harvey, Ged Marsh, Roy Barrow, Jeff Gormley. (Courtesy: Brian Peers)

On a more sombre note Whittle ruminated first on the disappearance of the memory-jerking Hall of Fame gallery at City Road, followed ultimately by the decaying condition of the fabric of the time-honoured stadium itself.

"It was a great pity that a multi-national company or financial giant could not be persuaded to act as backer to carry the name of Pilkington Recreation forward. The hope must be that the projected move to Bishop Road proves to be a rescue package," said the 67-year-old former lynch-pin of the club's affairs.

It was certainly not for the glory and simply for the love of Recs' that Kevin acted out the roles of player-coach, secretary, treasurer, fund-raiser and 'Man Friday', during his tenure of office at what had to be self-sufficient City Road. It was a blessing he had an understanding better half in Sheila. As a diversion from the rigours of rugby league – but not quite – Kevin and Sheila were hosts at the Saints Restaurant for 13 years.

Setting the seal on this Whittle odyssey of oval-ball excellence Kevin and his cohorts such as Paul 'Buffer' Forber, Brian Fairhurst, Steve Peters, Uncle Tom Cobley and all, could not resist the temptation to launch a team in the rugby league hot-bed in Nutgrove circa 1995. By then the perennial Whittle was a mere lad of 54 summers and just thinking of retiring as a player.

St Helens Cup winners 1980

Back: Dave Manning, Tom Ashcroft (chairman St Helens RLFC), Kevin Whittle, Colin Whittaker (trainer), Bob Bolan, Les Bluck, Dave Rathbone, Bob Williams, Ian Lea, Billy Simmons; front: Steve Fenney, Brian Harvey, John McCabe, Jeff Gormley, Joey Hull. (Courtesy: Brian Peers)

Joey Hull races in for a superb solo try. (Courtesy: Brian Peers)

Dave Manning shows his handling skills in a National League match at City Road. (Courtesy Denis Litherland)

Billy 'Rufus' Hill sets up an attack. (Courtesy: Brian Peers)

11. 1982 to 1990: In the footsteps of legends

The 1982 National Cup victory marked the end of an unparalleled era of success for Pilkington Recs. "There are still a lot of expectations here from the success of the 1970s and 1980s," says John Rees, a Recs stalwart who joined the club in the under–10s in 1988 and was a key member of the first team some 20 years later. "We are still compared with the sides of yesteryear. The frustrating thing is that the legend of the 1970s not only makes people say 'not as good as', but also we are in many ways the team people love to hate."

The Recs still retained their famous fighting spirit however, although at times it would seem to be misplaced. They failed to distinguish themselves when they faced rivals Saints at Knowsley Road on 6 August 1982 in what was loosely described as a friendly. The incident-packed occasion was the testimonial match for Saints' long-serving winger Roy Mathias, with Recs being on the receiving end of a 51–7 drubbing, which was doubly notable for an eyeball to eyeball confrontation featuring the beneficiary and Pilkington skipper Kevin Whittle, plus the dismissal of the visitors' front-rower Ian Lea.

Those players who formed the core of that golden era gradually began to move away or retire. Some departed for the professional ranks for a last hurrah. Peter Glover and John McCabe joined Huyton, with McCabe adding to his legendary status in the amateur game by enjoying further success with the fledgling Thatto Heath club. Kevin Whittle set up Nutgrove ARLFC. Yet many still retained links with the Recs in various capacities: Billy Simmons, together with the inimitable Jethro Phillips and Andy Casey, became members of the coaching team at various times, as did Jeff Gormley, Joey Hull and Rufus Hill, who like Kevin Whittle played on well into their mid-30s and beyond at City Road. The seemingly evergreen Colin Whittaker also remained as a valuable part of the backroom brigade and Eric Frodsham, a Recs man through and through was a stalwart Committee member for many years. Denis Litherland eventually returned from St Helens RLFC to play once more at City Road and continued to be one of the most respected members of the club in 2007, with his grandson playing in the junior ranks.

Eddie Tinsley joined the Recs as a 16-year-old and played in the under-18s. "It was just down the road from where we lived and my dad worked for Pilks," he remembers. "And it was a really friendly club. There were just three teams at City Road in those days and we would train with the likes of Dennis Colbon, Jasper [Ian Jones] and Dave Rathbone. Colin Whittaker was also on the scene. In 1980–81 the under-18s and first team reached the Lancashire Cup final, both against Rose Bridge. We played at Central Park and lost 9–6. The first team won easily at Knowsley Road. One of our players, Brian Dunn, signed for Wigan as a result of that cup run. We were also the first team to beat Wigan St Pats for three years. The senior team was very talented and used to pick itself with names like Wright, Hull, McCabe, Gormley, Whittle and Rufus Hill. They didn't bring many youngsters through – they were a close-knit unit and kept themselves to themselves. But they all seemed to grow old together and it left a huge gap. Although it gave players like Bernard Bibby, Paul Giblin, Mick Roughley, Paul Roberts and me the opportunity to keep the Recs flame burning, it was a tough ask – after all, this was Pilks, the team everyone wanted to beat.

When Frankie Barrow set up Thatto Heath, he invited me down there. They seemed to take on Recs' mantle of success locally for the rest of the 1980s and early 1990s, with Johnny McCabe coaching them."

Although it was an understandably difficult task to follow in the footsteps of legends, the club was as determined as ever to maintain its high standards on the playing field. There were changes behind the scenes at City Road, with long-serving chairman Roy Britch standing down, replaced by former secretary Brian Woodward. International hooker Jeff Gormley and Andy Casey took up the coaching reins in place of Kevin Whittle. The team finished runners-up in the North West Counties Premier Division in 1982–83, yet not being able to defend their BARLA national title – the competition that had given the Recs such a phenomenal reputation in the amateur game for more than a decade was a bitter blow for players and supporters. "We got our wrists slapped after the National Final," recalls Jeff Gormley, who was on the BARLA tour at the time and returned to become player-coach at City Road. "To try and repair relations, we played Milford in a friendly just to say there was no animosity and that the flare-up on the pitch was just a one-off. The big let down for me, however, was when we were allowed back in and we lost 26–15 at Dudley Hill in the semi-final in 1984."

Sadly on 22 December 1983 Lord Pilkington passed away in the Providence Hospital, St Helens, aged 78. Although he was the president of local rivals Saints, he always took an interest in the affairs of the Recs, together with his wife Lady Mavis Pilkington, who was a vice president of the club. David Pilkington, the son of Colonel Guy Pilkington, remained as club president at City Road.

In 1983-84, Recs were allowed back into the National Cup, but lost in the quarter final to Heworth.
(Programme courtesy Billy Simmons)

B.A.R.L.A. Whitbread Trophy
(QUARTER FINAL)
PILKINGTON REC'S
(St. Helens)
V
HEWORTH
(York)
at
City Road, St. Helens
on
Saturday, 7th April, 1984
K.O. 2-30 p.m.
20p
TODAYS MATCH SPONSORS
DEREK & BARBARA
WINDLE CITY CLUB

A new beginning

The annual report for the Pilkington Recreation Club in 1986 gave the following teams for the rugby league section:

1 team in the N.W. Counties First Division
1 team in the N.W. Counties Second Division
Junior team (depending on numbers available)
1 team (one of 10 in the country) in the BARLA National League.

It was the last of these which was of great interest. In 1986–87, the amateur game was overhauled with the creation of a new National League, which was to include the cream of the BARLA teams. Pilkingtons – champions of the North West Counties First Division the previous season – proudly took their place in the new top division with nine other clubs. "We were admitted to the new league because we satisfied all the criteria BARLA were looking for," remembers Billy Dillon, a long-serving Recs player and administrator. "We had superb facilities, including an enclosed pitch and a clubhouse with a friendly atmosphere – if you wanted a model of what BARLA wanted, it was there at City Road." Under the expert guidance of coach Billy Benyon, the team made an excellent start in the Slalom Lager-sponsored National League by beating West Hull 11–10 with full-back Niel Wood scoring the first points with a drop-goal. Alun Allcock scored the club's first try in the new competition. West Hull had a man sent off in each half.

Pilkington Recs celebrate their 1986 St Helens Cup victory.
Back: Ian Thomas, Gary Fletcher, Steve Fenney, Paul Hankinson, Frank Tinsley, Eric Frodsham, Andy Fairclough, Geoff Grimes, Les Bluck, Dave Manning, Alan Alcock, Colin Whittaker, Ged Marsh (coach), Paul Giblin, Jimmy Seddon; front: Dave Price, Bernard Bibby, Ian Stanley, Dave Harrison, Niel Wood, Jon Parsons. (Courtesy Denis Litherland)

Recs were starting their youth development at this time, with Niel Wood and Ray Ryan advertising for players from under-11 to under-17 levels. The club also enjoyed the luxury of a third team.

Although the first away match was lost in injury time at Heworth, Recs were near-invincible at City Road. In the Lancashire Cup, Recs met Thatto Heath in the semi-final, drawing a crowd of 1,500 to Sherdley Park, including the Mayor of St Helens, who was presented to both teams before kick off. Despite a 14–0 deficit at half-time, Recs won a pulsating encounter 16–15, with a last-minute try from Eric Frodsham, converted by Wood. "A breathtaking advert for amateur rugby league played in a remarkable atmosphere," wrote *Open Rugby* magazine.

The Final at Knowsley Road on a bitterly cold December evening was hardly conducive to good handling. It proved to be one to forget for the Recs in their record-breaking ninth final appearance, as opponents Blackbrook, from the North West Counties Premier Division, won 12–5 and qualified for the first round of the Challenge Cup. Blackbrook eventually lost 74–6 to Castleford in a weather-affected fixture switched to the under-soil heating of Headingley.

It had been a tense autumn in St Helens, with the possibility of a takeover of Pilkingtons by BTR, an industrial conglomerate. Chairman Anthony Pilkington urged shareholders to reject the takeover bid. Indeed, according to the local press, Pilkingtons were regarded as "conscientious employers with a private welfare state second to none." *The Reporter* gave dire predictions for the town's future: "St Helens, a town built proudly on glass and coal, would end up like the forgotten steel towns – a ghastly, ghost world falling apart through financial neglect, the epitome of desolation in a deprived and industrially degraded North West." Questions were asked in the House of Commons about the company's situation.

Despite the gloom and doom, Recs beat Ealing 48–12 in the BARLA National Cup, at the Polytechnic Stadium home of Fulham RLFC in Chiswick. Featherstone Miners Welfare fell in round three at City Road, with forward Alun Allcock in barnstorming form, before hopes ended at Millom. In the new year, Frank Wilson was appointed coach to replace Bill Benyon, who had accepted the coaching position at Leigh. Recs' league form continued to be impressive and by the middle of April they stood proudly at the top of the league after a magnificent one-point victory at rivals Millom. There were just six minutes remaining in Cumbria when Gary Fletcher broke through on a diagonal run before switching the ball back inside for the supporting Geoff Grimes, who promptly sent front-rower Paul Hankinson over by the posts. Niel Wood edged Recs into a 7–6 lead with the conversion and sealed a fantastic victory.

By late April, however, Recs' nine-match unbeaten run came to an end at West Hull and with it their hopes of the inaugural championship as Yorkshire rivals Heworth snatched the advantage with a late run, winning their games in hand. Heworth won the title on points difference. After a demanding season, Parkside beat the Recs in the semi-final of the St Helens Cup.

Slalom Lager National League Top Three 1986–87

	P	W	D	L	Pts
Heworth	18	14	0	4	28
West Hull	18	14	0	4	28
Pilkington Recs	18	13	0	5	26

The Recs had played a part in one of the most memorable winter seasons of sport witnessed in the town. Full-back Niel Wood was Slalom Lager National League player-of-the-year, topping the kicking charts with more than 200 points. Steve Fenney and Gary Fletcher were also members of the competition's Team of the Year. Dave Carsley, Paul Hankinson, Vic Speakman and Dave Manning had also featured in *Open Rugby's* National League Team of the Month during the season. Ironically, Frankie Barrow's Thatto Heath outfit marched on to victory in the National Cup against Heworth at Headingley, with former Recs skipper John McCabe playing a dominant role and winning a record fifth National Cup winner's medal. Pilkington employee and amateur boxer Johnny Lyon won a record sixth ABA title and the Saints went to Wembley only to be defeated 19–18 by a supposedly over-the-hill Halifax outfit in the Challenge Cup Final. One week before came the greatest achievement of them all, however, when St Helens Town – the club formed as a rival to the powerful St Helens Recs football team at the beginning of the century – beat Warrington Town 3–2 in the FA Vase at Wembley. As for Pilkingtons, the gloom was dispelled. The proposed take-over from BTR was shelved when the company's pre-tax profits of £250m were announced in the New Year. "The World's Leading Glass company," claimed one advert. "Together we've kept it that way!"

After a meeting in the George Hotel, BARLA proposed the formation of a second division for National League clubs, beginning in 1988–89, with two-up and two-down. The bottom clubs in the second division were to apply for re-election to the League.

The 1987–88 season began promisingly. In what was almost a carbon-copy of the previous campaign, Recs found themselves with a five-point gap at the top of the league in December 1987, after a thrilling 20–17 victory over Dudley Hill at City Road. They remained in top spot until the final stages of the season, when Milford, coached by Allan Agar, overtook them with matches in hand. It was another frustrating end to a season that had promised so much, with a 6–4 defeat at the hands of Wigan St Jude's in the National Cup another bitter pill to swallow. Points machine Niel Wood once again was rated the best full-back in the league, with Hankinson, Speakman, Jackson and skipper Dave Manning also showing top form.

Scrum-half Johnny Smith had left St Helens at the end of the 1985–86 season and after a dalliance with Thatto Heath and a brief return to the professional ranks at Leigh, joined the Recs in 1988–89, a club that 20 years later, still remains close to his heart: "Ray Ryan was the chairman and Frank Wilson was the coach when I came to City Road. My first game was against Egremont, who had this lad John Brocklebank at scrum-half who was a BARLA international. They said that I had got something on my plate with him, but I held my own and even got the man-of-the-match award from the sponsors. I then got a player-of-the-month award and started to really enjoy my rugby.

We weren't a bad side with the likes of Niel Wood and my half-back partner Eric Frodsham. We had players like Brian Dunn and Gary Fletcher, who signed for Warrington originally and came to us from Blackbrook. It was a real former Saints enclave at Recs. Apart from the coaches [Benyon, Wilson and Mantle] I was one of the first there from Knowsley Road. Denis Litherland came back after me. There was Shaun Allen, Chris Arkwright and Barrie Ledger, although he had a bad injury and he packed in. Then there was Steve Fenney and Phil Price - his brother Dave was a good 'un too. How he didn't get picked up by the professional clubs I'll never know. He was my stand-off after Eric Frodsham."

Recs began the 1988–89 campaign in the newly-named Rodstock National Amateur League Division One with three victories. By December, the side was top of the table with 13 points from 10 matches, with second-rower Andy Crehan in outstanding form. By the end of the campaign, however, the team had slumped to third from bottom, with no further wins, including a shock 25–8 National Cup exit at the hands of Westgate Redoubt of Wakefield in the third round. Some club members were deeply concerned about the club's long-term future in the competition. "The club was struggling to attract players to play in the National League because of the travelling and the players that were there were also getting fed up of the travelling," remembers Johnny Smith. "It was hard giving up a Saturday morning to go to West Hull and getting nothing financially out of it. We always entered the National Cup. Some years they would say: 'we'll never win it again, we're not strong enough', but we thought it was a matter of tradition. The cost of the coach or whatever didn't matter."

Recs' indifferent record in the National Cup continued in 1989–90 with a 28–12 defeat by Dudley Hill at City Road. The team found wins hard to come by in the league, finishing third from bottom, two points above Milford and Lock Lane, who were both relegated. There was one good reason to celebrate, however, when front-rower Paul Hankinson was selected in the BARLA Great Britain squad to tour the Cook Islands, Western Samoa and Tonga. Unlike their professional counterparts, the amateurs relied on their clubs' fund-raising activities for travel and equipment for the five-week tour, which came to almost £2,000 per player.

The 1990–91 campaign saw a further decline in playing standards, with the Recs managing just three wins. Coach Billy Simmons faced a tough task as the team finished bottom of the table, eight points behind fellow-strugglers West Hull. As relegation into the Second Division beckoned, after much deliberation the club elected to withdraw from the National League and return to the North West Counties competition. Clearly, the limited finances at the club were being stretched to breaking point and playing resources were starting to dwindle, as Jeff Gormley points out: "People were having time off work and they couldn't afford it. They cried off some matches and probably also didn't train on a Thursday, so it became more and more difficult to run a team in the National League."

The club would begin the 1991–92 season in the North West Counties First Division, the second tier of that competition. "This was an agreement between BARLA and the local competition," recalls Billy Dillon. "We had to start in a division lower, we couldn't just return back to the Premier Division. It was a chance for us to re-group and put the club on a sound footing once more." It was a tough time for everyone at City Road. Despite sponsorship from the likes of Whitegates Estate Agency, the club accrued debts of several thousand pounds during the latter stages of their National League existence and the committee was put under increasing pressure. Several players left the club for a variety of reasons. Dave Carsley and Alun Allcock retired and powerful front-rower Paul Hankinson joined rivals Thatto Heath. Trying to replicate the success of the previous decade was becoming an increasingly difficult task.

Dave Manning – reeling in the years

It was fitting that many former Recs greats were in the crowd at Widnes St Maries to see the team lift the North West Counties Premiership trophy in 2008. Dave Manning wouldn't have missed it for the world. A former rugby union player, Dave, also known by the nickname 'Arthur' at City Road, played for Ruskin Park, West Park and Orrell before turning out in the Shaw Cup at Leigh in 1976–77, where teams included six registered rugby league players, plus anyone else who wanted to play. It was a way of attracting players to the XIII-a-side code and Dave was hooked.

"Believe it or not I got straight into the Recs' first team in the second-row," he remembers. "When I started, I was a grafter. I used to try and do my fair share of tackling and support play. Although there were several creative players in the side, like Sid Wright, Simmons, McCabe and Jeff Gormley, I never felt overawed. They made me feel welcome and perhaps they needed some new blood in the team because they were all coming to the end of their careers together. Mind you, it was a close-knit affair in those days. They all mated round together and worked together. They used to say the team used to get picked at Triplex on the afternoon shift."

When the team of the 1970s had largely broken up, Dave was appointed captain, where his vast experience was a tremendous help to the younger players. "I also started to become more creative and do a bit more ball-handling," he recalls. "In the first season in the National League we nearly won the competition, but just failed after West Hull beat us. Those days were hard to sustain because players had to miss work. Some missed the games and that was the problem. We had too many players missing matches. Fortunately, in the North West Counties today, travelling long distances is rare."

For Dave, the game that really stands out is the one against Wigan in the John Player Trophy in 1979–80. "We were beaten 18–9 at Knowsley Road and I only remember the game vaguely, because I got knocked out," he grimaces. "And then I scored a try which I didn't remember." Dave ended the season with the first of his two BARLA National Cup winners medals after a try-scoring performance against Dewsbury Celtic, although his second final, two years later, was memorable for the wrong reasons: "All hell broke loose in the last few minutes. Our last try killed the game off and they had no chance of winning. So they must have thought it was time for a bit of retribution and they cut up rough. Both sides got a two-year ban after that."

Dave fully enjoyed his playing career at the Recs, which went on well over 20 years. "Perhaps the old team just stayed on a little too long and they retired together," he recalls wistfully. "All the teams that we had dominated over the past 10 years then decided to take it out on our young lads. It was retribution all over again."

Dave was captain when news of the initial plans to sell City Road first appeared in 1990: "Part of the original plans included a Peugeot garage opposite Skippers Ford garage." He reveals: "They were going to put a dealership there. It sounds daft but when you get two car dealerships together it is better than one. It attracts custom. The main office unit was Peugeot... that was the pivotal development. They then started taking soil samples in 2004 and the land was put up for sale, for residential development. I wouldn't say it is exactly prime land for house building. The best future set up [for the Recs] would revolve around the cricket club, because you are keeping the club in the catchment area of Windle. The whole idea is go to the cricket club and build extra changing rooms so that we can play at Bishop Road. Where you play your rugby, you want to go back for a drink afterwards, but everything is still in the balance."

Dave is enthusiastic about the prospects of the current Recs' team and the future of the club itself. "They have a solid core of lads who have come through the ranks, such as John Rees, Andy Lyons, Neil Morris, Peter Cahalin and Andy Burns and a first-rate coach in John Ledger. Some people have suggested we revert back to the name St Helens Recreation when we leave City Road. I think that would be superb. I've played at Pilkington Recs for an awful long time. But something like that would signify the birth of a new era, yet at the same time would refer back to the history of the club."

Recs hooker Andy Fairclough in action against Egremont in 1986.
(Courtesy *Rugby League Journal*)

Action at City Road in 1986-87. Dave Manning prompts. Other Recs players from left to right:
Andy Fairclough, Steve Fenney Paul Hankinson and Niel Wood.
(Courtesy *Rugby League Journal*)

12. 1990 to 2000: At the crossroads

Recs' final season in the National League had been blighted by news which threatened the very existence of the club itself. Although the town as a whole had been jubilant when the proposed take-over of Pilkingtons by the financial conglomerate BTR had been thwarted in 1987, there were serious implications for Pilkington Recs Rugby League Club. In July 1990 came the announcement that Pilkingtons were prepared to sell the 45-acre City Road site. A meeting was arranged at City Road when these plans were revealed for both the rugby league and bowling sections. Needless to say the members were quite staggered at the proposals. "When we met them at the club they assured us that alternative accommodation would have to be found first," recalls former Recs secretary Albert Garner. "We went round the town with them, looking for alternative sites, but most were entirely unsuitable for our needs and the whole thing was totally unrealistic."

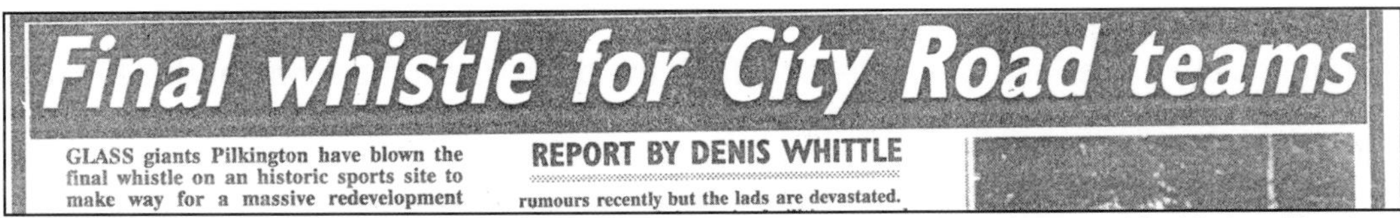

Final whistle for City Road teams

GLASS giants Pilkington have blown the final whistle on an historic sports site to make way for a massive redevelopment

REPORT BY DENIS WHITTLE

rumours recently but the lads are devastated.

The nightmare begins! Speculation about the sale of the City Road site began with this headline in the *St Helens Star* in July 1990. (Courtesy *St Helens Star*)

Billy Dillon, a former player, chairman and current secretary (at the time of writing) of Pilkington Recs explained the effects of the proposed takeover on the company: "Ruskin Leisure came about after the proposed takeover by BTR [which did not happen]. If they came in, they might take Pilkingtons, but all the land was leased out to other companies. Ruskin Leisure was given City Road and Ruskin Drive. It was a way of protecting assets. Ruskin Leisure was backed by Pilks for about five years until it became a company in its own right. As soon as the five years were over, we were hit hard and things have been made increasingly difficult for us at City Road. It has been difficult for us to get a Lottery grant for two reasons. If you mention you are Pilkingtons, they assume you are connected to the firm as it was; secondly, we have never had a lease on the land. I went to see the properties director at Pilkingtons head office to see if he would be prepared to let Pilkington Leisure lease the land to us, which he refused point blank. He then got out a load of plans and drawings – this would be in the early 1990s and there was also a proposed new road to link up with the East Lancs [Road], which would have cut through the pitches at City Road.

The new infrastructure was connected with the office park development, which never got off the ground. Whether the thing failed because the road never got put through, or whether money got tight, at the back end of the 1980s or 1990s, I don't know."

Although little happened regarding the sale of the ground, the threat of eviction from City Road marked the beginning of the end of a glorious era for works sports in St Helens. Gradually the town was losing its manufacturing base, with the demise of UGB and Beechams in the 1990s. The numbers employed by Pilkingtons had decreased, with the company announcing 747 job losses in St Helens in October 1991, partly as a result of changing technology and competition from the global market. The need to satisfy shareholders was paramount and recreation provision became of secondary importance. Playing fields were sold off for other purposes – usually housing – and tertiary or service industry had replaced manufacturing. It is significant that the town's largest employer in

2008 was the local authority. Pilkingtons itself remains in St Helens, but is now owned by Nippon Sheet Glass, who made the £1.8 billion purchase of the former family firm to extend its own position in the global glass market – changing times indeed.

Bouncing back

The Recs' return to the more parochial and less financially demanding North West Counties league was welcomed by many and provided stability for a club that faced life at the crossroads. After spending the 1991–92 season in the First Division, the Recs finished as Champions and were promoted into the Premier Division. Local rivals Thatto Heath won the Premier Division championship in 1990–91, one of four titles won by the club in the 1990s. which would have a knock-on effect at City Road, as Johnny Smith explains: "Thatto Heath began attracting players – that was a problem. It was difficult for us because players would pack in at local professional clubs and they would go to Thatto Heath, who were a side capable of winning the BARLA Cup."

Unfortunately, the Recs were relegated from the top division at the end of the 1993–94 season. By June 1994, a new structure was announced under the chairmanship of Joe Dillon. Shaun Allen and Johnny Smith were to be joint first team coaches. Denis Litherland would continue in charge of the 'A' team. The on-going junior development was in place with Barry Diggles in charge of the under-8s, Ralph Rawsthorne coached the under-10s, Barry Hasleden and Keith Ford ran the under-12s and Phil Lee oversaw the under-16s.

Down to the Wire

Ironically, Pilkingtons came under fire from supporters of St Helens RLFC as a result of its continuing sponsorship of rugby union in the shape of the Pilkington Cup competition. "We must be the only club in the league which does not have major sponsorship from the town's major employer," commented one Saints shareholder. A Pilkington spokesperson replied that the sponsorship provided them with maximum exposure to their national and international customer base. Meanwhile, the rugby league arm of the Pilkington Recreation club had stabilised their position in the North West Counties First Division after their recent demotion. There was a chance for glory in the Hays Chemicals St Helens Cup competition at the end of 1994–95, however, when the Recs reached the Final after a convincing 24–7 victory over UGB, including a 60-metre try from stand-off Brian Garrity.

Recs faced deadly rivals Blackbrook at Knowsley Road, who were enjoying a successful season in the Second Division of the National League and began as favourites. It was a superb spectacle for the large crowd, laced with excitement and drama at every turn. A penalty and two drop goals from scrum-half Mark Jackson gave Recs an early advantage, yet Blackbrook fought back with a penalty and try from Ian Callaghan. In what was becoming a see-saw battle, Jackson levelled the scores with a further penalty and then created the opening for stand-off Brian Garrity to touch down and added the goal to give the City Road boys a 12–6 lead at half time.

Although Recs continued strongly after the interval, Blackbrook replied with a further Callaghan try and the same player levelled the scores shortly after with a penalty. Blackbrook's Dave Ryan put Jason Mitchell in under the posts, with Callaghan's conversion giving them a six-point advantage. Both sides had chances to increase their tally, but Blackbrook looked set to hold on until a minute before the end when Mike Pilling galloped

Pilkington Recs 1994–95. Back: Johnny Smith, Jimmy Dooley, Bill Chester (chairman), Chris Arkwright, Andy Crehan, Ian Thomas, David Pilkington (president), Mike Dennett, Colin Whittaker (vice president), Stuart Wilson, Paul Parnell, Chris Gearing, unknown, Mark Leadbetter, Darren Haigh, Shaun Allen; Front: Dave Manning, Ian Connolly, Jeff Hornby, Mal Jackson, Mike Pilling, Keith Grimes, Andy Traverse, Denis Litherland. (Courtesy Denis Litherland)

Pilkington Recs first and second team squads circa 1995-96.
Back: Mark Jackson, Steve Fenney, unknown, Phil Ashall, Chris Gearing, Dave Manning, Paul Parnell, Dave Harrison, Barney Eastwood, Mike Cooper, Joe Ball, Ian Thomas, Glen Pilling, Shaun Allen;
Middle: unknown, Phil Chisnall, Mick Pilling, Andy Swift, Dave Corless (sponsor and chairman), Dave Chisnall (coach), Alan Maleedy, unknown, Paul Dickinson, Keith Wills.
Front: unknown, Andy Holmes, Jason Ledger, Craig Burrows, Shaun Baker, Tony Lloyd, Jeff Albin.
Mascots: Dave and Ryan Corless.

Pilkington Recs under–18s 1995-96. Back: Paul Hankinson (coach), Eric Frodsham (coach), Jamie Smith, Dave Perry, Tony Boulton, Nick Cammann, Peter Cahalin, Anthony Marsh, John Rees, Joey Briers, Neil Morris, Peter Smith (Kit) 'Big John' the Butcher, Andy Lyons; front: Ste Briggs, Gareth Roberts, Iain Phar, Jamie Grice, Sponsor (CIE Windows), Paul Nicholson (capt), Steven Smith, Scott Adams, Andrew Kilmurray. Mascot – Jon Frodsham. (Courtesy Denis Litherland).

over for a touchdown, Jackson's conversion sending the game into extra time, delighting the City Road fans in the main stand.

Jackson gave Recs the lead with a penalty in the first period of extra time, but Blackbrook staged a late, late show to take the trophy with a converted try from Mark Flinders, together with a drop-goal from Callaghan. Scrum-half Mark Jackson was in the thick of the action for Recs throughout and his varied passing and kicking game kept the visitors constantly on the back foot. Chris Gearing earned the plaudits for a hard-working display in the forwards.

The highlight of the season was the performance of the under–18 team, who won North West Counties Premier League title, coached by Eric Frodsham and Paul Hankinson, including the likes of John Rees and Andy Lyons, who were to feature in the Recs open age team more than a decade later.

The yo-yo Recs

The St Helens Cup defeat was a further blow for morale and the club was to spend the second half of the 1990s desperate to establish themselves once more in the Premier Division without success.

However, by the 1995–96 campaign, the Recs enjoyed excellent coverage in the local press for their full range of teams from open age down to under-7. The Recs lottery was also in full swing with a £1,000 first prize. Such fund-raising was essential with difficult draws in the National Cup, including a visit to London-based Surrey Heath, where the Recs won 64–6.

There was jubilation for the club at the end of 1996–97 with promotion back to the Premier Division. A tough campaign reached a climax with Recs' superb victory at Orrell St James in April that cemented their place back in the Premier Division. The newspaper report in the *St Helens Star* on 17 April 1997 conveys some of the excitement of a magical afternoon for the City Road boys:

Going Up!
Orrell St James 14 Pilkington Recs 37

This victory against third-placed Orrell ensures Recs of promotion to the Premier Division of the Burtonwood Brewery North West Counties League next season. The win was all the more pleasing in view of the patched-up side that Recs were forced to field on the day, which included coach Shaun Allen slotting in very comfortably at prop forward.

An early penalty goal from Mark Jackson helped to settle Recs' nerves and after 15 minutes they registered their first try when, after a good drive from Shaun Allen, ever alert hooker Craig Burrows plunged in for a try from acting-half. Jackson's conversion opened up an 8-point gap. Midway through the half, a well-taken drop-goal from Jackson kept the score moving along.

Just as Recs looked set for a 9-point interval lead, Orrell did well to keep the ball alive to cross for an un-converted try through their right-centre. However, an instantaneous response from the visitors proved a hammer blow, as good yardage through one-out rugby set up the position for a repeat score from Burrows, who burrowed through again. Jackson's goal stretched the scoreline to 15–4 in Recs' favour.

Orrell started more strongly after the break and they reduced the deficit through a converted try. With the homesters enjoying their best period of play, Recs did well to score with one of their raids as stand-off Litherland sliced through to feed the supporting Darren Haigh who scored. Minutes later, the homesters crossed wide out for their third try to again worry the visitors.

Recs lifted their game in the last ten minutes to cross for three converted tries to sink Orrell's own promotion hopes. At this stage of the game, substitutes Nicky Leyland, Brian Garritty and Mark Leadbetter played important parts.

First Litherland teased the home defensive line before straightening up to score beneath the posts, beating three defenders on the way. Next, Nicky Leyland crashed through for a try by the posts. Finally, a spectacular run by Garritty saw him feed the supporting Leadbetter, who held off a tackler on his way to his first try in the first team this season. All three tries were converted.

The Mike Wilson, Painter and Decorator Man of the Match was Craig Burrows

Alas the joy of promotion was tempered somewhat, 12 months later, as the Recs once again found themselves in the First Division. It was a difficult campaign, punctuated by the death of former chairman Bill Chester at the end of January 1998 at the age of 70 after many years of poor health. Beginning at Blackbrook, Bill was invited to join the Recs and his vast knowledge and enthusiasm saw him willingly take on the chairmanship of the club for several seasons. He took great pleasure in the Recs' legendary Challenge Cup. Blackbrook chairman Harold Swift talked of Bill's "massive contribution to the amateur game in St Helens and further afield." Great administrators, like great players, are undoubtedly the life-blood of a successful rugby league club and Bill Chester was no exception.

Pride of the Recs – 50th anniversary

On 4 July 1999, the Pilkington Recreation Rugby League Club celebrated its 50th anniversary at Knowsley Road with a parade of past and present teams before the Saints versus London Broncos Super League match. The club that had begun with just a single

The Recs team at Keighley Albion in 1999–2000. Back: Jeff Albin, Jason Ledger, Graham Cranny, Andrew Kilmurray, Mike Dennett. John Rees, Neil Morris, David Archer, Chris Hillan; front: Darren Haigh, Mark Forber, Ian Connolly, Andy Fairhurst, Neil Morris, David Archer, Chris Hillan. (Courtesy Denis Litherland).

open age outfit in 1949 could now boast no less than 13 teams – a marvellous achievement. The parade was led by two members of the under-9 squad, Danny Lynch and Matthew Holding, whose father Neil had played for Recs before finding fame with the Saints several years later. The parade also featured a cross-section of great players and officials from the different eras, including Les Corns, Ronnie Barton, Geoff Irwin, Denis Litherland, Eddie Prescott, Bob Williams and Joe Dillon. To complete the celebrations, on 25 February 2000, the club held a celebration dinner at its City Road headquarters, hosted by Sky Television's Eddie Hemmings and Mike Stephenson.

Club officials at the time of the 50th anniversary celebrations were as follows: president: David Pilkington CBE; vice president and chairman: David Corless; treasurer: Mrs S. Rawsthorne; secretary: Ralph Rawsthorne; PRO: Mr N. Swift; social secretary: Mr D. Lane; committee: Mrs G. Lane; Mr J. Parr; Mr S. Allen; Denis Litherland and Mr J. Dillon.

Promotion to the top flight was secured in 1999–2000, under coach Eric Frodsham and the club looked ready to establish itself as Premier Division challengers in the new millennium. Yet given the always uncertain situation regarding their City Road home, the Recs had proposed a possible link with Liverpool St Helens RUFC at Moss Lane on the other side of the East Lancs Road. "LSH were in a bit of a sticky financial situation at the time," remembers Billy Dillon. "Our younger teams had a base there already, which suited us. Their chairman [the Late] Alan Walker wanted the two clubs to merge. Dave Corless and I put a package together where we were going to put money into LSH. It was a big sell on our part and we went to a meeting with Alan and things were apparently going smoothly. But the whole thing was destroyed with Sporting Club St Helens coming along [St Helens RLFC, St Helens Town and Liverpool St Helens RUFC were to make up the proposed new organisation – keeping their separate team identities].

There was a big meeting at Moss Lane and they went along with the Sporting Club idea. If that had not happened, Pilks would have been at LSH. There is another piece of land opposite the LSH clubhouse at the back, which would have been available to put more pitches on. Eventually, of course, Saints paid off LSH's debts, put Eric Hughes in as coach and paid the players, but the 'sporting club' concept fizzled out in the end.

The Recs had to explore any avenue open to them. Our thinking was that some time along the line the club would have to move and things were being made difficult for us financially to stay there [at City Road]."

As the new millennium dawned, however, the Recs were still playing on the hallowed turf of City Road and their great spirit continued to prevail in the face of adversity.

Denis Litherland

A flying winger who first trod the hallowed City Road turf in the 1970s before joining Saints is still very much an integral part of the Pilkington Recs' scene, albeit at grass roots level. Happily recovered from a hip operation, loyalty-personified Denis Litherland is an important cog in the club's junior movement, in which at the time of writing his grandson Jack is a regular choice in the under-10 line-up. Several other stars of yesteryear, including John Ledger and Geoff Phillips, are also fully committed to the club's coaching cause which, despite City Road being scheduled for possible house-building, can only auger well for Recs' long-term playing future.

Denis lives at Moss Bank with his wife Lorraine. His nephew Roy also kept the family Rugby League flag aloft in playing for Halifax as a half-back. Born in the town centre in 1958, Denis first played his rugby at Central Modern School, before starting amateur rugby league with Haresfinch Social Club in the St. Helens League. The mid–1970s found him heading for City Road where he quickly became an automatic selection in the senior side, as a winger, full-back or centre.

Arguably his best game for his beloved Pilks was against Wigan in 1979. In that same season 6 feet 13 stone Litherland also starred in the Recs team that won the National Cup. Small wonder then that Saints spotted his burgeoning talents and, after being chatted up by chairman Harry Cook, the 20-year-old became a Saint for whom he made 144 appearances, including 21 on the bench, and scored 38 tries, despite living in the shadow of Les Jones, Roy Mathias and Barrie Ledger.

The whistle finally blew on eight eventful years at Knowsley Road in 1987 and he needed no second asking to return to City Road. Another abiding memory of his time with Saints being when he played in Mathias's testimonial match – against Pilkington Recs. Incidentally, he was nicknamed 'Nellie Pledge' (of BBC Television's *Nearest and Dearest* fame) by team-mate Eric Frodsham because Litherland – like Nellie – is also employed in the chutney and vinegar trade. Having played both amateur and professional rugby league, Denis readily conceded that players in the paid ranks are generally fitter and faster. But, nonetheless, he named a number of the Recs squad of his day who could have made it with the big boys of rugby league: "Second-rower Kevin Whittle and centre Rufus Hill both wore the Swinton jersey", remembered Litherland, "and why loose-forward Sid Wright and hooker Jeff Gormley failed to take the professional ticket I will never know."

Denis is not looking forward to the day when he finally trudges away from the ground he first entered as a player as long ago as 1976 and prior to that as an enthusiastic youngster. "I believe it should not be demolished to make way for residential development," he declared. "At the end of the day it is all about money," added Denis. "However ingrained habits and loyalties don't go away overnight and, despite the changing problems etc, many of the old guard still make the weekly pilgrimage to City Road on Saturday afternoons and also on training nights. The pavilion is virtually derelict and could become a sitting target for vandals, and in this respect we are extremely grateful to St Helens Cricket Club for the social facilities they have made available to us. Taking an optimistic peep into the crystal ball, I believe that time-honoured Pilkington Recs RLFC might live on at a new pitch at Bishop Road when the bulldozers have started to raze City Road to the ground," concluded an undeterred Denis Litherland.

Denis Litherland (left) and Geoff 'Jethro' Phillips - two Recs greats who still can't keep away from City Road.

Three Recs legends: John Forster, Billy Simmons and Eric Frodsham in 2007.

13. 2001 to 2007: Requiem for the Recs?

Over the years, Pilkington Recs has engendered a fierce sense of loyalty from players, administrators and supporters alike. John Rees is typical in this respect. For him, there has only ever been one place to play his rugby – at City Road, in the famous red-amber-and-black. He has been a Recs man for almost 20 years and no-one is better qualified to review the club's progress since the dawn of the millennium. The forceful second-rower is now a well-respected committee member, in addition to his responsibilities on the field. He talked about his commitments to his beloved Recs in July 2007: "I was from Haresfinch originally and it was handy for me – I used to walk down the East Lancs Road. I started at Recs in the under-10s with coach Barry Diggles in 1988–89. A couple of my mates from Parish Church Primary School decided that they wanted to have a go at playing rugby and it took off from there really. I've remained at Recs for 19 years. When I started we were the only junior team at the club, unlike today. Since then the club has gone from strength to strength. Andrew Canovan and Gareth Davies were contemporaries of mine. I went into the under-18s, with coaches Eric Frodsham and Ian Hankinson and spent two years there but I missed a season with back surgery.

"My first game at open age was in the second team. I had just returned from back surgery and we played one of the Leigh teams. I briefly remember scrum-half Johnny Smith putting me in under the posts. Eric Frodsham had done the under-18s and had moved up to open age. He called me up into the firsts after two games. That was in the North West Counties First Division. When I made my debut, some of the old Saints pros were still there – Johnny Smith, Shaun Allen and Chris Arkwright had had a season with us and packed in just before I stepped up. Barrie Ledger made a few appearances when Arkie was there too and helped us with our sprint training. We played two seasons in the First Division and then we got promoted in my second season, 1999–2000. We had four seasons in the Premier Division and were then relegated again, spent one season in the First Division, before getting back to where we are now.

In the 2000–01 season, Chris Arkwright was our coach. He knew what he was talking about and introduced three-times-a-week training on Monday, Wednesday and Friday. He said we needed to do that to be a successful Premier League side. Friday was for the first team only, when we used to do the game plan. Unfortunately, some of the lads there didn't really give him the respect he deserved. There were a few who didn't like training three times a week and so they didn't. It's a real shame that he didn't get that true commitment from the lads as a whole. But we finished third from bottom and avoided relegation.

The club then approached Kevin Thompson, who came with a great reputation from Haydock. He was more a 1970s or 1980s type of coach, who would shout at you and wind you up to try and get the best out of you. Under Kevin, a lot of players left because they didn't agree about how he coached us. We finished in the relegation places two years on the run and stayed up by default twice. At the end, he lost the dressing room – which can happen. It was towards the end of 2003–04 when [chairman] Ralph Rawsthorne relieved him of the coaching duties after we lost 30–0 to Haydock. John Ledger stepped in and nearly saved us. It was only by pure bad luck that we had to play Simms Cross twice, who had to win twice to win the league. They were a champion side. In both matches we led at half-time but lost them both and went down. We bounced back the following season, losing only one match, away at Roose Pioneers, which made us realise we weren't invincible.

Pilkington Recreation 2003–04. Back: Andy Lyons, Ricky Shaw, Graham Cranny, Dave Scott, Simon Grayley, Neil Morris, David Archer, Darren Haigh, Andrew Kilmurray, Andy Traverse, Barry Pope, Craig Burrows; front: Kevin Thompson (coach), Ste Smith, Andy Fairhurst, John Rees, Stuart Foster, Steven Rawsthorne, Chris Bailey, Mark Ashton. Mascot: Ben Burrows (Photo: Bernard Platt)

Pilkington Recs 28 Haydock 8 in the Lancashire Cup clash at City Road on 10 September 2005.
Recs are in their new kit sponsored by Cor Developments.
The trophy is the North West Counties First Division Championship.
Back: John Ledger (coach), Peter Cook, Andy Burns, Ricky Shaw, Mike Loughlin, Stuart Mansfield, Graham Cranny, Neil Morris, Mark Ashton, Ralph Rawsthorne (chairman); front: Chris Bailey, John Ford, Andy Fairhurst, John Rees, Steven Rawsthorne, Tim Critchley, Andy Lyons, Barry Pope.
(Photo: Bernard Platt)

Although I played for Lancashire in my first year of open age rugby, I was selected again in 2006–07. Our full-back Mark Ashton got the call-up for the second game and he was the best player on the day. He has played for Lancashire, Great Britain under-21s, under-23s and has fully justified his selection for the BARLA tour at the end of the season. Those selected for representative rugby were originally thin on the ground, but now, hopefully, success will breed success.

"I went on the Recs committee to make sure the open age players had a voice. The junior sections were blossoming and a lot of energy was going in there, but the open age section must never be ignored. When I started to help out, about three years ago, it was when the ground at City Road was being put up for sale. Now there are four of us on the committee – effectively it's Ralph, me, Dave Lee and Dave Roughley. That's the backbone. Then there's treasurer Andy Lyons, who is an accountant and John Ledger as head coach. It's incredibly streamlined. We get things done and it's not too unwieldy. We deal with so many other organisations, such as Pilkingtons, Sport England, the RFL that there's no point in having any more people involved.

The future's good when I think of all the teams we have here now. The junior section has produced such good quality rugby and such good players, such as Andy Lyons, Neil Morris, Mark Forber who are in their late 20s and the younger lads – Ste Rawsthorne, Mark Ashton and John Ford. I think our club tries to reward longevity and loyalty to the cause. We have a special tie for long-serving players. Our biggest rivals are Blackbrook and Simms Cross, but we'll see. I don't know how long I'll continue playing – perhaps until my body says I can't. My back's in really poor condition. I've got three bulging discs and trapped nerves, but I've got a brilliant physio, who really looks after me. Maybe I've got three or four seasons left. I already coach the under–18s with a few other open age players. The second team has always been strong and with a decent Lancashire Cup draw for us – that's what we need."

The end of an era

The club had been living with the spectre of having to leave its City Road home since July 1990, when the initial plan to develop the site into office units fortunately failed to come to fruition. Early in 2004 rumours spread that there was to be another attempt to sell the land, fuelled by a survey of the whole site, which included the pitches, bowling greens, Windle City Social Club and the car park. According to a Pilkingtons spokesperson in the *St Helens Star*, this was part of a review of the Cowley Hill and City Road factory site: "We are assessing the immediate and surrounding areas also owned by Pilkingtons and samples are currently being taken from the ground. At this stage, there are no plans for development. If and when there are, there would be full discussion with all parties involved in the usual way. Ruskin Leisure was consulted regarding the samples taken from the recreation site."

By the end of September 2004, however, the die was cast with the announcement that there were indeed plans for the sale of the City Road site. The initial plan was for the rugby league section to move over to the existing complex at Ruskin Drive, but the move never transpired. In the *St Helens Star* in early November, Ralph Rawsthorne, chairman of Pilkington Recs came out on the offensive, claiming that no consultations had been forthcoming concerning the future of the City Road site. In early November, St Helens North MP Dave Watts urged Pilkingtons to reconsider their plans for 400 homes in a letter to the company's chief executive Stuart Chambers. Despite promises of up-grading Ruskin Drive, opponents said the upgrade would not adequately compensate for the loss of vital community sports facilities. Watts urged Pilkingtons to use funds generated from the prospective sale to maintain sports facilities in the area. At the time, there were more than 250 players at the club, with all the junior teams. The loss of the floodlit training pitch in particular, used by team members, would in itself be a huge blow to community sport.

Mr Watts wrote to St Helens Council asking them to reject any plans which did not maintain sports facilities in the area. Pilkingtons blamed declining membership at the Windle City Social Club as the reason for the proposed closure. Ideally, the Recs would like to remain as close to their catchment area as possible – preferably in Windle City itself. St Helens Cricket Club has been proposed as a new base for the club, but finding additional accommodation for teams already using the playing fields at next door Bishop Road would cause inevitable knock-on effects. Victoria Park was also mentioned, although development of pitches on that site was rejected.

By January 2008, no-one could give appropriate safeguards for the long term future of the Recs. The land was still up for sale, but planning permission was recently rejected by the Council and it was back to square one. It is a classic case of hard-nosed economics versus much needed social provision. These are constantly changing times so cool heads all round are needed. Much compromise will be required if Pilkington Recs are to be allowed to maintain their community leisure provision in the long term.

One thing in the club's favour, however, is the Sport England legally binding dictum that states that existing sports grounds cannot be sold off unless like-for-like provision is found within the local community. "It would be easy, for example, for the Recs to be located at a site over the East Lancs Road," says under-18s manager Andy Foreman. "We would get pitches and changing facilities, but no social club provision which is so important for us. This is why the cricket club is important in the equation, in this respect. The main stumbling block is pitches at Bishop Road, adjacent to the cricket club. They are already being used by various football teams – mainly open age – at the moment. But the acquisition of this area would mean that we would become more inclusive as a club – something that we have wanted for many years, ever since the younger age groups were developed by the club."

So near... yet so far

Following the club's relegation in 2003–04 and the controversy regarding the possible loss of City Road, the open age team fought back brilliantly by losing just one match during the whole of the next league campaign in the First Division to finish as worthy Champions. At the end of the 2004–05 campaign the chance for further glory came with a St Helens Cup Final against Conference side Thatto Heath at Blackbrook.

Thatto Heath scored first, with a try from Webster, but Recs hit back courtesy of a superb one-on-one ball steal from Mark Ashton, who scampered over for a try which Barry Pope converted. Recs went ahead after Steven Rawsthorne and Chris Bailey combined to send centre Andy Traverse under the posts for Pope to add his second conversion. Although Thatto replied with a Dave Hull try, Recs maintained their four-point advantage when hooker Andy Fairhurst sent centre Andy Lyons over out wide. Pope goaled from the touchline and Recs held their 18–8 advantage until half-time.

Early in the second half a disallowed try from Mark Ashton triggered a concerted Thatto fightback. Front-rower Dootson crashed over under the posts and Woods' goal cut the gap to four once more. A Pope penalty extended the lead to a converted score but Thatto hooker Dave Scott scampered over and Woods' conversion levelled the contest at 20–20. As time ran out a strong run by John Rees took Recs back into drop-goal range, but Pope's effort went agonisingly wide.

There were just three minutes remaining when Thatto skipper Mike Woods chipped over. The bounce beat Ashton and Woods followed up for the winning try. Although it was a terrific disappointment for the Recs, they had contributed to a showpiece final. Steven Rawsthorne, Neil Morris and Andy Burns had been superb throughout and with just a little more luck Mark Ashton could have registered another four-pointer.

It was to be another three years before the Recs would compete in another knockout final but they would undoubtedly draw on the experience from this encounter to put them in good stead for the future.

A shock to the system

The Recs mourned the passing of two players from the modern era in 2003 – Ste Traverse and Dave Lang, both popular clubmen and still sadly missed at City Road. In November 2005 a link with the National Cup winning sides of the early 1980s was also broken with the untimely death of 54-year-old Bob Bolan, a superb threequarter, who had come through the under-18s at City Road with his close friend Eddie Cunningham.

Like many Recs players before him, Bob was a licensee. His last pub was the Cherry Tree in Parr and his two brothers were also connected with the club. "Harvey was our touch-judge and secret weapon," remembers Eric Frodsham, "While Bob's other brother David played in the second team. It was such a shock for all of us when we heard he had passed away."

There was another blow to the very fabric of Pilkington Recs ARLFC on Saturday 31 March 2007, when the Windle City Social club was closed down after the final game of the season against local rivals Blackbrook – a decision made by Ruskin Leisure. To mark the occasion, there was a special dinner at the club after the match featuring a host of former past and present players, in line with chairman Ralph Rawsthorne's desire to "See the old girl off in style". Only changing facilities remained for the club for the 2007–08 campaign, despite having to cater for the full range of teams from the different age ranges. They were indeed challenging times at City Road.

Completed in 1964, with changing rooms added some years later, the club had not always been the preferred meeting place for the rugby league team, as Jethro Phillips remembers: "We used to have training Tuesday and Thursday, 6.45pm, finish at a quarter past eight, shower and have a drink in the club. Then we all went our different ways. Some went up Thatto Heath, Carr Mill or wherever. The club used to shut early on match days. Only Ruskin Drive was able to open all day, because of all the sports there. We used to finish at four and by the time we were out of the shower we just had time for the last pint. Both teams would then go to the Park Hotel and the licensee Roy Skerry would put a bit of food on, a few plates of sandwiches and pies. We all had a few pints and away we went."

Obviously, as Billy Simmons explains, this was to the detriment of the Recreation Club facilities: "Recreation secretary Ken Griffiths eventually got wind of the situation. Obviously by the early 1970s we were becoming a successful team with a lot of people watching us. So Ken was watching, say, 600 to 800 people coming down to Pilks, watching an amateur team and going away and not using the facilities.

So he then got the club to open all day. We had some great nights there. [Club president] Mr David [Pilkington] was brilliant with us. There was one occasion after a big match when the company had put money over the bar, so it was free all night. He said to those waiting on 'keep the bar open' and he paid the remainder."

Lock-in

One person in particular did not want to leave the club on its final night. Recs front-rower Neil Morris found himself locked in the building and got a lift home from the police after setting the alarms off. The closure of the Windle City club left the Recs without a social base, although St Helens Cricket Club was used for post-match conviviality during the 2007–08 campaign, perhaps a sign of future plans for this most enduring of rugby league clubs.

The end of City Road

City Road for sale! The notice outside the Recs ground on 31 March 2007 (Courtesy Pilkington/Ruskin Leisure)

The site of the former grandstand at City Road has changed immeasurably since its halcyon days in the 1920s, now occupied by a line of trees and the pylons for the training lights. Pilkingtons Cowley Hill works is in the background. (Courtesy Pilkington/Ruskin Leisure)

The Windle City Social Club is photographed on its final day on 31 March 2007.
The dressing rooms (right) still remain operative, but the site was increasingly dilapidated.
(Courtesy Pilkington/Ruskin Leisure)

Left: The special programme produced to celebrate 43 years of the Windle City Social Club.

Below: Recs' John Rees tackling against Blackbrook in 2007.

Recs players celebrate after the defeat of Blackbrook in the last home game of 2006-2007.

14. 2007 to 2008: Recs in microcosm

Down the years the name Frodsham had a familiar ring at Saints with no fewer than five brothers on the books before the war, including 1928 tourist centre Alf, who later became club coach. That quintet were raised in Pigot Street and were followed to Knowsley Road by full-back Eric in 1946, plus trialist forward Peter and stand-off Tommy in the 1990s, none of whom were related.

Then came a lengthy pause, with fans looking in vain for the name 'Frodsham' in Saints team selections until – hey presto! – a giant 18-year-old forward recently appeared on the Super League scene. Gareth Frodsham put pen to paper on a three-year contract after making his way through the ranks at the prolific Pilkington Recs nursery.

He was first taken to City Road as a six-year-old mascot by doting dad Eric, who was 'part of the furniture' at the ground both as a player and official, and it soon became apparent that Frodsham junior had taken to rugby league like a duck to water. A former pupil of Blackbrook St Mary's and St Augustine's schools, Gareth lives at Laffak where, along with dad, his greatest fans are proud mum Liz, brother Jonathan, and sister Charlotte.

The house is festooned with trophies and photographs of Gareth's burgeoning oval ball career, which includes captaining England against Wales at under–16 level in 2005 and in France 12 months later. Travel-wise the highpoint arrived in touring Australia with the Academy squad in 2007. Given such a soaring pedigree, and supported by Academy gurus Mike Rush, Derek Traynor and Eric Chisnall, young Frodsham needed no second asking when Saints urged him to cross the Rubicon from City Road to Knowsley Road.

Nowadays a strapping 6 feet 2 inches, 16 stone finely-tuned athlete, dark-haired crew-cut Gareth has never been happier since becoming a Saint. As for his role in the team's scheme of things he said: "making the hard yards, being first receiver, tackling stints – it all comes the same to me because I am enjoying myself." As for fitness levels Gareth knew what to expect on touching down at Knowsley Road: "Obviously they are much higher than in the amateur game, and what with intense training programmes and careful diets I am feeling tremendous" he chuckled.

A good friend of Kurt Haggerty (son of Roy and another former Recs player to sign for Saints), Gareth is grateful for the help and encouragement received from Saints coach Daniel Anderson during his time at the club, his team-mates, and of course his dad who is now in charge of scholarship courses at Knowsley Road.

Simply the best

Gareth was indeed the first player to come 'through the system' at City Road and sign full-time professional forms for a Super League club and looks to have a promising future ahead. What about the club he left behind?

The under–9s, 10s and 11s, while not playing in competitive leagues have been successful. The under–12s won the Lancashire Cup and North West Counties Cup by record margins and were still unbeaten at the end of the 2007-08 season. They had not been beaten since they were under–7s. They toured France in June 2008 – the first overseas tour for any junior team in the club's history. Both under–13 teams finished strongly in their respective leagues in 2007-08, while the under–15s had their highest league position ever. The under–16s were promoted to the Premier Division and the under–17s reached their first Final, in the BARLA Lancashire Cup, but were beaten 16–8 by Hindley.

Young guns

Gareth Frodsham the latest in a long line of Recs-Saints!
(Courtesy Bernard Platt)

Man-of-the-match Jonathon Peers offloads in the North West Counties Challenge Cup Final 30–0 win against Oldham St Anne's under-18s on 16 March 2008 at Clarrington Park, Wigan
(Courtesy Tommy Morris)

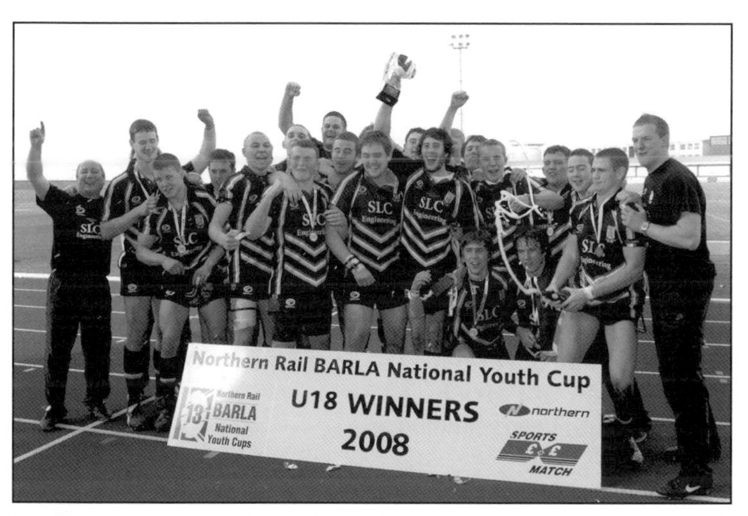

Pilkington Recs under–18s celebrate their National Cup victory at Hunslet.
Left to right: Andy Foreman (manager), Gary Trueman (physio), Mark Briody, Owen Livesey, Shaun Forber, Will Abbott, Mike Wilson, Stephen Lane, John Rees (coach), Ryan Liptrot, Paul Knapper, Alex Kean, Jonno Peers, Greg Smith (captain), Kelvin Duffy, Robbie Foreman, Kurtis Marsh, Danny Lynch, Tom Connick, Ian Marren, Andy Ranson, Danny Filson, Steve Edgerton (coach)
(Courtesy Tommy Morris)

Recs under–12s – North West Counties Cup winners 27 April 2008 at Fylde Rugby Union club
Back: Jack Birchall, Callum Murphy, Josh Springford, Liam Forsyth, Mike Hewitt (coach), Kurt Riley (captain), Darren Riley (coach), David Hewitt, Liam Parr, Connor Davies, Ross McCauley; front: Ryan Briggs, Daniel Byrne, Matthew Whitley, Callum Savage, Connor Davies (mascot), Chris Carberry, Thomas Davies, Bradley Ramejkis, Connor Davies, Niall Allen
(Courtesy Darren Riley)

The Recs under–18 team enjoyed a fantastic season in 2007–08, with a two-trophy haul, including the club's first national cup final success since the early 1980s. This was reflected in the selection of six players for Lancashire during the season: full-back Danny Filson, half-backs Greg Smith and Danny Lynch, plus forwards Tom Connick, Mark Briody and Jonathon Peers. Ian Marren and Ben Gravener also received a call-up for the England Students under–19 squad. On 16 March 2008, the team steam-rollered Oldham St Annes 30–0 to pick up the North West Counties Challenge Cup in the Final at Clarrington Park, Wigan. There was even more success to come in the National Cup Final, against Wigan St Patrick's – a real pulsating affair on a memorable afternoon in Hunslet's South Leeds Stadium.

Northern Rail National Youth (under–18) Cup Final
Pilkington Recs 16 Wigan St Patricks 12
Monday 5 May 2008 at South Leeds Stadium

Although Recs dominated the early exchanges, it was St Pats who took the lead when winger Boardman picked up a towering bomb from Greg Smith and ran 70 yards to the line. Scrum-half Schmekel added the extras. Before the break another kick from Smith, this time of the grubbing variety, was seized upon by centre Sean Forber, who made the touchdown. Mike Wilson's goal levelled the scores and Recs took the advantage after the break, with Forber's second try, following a brilliant run from winger Owen Livesey.

Wilson's conversion hit the post, yet the Recs maintained their dominance in what was becoming an enthralling spectacle. In the 70th minute, Greg Smith spotted a gap in the St Pats defence on the last tackle and shimmied his way over. Wilson converted once more. Following the sin-binning of St Pat's prop Mike Nicholls with just five minutes to go, a try from Wilson was disallowed for a forward pass. The Wigan side threw everything at the Recs and scored a try from Banks which Charnley converted. At 16–12, it was a panic time after Recs restart kick went out on the full and gave St Pats one last chance to claim victory. Just as centre Mark Bayman looked certain to score, he was tackled. His attempted off-load to his winger went to ground and the Recs celebrated a double trophy success.

Skipper and stand-off Greg Smith lifted the trophy aloft after a marvellous display, which earned him the man-of-the-match award, capping a great afternoon for his team-mates and coaches Steve Edgerton and John Rees. Plaudits must also go to winger Owen Livesey for his dedication to the Recs. He had previously lost in two previous national finals for Blackbrook, both against Wigan St Patricks at under–14 and under–16 levels. A talented judo exponent, he took part in a tournament in Sweden on the Saturday before the National Final and despite being only 16, won a silver medal in the open age competition. He was so determined to get a winner's medal this time around that his father booked him home on an earlier flight, arriving home 24 hours before the match.

Pilkington Recs: Danny Filson, Mike Wilson, Stephen Lane, Sean Forber, Owen Livesey, Greg Smith (capt), Danny Lynch, Rob Foreman, Ryan Liptrot, Mark Briody, Kurtis Marsh, Alex Kean, Ian Marren. Subs: Jonathon Peers, Tom Connick, Will Abbott, Ben Graveney.
Scorers: Tries: Forber 2, Smith; Goals: Wilson 2,
Wigan St Patricks: Charnley, Boardman, Bayman, Gannon, Hart, Banks, Schmechel, Nicholls, Clarke, Newton, Spencer, Molloy, Sedgwick (capt). Subs: France, Barrow, Beeston, Richard Ackers, Chris Ackers.
Scorers: Tries: Boardman, Banks; Goals: Charnley, Schmechel.
Half-time: 6–6
Referee: Michael Reid
Attendance: 600

Left: Danny Davies makes a break against Blackbrook in the North West Counties Premier Division at City Road. Mark Ashton backed up to score under the posts.

Middle: Full-back Mark Ashton scores one of his three tries in the North West Counties Premiership semi-final against Blackbrook. Other Recs are Mark Forber, Mark Rigby and Ricky Shaw.

Right: Recs' scrum-half Danny Lynch in action against Wigan St Patricks in the National Final at Hunslet. (Courtesy Tommy Morris)

Pride of the Premier League

Members of the North West Counties Premier League, the Recs open age team promised much for the 2007–08 campaign. Full-back Mark Ashton was an integral member of the side, with his pace and broken field running. The threequarter line consisted of Andy Lyons - one of the fastest centres in the league, together with Nigel Pratt, Mark Rigby, Danny Davies and goal-kicking winger Barry Pope. Recs were strong in the half-back positions, with Jamie Smith at stand-off, another who came through the ranks; Ryan Rogers is a scrum-half who can change the course of a match with his variation of passes and Mark Forber is a great organiser and handy goalkicker.

The forwards were enthusiastic and hard-working, none more so than front-rower Neil Morris, who seemed to top the tackle count every match and finish like a threequarter. The strong-running Andy Burns, Ricky Shaw and former Blackpool Panthers prop Richard Rafferty give the team a vital go-forward' platform, with Peter Cahalin calling the shots at hooker with his incredible work-rate. John Rees used his size and power to great effect in the second row; John Ford was a particularly solid hitter, with Gary Philbin, Chris Bailey and Andy Fairhurst capable of stepping in and providing a consistent approach when needed. Locking the scrum is captain 'Sam' Rawsthorne – a tremendously talented player, strong and with great vision. The club increased its forward power by signing second-rower Adam Fogarty from Ruskin Park RUFC, a strong runner who looked forward to touring with the British Police in October.

Former captain Dave Manning was fulsome in his praise of the current side: "I watch them train and join in a little bit now and then. There are several lads, like Sam Rawsthorne, who I rate very highly indeed – and such a lot of them have come through the ranks, which says a lot about the status of the club. John Ledger, too, is an excellent coach. He possesses good man-management skills, was innovative and really had the team buzzing. John fully understood the way in which Pilks Recs should play their rugby and he's gradually brought some of his own ideas, in the Recs style of rugby, with perhaps a little more defensive bite."

Rugby record breakers

Although league progress was encouraging in 2007–08, Lancashire Cup hopes evaporated at the hands of eventual winners Bank Quay Bulls in the semi-final at City Road – a huge disappointment for the large crowd. In one of the earlier rounds, however, the team ran riot against Third Division Heysham Atoms to the tune of 106–4, including an amazing 54-point haul from winger Barry Pope. It was the largest individual points total in the club's history, although Barry might well have been preceded in the early 1960s by centre Ernie Forber, who let the chance to notch the half-century pass him by on two occasions: "I had the chance to do it twice in the same season," he recalls. "In one of the games I had just scored a try and came back from about 70 yards. Eric Tierney caught it from the restart and went all the way through them for another try. I said 'You take it, I'm buggered!' That was a 47 pointer for me. Later I got a 49 pointer, but never the half-century."

The Recs produced one of the greatest come-backs ever seen at City Road with a fantastic 34–30 victory over Kells in the preliminary round of the National Cup, after being 30 points down at half-time, with Ryan Rogers' appearance after the break galvanising the team to an unlikely victory. Unfortunately the side fell in the First Round proper at Stanningley, but could look at two further avenues – the Premier League and North West

Counties Premiership as a means of further honours. Their key to success seemed to lie with a series of matches against Blackbrook. In the league at City Road, the visitors were swamped by a superb display of attacking rugby, as the Recs triumphed 34–24. The return league match at McDonald Avenue saw Blackbrook exact revenge with a backs-to-the-wall 14–12 victory, despite Recs' domination of territory and possession in a tense second half. The defeat effectively put league honours out of sight for John Ledger's boys.

Yet in the North West Counties Premier Cup semi-final, once again at Blackbrook on 23 February, the Recs emerged victorious to the tune of 36–26. Scrum-half Ryan Rogers effectively controlled the game with his astute kicks and long passes. Tourist full-back Mark Ashton chimed in with a hat-trick of tries, as the Recs spirited scrambling defence in the second half did much to secure the result. Blackbrook's season was all but over and the sheer jubilation of the Recs' players after the final whistle summed up their delight at beating their deadly rivals, who had made the final on the last three occasions.

Although a closely fought 24–18 defeat at Bank Quay Bulls effectively ended title hopes, further wins at Simms Cross and Golborne Parkside ensured the team finished runner's up in the Premier Division, behind the Warrington outfit. The focus then switched to the North West Counties Premiership Final, against Simms Cross, the BARLA National Cup winners 2007, at nearby St Maries on 19 April 2008.

North West Counties Premiership Final
Pilkington Recreation 18 Simms Cross 12
Saturday 19 April 2008 at Widnes St Maries ARLC

For the Recs players it was a chance to lay their hands on a knock out trophy for the first time since the St Helens Cup win in 1986. Perhaps the burden of expectation lay heavily on the shoulders of the City Road boys. In front of a large and vocal crowd, the Recs enjoyed an encouraging share of territory and possession early in the match, but seemed tense and rarely showed their normal fluency in attack. Indeed it was Simms Cross who created one of the clearest chances of the half, when Recs full-back Mark Ashton produced a stunning last-ditch tackle on winger Wareing. The Widnes side took the lead in the 26th minute with a penalty from Billington, although Recs went desperately close soon afterwards when Ashton grounded short after one of his trademark runs. The deficit remained at two points until half-time.

After the break the game became a more open spectacle, but it was Simms Cross who took the initiative with two tries in quick succession. In the 44th minute winger Billington made the most of an overlap on the right and shortly after stand-off Hunt burst through on halfway and sent fellow paceman Wareing under the posts. Billington's conversion opened up a 12-point lead and the Recs were reeling.

It was time for the players to dig deep and fight back. Coach John Ledger added to the mix, by introducing the experienced Mark Forber at stand-off, with Jamie Smith switching to centre. It proved to be a crucial turning point, as the Recs piled on the pressure. Simmies looked somewhat rattled and ended up with a player in the sin-bin and the Recs took full advantage. It was skipper Steve Rawsthorne who set the ball rolling, after a mesmerising dummy run-around with scrum-half Ryan Rogers saw Forber dive through a yawning gap under the posts. Barry Pope's conversion was a formality as the team's self-belief grew immeasurably.

Eight minutes later, the come-back continued, when Jamie Smith's incisive break on the right saw Mark Rigby power his way to the line un-opposed. Pope's kick levelled the scores.

Simms Cross's full-back ended up in the sin-bin as the Widnesians' discipline deteriorated further – a big plus for the Recs. Sensing victory, the Recs swept into the attack with renewed vigour. The breakthrough came in superb style in the 69th minute when man-of-the-match John Rees punched a hole through three defenders in centre field and drew the last defender before handing on to the ever-willing Neil Morris, who finished in style between the posts after a 40-yard dash to the line. Barry Pope's conversion completed the turnaround and the end of a scintillating 13 minutes of rugby and a transformation in fortunes that was certain to become etched into Recs' folklore.

Although an attempted drop-goal from Forber went wide, the Recs' scrambling defence worked overtime to ensure victory was achieved. Skipper Steve Rawsthorne capped an emotional afternoon for everyone at City Road by lifting the trophy aloft. The club's senior players in particular had worked so hard for this success. Ricky Shaw had carried the ball up in powerful fashion, especially in the first half; Neil Morris showed great anticipation for his vital four-pointer and Mark Forber's timely introduction had done so much to put the team on the winning path. John Rees led the tackle count and made the incisive break that effectively won the match while the mid-field combination of Rawsthorne, Cahalin and Rogers dominating the second half. Andy Burns also tackled himself to a standstill. Yet most important of all, it was a marvellous achievement for the squad as a whole and it was not too long before the champagne began to flow. There were many sore heads amongst those connected with the famous old club on Sunday morning, but nobody cared in the slightest. Perhaps the club could now look forward to continued success and stability in the future.

Pilkington Recs: Mark Ashton, Mark Rigby, Nigel Pratt, Andy Lyons, Barry Pope, Jamie Smith, Ryan Rogers, Neil Morris, Peter Cahalin, Ricky Shaw, John Rees, Andy Burns, Steven Rawsthorne (capt). Subs: Mark Forber, Adam Fogarty, John Ford, Richard Rafferty

Scorers: Tries: Rigby, Morris, Forber; Goals: Pope 3.

Simms Cross: Keiron Kavanagh; Billington (1T, 2G), Geoghagan, David Percival, Chris Percival; Hunt, Myler; Iwan Brown, Walsh, Swain, Carmichael, Owain Brown, Waring (1T). Subs: John Nanson, Brendan Kavanagh, Price, Chris Nanson

Scorers: Tries: Billington, Waring; Goals: Billington 2.

Referee: Mr Walker

Half-time: 0–2

Attendance: 500 (est.)

Coach John Ledger believes that the Recs' trophy breakthrough was just the start of further success: "We are certainly in the ascendancy. We've been together for three or four seasons and the lads have a good understanding on the field. There are some great individuals, who also work as a formidable unit.

Although we play because we enjoy it, there is such great pride in the jersey. The important thing is that our youth structure – the best in the town in my view – will see several of the successful under–18s vying for places next year. The young lads who will be coming in will pick a lot up from the experienced players in the side."

John believes that appropriate foundations have been set for success to be sustained for the next five to six years, although he does have one burning ambition for the club. "If I was asked what I would really want for the team it is to be back in the Challenge Cup – that would be absolutely brilliant. If the lads continue to believe in their own ability, there is a promising future ahead on the playing side at Pilkington Recs."

The North West Counties Premiership Final

Above: John Rees with his man-of-the-match trophy.

Left: John Rees makes the crucial break that led to Recs' winning try. (Courtesy Tommy Morris)

Neil Morris scores the Recs final try. (Courtesy Tommy Morris)

Pilkington Recs North West Counties Premiership winners 2007–08
Back: Gary Trueman (physio), Adam Fogarty, John Rees, Gary Philbin, Barry Pope, Andrew Fairhurst, John Ford, Neil Morris, Nigel Pratt, John Ledger (coach); front: Chris Bailey (assistant coach), Ricky Shaw, Andy Lyons, Richard Rafferty, Mark Forber, Andy Burns, Mark Ashton, Danny Davies, Jamie Smith, Steven Rawsthorne, Peter Cahalin, Mark Rigby, Ryan Rogers
(Courtesy Tommy Morris)

Epilogue

Despite some magnificent achievements on the pitch during 2007–08, Pilkington Recs' major strength was in the number of teams run by the club – 12 in all – that can only be beneficial for the future. This provided a recognised pathway from the youngest age group to open age and the club is proud that lads who had come through the system were involved with professional clubs, including Gareth Frodsham and Kurt Haggerty at Knowsley Road. Just when supreme progress was being made, they were resigned to losing their spiritual home – the biggest blow of all. It was the place that other teams hated to travel to. From 2004 onwards Recs were embroiled in politics in the search for an amicable solution to the ground move. "We want to stay in Windle," said John Rees. "We've been here for over 100 years and we've served the community and want to continue to do so."

The future still holds a degree of uncertainty for even the most die-hard Recs devotee. More than ever, the members need to display that famous indomitable spirit, un-faltering resolution and un-rivalled tenacity that Tom Reynolds identified in the late 1920s to see them through. The eventual move from City Road, however, could signal a new beginning for the famous club, something that would be beneficial for the current players, who would be less aware of the legend of the great sides of the 1970s.

"The really important thing is to have a set-up where the pitches are together and we have room to develop, like Blackbrook and Bold," said John Ledger. "I believe that we will achieve this in the near future and if everything goes according to plan it will be great for the club and the community as a whole."

One aspect of the club's history remains as relevant today as it has always been. When interviewed for this book, players, officials and spectators past and present talk of the great feeling of camaraderie at the club, where everyone looks after each other. For many, like Johnny Smith, there is no place like it: "It was the best 14 years of my life socially and for enjoying my rugby. There was a terrific team spirit. My lad went down at five years of age and is currently in the under–18s. Naturally I want him to join the professional ranks, but if things don't work out I would love him to stay at Recs. He used to carry my bag home every night and I'll carry his. We enjoyed ourselves so much and let's face it – that's what it's all about."

This sign outside the entrance to the City Road ground says it all.
(Courtesy Pilkingtons/Ruskin Leisure).

Appendix: Statistics and records

Rugby union

Recs' playing record 1890–91

		Venue	Recs			Opponents			Result
			G	T	M	G	T	M	
4 Sept	Suttons Team	H	4	3	2	0	1	0	W
6 Sept	Mossley	A	2	1	2	0	0	0	W
13 Sept	Holbeck	H	6	1	2	2	0	3	W
20 Sept	Leigh	H	2	1	5	0	1	3	W
27 Sept	Aspull	H	3	1	2	1	0	2	W
4 Oct	Barrow	H	2	5	9	1	1	1	W
11 Oct	Morecambe	A	4	1	2	0	2	0	W
18 Oct	Stockport	H	2	1	4	1	0	2	W
25 Oct	Warrington	H	2	3	1	1	0	0	W
1 Nov	Kendal Hornets	A	0	0	4	0	1	1	L
8 Nov	Swinton	H	2	0	1	1	1	3	W
15 Nov	Brighouse Rangers	H	0	2	4	0	0	1	W
22 Nov	Lancaster	H	1	2	5	1	0	0	W
6 Dec	Barrow	A	2	1	3	0	0	2	W
13 Dec	Broughton Rangers	H	2	3	2	1	0	0	W
25 Dec	Crompton	H	1	1	0	1	0	0	W
27 Dec	Stockport	A	1	1	1	1	1	0	D
1 Jan	Millom	H	1	2	4	1	1	1	W
3 Jan	Swinton	A	0	0	1	0	1	1	L
10 Jan	Oldham	H	1	1	5	0	0	1	W
17 Jan	Tyldesley	H	1	1	4	1	0	2	W
24 Jan	Crompton	A	0	0	4	0	0	2	D
31 Jan	Millom	A	0	1	0	0	0	2	W
7 Feb	Brighouse Rangers	A	1	1	1	0	3	4	D
10 Feb	Dewsbury	A	0	0	2	0	3	4	L
14 Feb	Mossley	H	2	3	3	0	0	1	W
21 Feb	Lancaster	A	2	3	7	0	0	0	W
28 Feb	Holbeck	A	0	1	1	0	1	5	D
7 Mar	Kendal Hornets	H	1	4	3	0	0	1	W
14 Mar	Morecambe	H	1	3	2	0	1	2	W
21 Mar	Warrington	A	0	1	0	1	1	6	L
27 Mar	Dewsbury	H	1	1	5	0	1	3	W
28 Mar	Runcorn	A	0	0	4	0	2	3	L
30 Mar	Heckmondwike	H	1	0	3	0	1	0	W
4 Apr	Broughton Rangers	A	0	3	5	0	0	0	W
9 Apr	Warrington	H	0	2	1	0	1	0	W
11 Apr	Leigh	A	0	0	1	4	0	2	L
18 Apr	Runcorn	H	0	3	3	0	1	0	W
20 Apr	Tyldesley	A	0	1	3	1	0	4	L
25 Apr	Aspull	A	2	1	3	0	0	1	W
30 Apr	Scottish Colleges	H	2	3	5	0	0	0	W
			52	**62**	**119**	**19**	**25**	**63**	

Recs 'second class' fixtures 1895–96

		Venue	Recs			Opponents			Result
			G	T	P	G	T	P	
21 Sep	Swinton	H	0	1	3	1	0	5	L
28 Sep	Rochdale St Clements	H	0	2	6	1	0	5	W
9 Oct	Leeds Parish Church	H	1[1]	0	4	0	0	0	W

19 Oct	Leeds Parish Church	A	0	0	0	2	5	23	L
26 Oct	New Brighton	A	0	1	3	0	1	3	D
Nov 2	Salford	A	1	1	8	0	0	0	W
9 Nov	Lancaster	A	1[2]	0	4	0	1	3	W
16 Nov	Altrincham	H	1	1	8	0	0	0	W
23 Nov	Liverpool	H	0	1	3	1	0	5	L
30 Nov	Holbeck	A	2	1	11	0	0	0	W
7 Dec	Birkenhead Wanderers	H	3[1],[3]	0	15	0	0	0	W
14 Dec	Sale	H	0	2	6	0	0	0	W
21 Dec	Birkenhead Wanderers	A	0	0	0	0	2	6	L
26 Dec	Dalton	H	1	1	8	1	0	5	W
28 Dec	Salford	H	0	0	0	0	0	0	D
Jan 1	Walkden	A	0	0	0	0	0	0	D
4 Jan	Rochdale St Clements	A	0	1	3	1	0	5	L
11 Jan	Pemberton	A	1	2	11	0	2	6	W
18 Jan	Altrincham	H	1[3]	0	4	0	0	0	W
22 Jan	Liverpool Old Boys	A	0	2	6	1	0	5	W
1 Feb	Liverpool	A	0	2	6	0	0	0	W
8 Feb	Birkenhead Wanderers	A	1[1]	0	3	1	2	11	L
15 Feb	Altrincham	A	1[2]	0	4	1	1	8	L
22 Feb	Birkenhead Wanderers	H	2[1]	1	11	1	0	5	W
29 Feb	New Brighton	H	1	1	8	0	0	0	W
7 Mar	Sale	A	1	3	14	0	0	0	W
14 Mar	Liverpool Old Boys	H	0	1	3	0	0	0	W
21 Mar	Liverpool	A	1[2]	3	13	0	0	0	W
28 Mar	Liverpool	H	2	2	16	0	0	0	W
3 Apr	Walkden	H	1	1	8	0	0	0	W
6 Apr	Holbeck	H	2	1	13	1[2]	1	7	W
11 Apr	Swinton	A	1	1	5	0	1	3	L
23 Apr	Crompton*	H	1[2]	0	4	0	1	3	W

* Played under Northern Union rules; [1] Penalty goal; [2] Drop goal; [3] Goal from a mark

County and international representatives 1890 to 1898

Surname	Forename	Date	Opposition	Venue
England				
Pyke	James	02/01/1892	Wales	Blackheath
Pilkington*	William	12/03/1898	Scotland	Edinburgh
*Recs and Cambridge University				
The North				
Pyke	James	19/12/1891	South	Jesmond
Lancashire				
Pilkington	James	22/03/1890	Ulster	Belfast
Fildes	Peter	08/11/1890	Cheshire	Birkenhead
Pyke	James	22/11/1890	Westmorland	Kendal
		29/11/1890	Yorkshire	Manchester
		10/01/1891	Devon	Exeter
		24/01/1891	Durham	Manchester
		16/02/1891	Surrey	Manchester
		28/02/1891	Cumberland	Manchester
		09/03/1891	Ulster	Manchester
		14/03/1891	Gloucester	Manchester
		18/04/1891	The Rest	Manchester
		04/11/1891	Cambridge University	Cambridge
		07/11/1891	Cheshire	Whalley Range
		21/11/1891	Cumberland	Whitehaven
		28/11/1891	Yorkshire	Huddersfield
		21/12/1891	Cambridge University	Whalley Range
		24/10/1892	Glamorgan	Whalley Range

Seddon	James	18/03/1893	Glamorgan	Swansea
		20/03/1893	Devon	Exeter
		11/01/1896	Durham	Fallowfield
		19/02/1896	Glamorgan	Salford
		14/03/1896	Devon	Whalley Range
Crossley	James	19/02/1896	Glamorgan	Salford
		29/02/1896	Northumberland	Newcastle
		14/03/1896	Devon	Whalley Range
Pilkington*	William	02/03/1895	Devon	Exeter
		04/03/1895	Glamorgan	Cardiff
		02/11/1895	Cheshire	Swinton
		09/11/1895	Westmorland	Kendal
Traynor	David	19/02/1896	Glamorgan	Salford

*Recs and Cambridge University

West Lancashire and Border Towns

Pyke	James	27/11/1886	Westmorland	Kendal
		02/01/1888	Westmorland	Aspull
		26/04/1888	Westmorland	Kendal
		06/02/1889	SE Lancs	Wigan
Pilkington	James	21/04/1887	Westmorland	Widnes
		02/01/1888	Westmorland	Aspull
		06/02/1889	SE Lancs	Wigan
Parr	William	21/04/1887	Westmorland	Widnes
Lund	William	02/01/1888	Westmorland	Aspull
Seddon	James	06/02/1889	SE Lancs	Wigan
Smith	Albert	04/05/1889	SE Lancs	Leigh
Dolan	James	04/05/1889	SE Lancs	Leigh
Fildes	James	04/05/1889	SE Lancs	Leigh

Association football

League matches

1899–00 Joined Lancashire Combination
1902–03 Joined Lancashire League
1903–04 Re–joined Lancashire Combination as founder members of new Division 2
1904–05 Lancashire Combination Division Two Champions
Promoted to Division One
1911–12 Lancashire Combination runners–up

Season	League	P	W	D	L	F	A	Pts	Position
1899–00	Lancashire Combination	30	7	4	19	37	83	18	16/16
1900–01	Lancashire Combination	34	16	8	10	79	06	40	5/18
1901–02	Lancashire Combination	34	17	3	14	80	64	37	7/18
1902–03	Lancashire League	22	13	1	8	51	41	27	5/12
1903–04	Lancs Comb. Division 2	34	12	8	14	47	47	32	11/18
1904–05	Lancs Comb. Division 2	34	22	6	6	91	32	50	1/18
1905–06	Lancs Comb. Division 1	38	17	10	11	74	69	44	4/20
1906–07	Lancs Comb. Division 1	38	15	6	17	75	75	36	14/20
1907–08	Lancs Comb. Division 1	38	14	6	18	67	73	34	14/20
1908–09	Lancs Comb. Division 1	38	20	7	11	73	60	47	4/20
1909–10	Lancs Comb. Division 1	38	13	8	17	58	69	34	16/20
1910–11	Lancs Comb. Division 1	38	15	6	17	66	57	36	13/20
1911–12	Lancs Comb. Division 1	32	19	6	7	96	49	44	2/17
1912–13	Lancs Comb. Division 1	34	16	4	14	72	56	36	8/18

FA Cup

Date	Rd	Home Team	Score	Away Team	Score
04/10/1902	Q1	St Helens Recs	2	Earlestown	0
18/10/1902	Q2	St Helens Recs	3	St Helens Town	0
01/11/1902	Q3	St Helens Recs	18	Rhyl	0**
15/11/1902	Q4	St Helens Recs	2	**Burslem Port Vale**	1*
29/11/1902	Q5	Glossop	5	St Helens Recs	0
03/10/1903	Q1	St Helens Recs	4	Earlestown	3
17/10/1903	Q2	Ashton Town	0	St Helens Recs	1
31/10/1903	Q3	Nantwich	1	St Helens Recs	1
04/11/1903	Q3 (Rep)	St Helens Recs	2	Nantwich	3
01/10/1904	Q1	Earlestown	2	St Helens Recs	2
01/10/1904	Q1 (Rep)	St Helens Recs	1	Earlestown	2
07/10/1905	Q1	St Helens Recs	1	Brynn Central	0
28/10/1905	Q2	St Helens Town	0	St Helens Recs	1
18/11/1905	Q3	St Helens Recs	1	Earlestown	5
22/09/1906	PR	St Helens Town	2	St Helens Recs	1
21/09/1907	PR	St Helens Recs	2	St Helens Town	1
05/10/1907	Q1	St Helens Recs	7	Fairfield	0
19/10/1907	Q2	St Helens Recs	7	Stalybridge Rovers	1
02/11/1907	Q3	St Helens Recs	4	Atherton	0
23/11/1907	Q4	St Helens Recs	2	Haslingden	1
07/12/1907	Q5	St Helens Recs	1	**Chesterfield**	4*
19/09/1908	PR	Buxton	2	St Helens Recs	3
03/10/1908	Q1	St Helens Recs	3	Altrincham	1
Walk–over	Q2	St Helens Recs		Chorley	
07/11/1908	Q3	Northern Nomads	2	St Helens Recs	1
18/09/1909	PR	Hyde	1	St Helens Recs	0
17/09/1910	PR	St Helens Recs	4	Newton–le–Willows	1
01/10/1910	Q1	St Helens Recs	5	Macclesfield Town	1
15/10/1910	Q2	Hooley Hill	0	St Helens Recs	0
19/10/1910	Q2 (Rep)	St Helens Recs	4	Hooley Hill	0
05/11/1910	Q3	Rochdale	1	St Helens Recs	0
03/09/1911	Q1	St Helens Recs	2	Hurst	0
14/10/1911	Q2	Altrincham	2	St Helens Recs	2
Walk–over	Q2 (Rep)	St Helens Recs		Altrincham	
04/11/1911	Q3	Heywood United	3	St Helens Recs	2
28/09/1912	PR	St Helens Recs	1	Heywood United	1
02/10/1912	PR (Rep)	St Helens Recs	1	Heywood United	3

Q – Qualifying Round; PR – Preliminary Round; (Rep) Replay
* Football League clubs (Division Two)
** Only three clubs have ever scored more than 18 goals in the competition

Lancashire Cup

Date	Rd	Home Team	Score	Away Team	Score
	QR1	St Helens Recs	Bye		
13/09/1902	QR2	Accrington Stanley	4	St Helens Recs	1
28/11/1903	QR1	St Helens Recs	4	Black Lane Temperance	1*
12/12/1903	QR2	St Helens Recs	1	Oswaldtwistle Rovers	0
09/01/1904	RD1	St Helens Recs	0	Everton	1
21/09/1905	RD1	St Helens Recs	3	Everton	2
02/10/1905	RD2	St Helens Recs	1	Blackpool	1
09/10/1905	RD2 (Rep)	Blackpool	1	St Helens Recs	0
17/091906	RD1	St Helens Recs	1	Rossendale United	1
24/09/1906	RD1 (Rep)	Rossendale United	3	St Helens Recs	1
16/09/1907	RD1	St Helens Recs	5	Chorley	0
30/09/1907	RD2	Blackpool	0	St Helens Recs	4
14/10/1907	RD3	Oldham Athletic	2	St Helens Recs	0

30/09/1908	RD1	Accrington Stanley	0	St Helens Recs	0
05/10/1908	RD1 (Rep)	Accrington Stanley	0	St Helens Recs	1
15/10/1908	RD2	St Helens Recs	0	Southport Central	2
11/10/1909	RD2	Liverpool	4	St Helens Recs	4
18/10/1909	RD2 (Rep)	Liverpool	1	St Helens Recs	3
01/11/1909	RD3	Accrington Stanley	3	St Helens Recs	3
08/11/1909	RD3 (Rep)	St Helens Recs	3	Accrington Stanley	0
22/11/1909	SF	St Helens Recs	0	Everton	2
12/10/1910	RD2	Chorley	0	St Helens Recs	2
24/10/1910	RD3	Burney	3	St Helens Recs	0
09/09/1911	RD1	St Helens Recs	3	Colne	0
02/10/1911	RD2	Barrow	5	St Helens Recs	2
23/09/1912	RD1	St Helens Recs	2	Rossendale United	0
07/10/1912	RD2	St Helens Recs	0	Blackpool	0
14/10/1912	RD2 (Rep)	Blackpool	3	St Helens Recs	1

* Abandoned – result stood

Professional footballers associated with St Helens Recs

Surname	Forename	Born	Birthplace	Posn	Recs	Internationals	Professional clubs
Bamber	Jack	1895	St Helens	WH	1911	England 2 F Lge 2	Liverpool; Leicester; Tranmere
Birchall	Jack	1876	Prescot	WH	1898		Liverpool; Blackpool; Blackburn R
Crelley	Jack		Liverpool	FB	1910		Everton
Cunliffe	Tommy	1886	Simms Ln E	W	1906		Blackburn R; Oldham
Dagnall	Walter	1883	Prescot	IF	1905/7		Hull C
Dalton	Edward		Manchester	FB	1910		Manchester U
Doig	Teddy	1866	Letham	G	1908	Scotland 5	Blackburn; Sunderland; Liverpool
Edelston	Joe	1891	Appley Bridge	WH	1912		Hull C; Manchester C; Fulham
Evans	Nolan		Ashton	FB	1909		Clapton Orient
Fairclough	Albert	1891	St Helens	CF	1911		Manchester C; Southend; Bristol C; Derby; Gillingham
France	Herbert			CF	1907		Blackburn Rovers
Hamblett	George				1908		Manchester C
Hodson	Jimmy	1880	Horwich	FB	1902		Bury; Oldham; Brentford
Hogan	Cornelius	1878	Malta	CF	1905		New Brighton; Burnley
Holden	Ralph	1890	Blundellsands	CH	1910		Liverpool
Hulme	Aaron	1883	Manchester	FB	1911		Manchester U
Jackson	William	1876	Flint	IF	1898	Wales 1	Newton Heath; Burnley
Kearns	Alfie	1877	Belfast	IF	1905	Ireland 16 Ire Lge3	Blackpool
Lee	Harry	1887	Preston	CF	1906		Fulham
Lester	Hugh	1891	Leligh (USA)	FB	1910		Liverpool; Oldham
Lofthouse	Jimmy	1894	St Helens	W	1911		Sheffield W; Rotheram; Bristol R; QPR
McDermott	Tommy	1878	Bridgetown	IF	1911		Everton; Chelsea; Bradford C; Gainsborough Trinity
Middlehurst	James	1892	Prescot	FB	1913		Hull C
Neve	Edwin	1885	Prescot	W	1905		Hull C; Derby C; Notts Forest
Platt	Jack	1880	Preston	IF	1911		Preston NE
Roughley	Edward	1880	Prescot	G	1905		Hull C
Storey	George	1877	Dudley	CF	1901		Everton; Bury
Welfare	Harry	1888	Liverpool	WH	1909		Liverpool
Wilkinson	Harry	1883	Bury	W	1906		Manchester U
Williams	David		Liverpool	CF	1911		Glossop; Notts C; Brighton & HA
Woods	Harry	1890	St Helens	IF	1908		S Shields; Newcastle U; Arsenal; Luton

Professional rugby league

Northern Rugby League

	P	W	D	L	Pts	F	A	Percent	Position
1919–20	28	13	3	12	29	329	196	51.79	11 from 25
1920–21	30	15	1	14	31	299	201	51.67	15 from 25
1921–22	36	19	1	16	39	417	315	54.17	12 from 26
1922–23	36	19	0	17	38	319	292	52.77	11 from 27
1923–24	32	19	0	13	38	363	255	59.37	6 from 27
1924–25	38	26	3	9	55	564	267	72.36	4 from 27
1925–26	36	23	2	11	48	437	278	66.66	5 from 27
1926–27	38	29	3	6	61	544	235	80.26	1 from 29
1927–28	36	24	0	12	48	499	251	66.66	5 from 28
1928–29	38	22	1	15	45	545	374	59.21	8 from 28
1929–30	36	17	3	16	37	355	414	51.38	13 from 28
1930–31	38	21	2	15	44	436	243		12 from 28
1931–32	38	18	1	19	37	523	523		13 from 28
1932–33	38	16	4	11	36	419	416		16 from 28
1933–34	38	16	1	21	34	442	524		18 from 24
1934–35	38	21	1	16	43	431	404		10 from 28
1935–36	38	11	1	26	23	261	483		26 from 30
1936–37	38	21	2	15	44	410	343		10 from 30
1937–38	36	15	1	20	31	353	471		22 from 29
1938–39	40	11	0	29	22	311	504		24 from 28
	726	**376**	**30**	**313**	**783**	**8,257**	**6,989**		

Lancashire County Rugby League

	P	W	D	L	Pts	F	A	Position
1919–20	22	8	3	11	19	213	171	7 from 12
1920–21	22	11	1	10	23	318	115	8 from 12
1921–22	22	12	1	9	25	202	162	4 from 12
1922–23	24	15	0	9	30	238	176	6 from 13
1923–24	24	13	0	11	26	268	199	6 from 13
1924–25	24	15	2	7	32	311	157	3 from 13
1925–26	24	14	2	8	30	254	177	5 from 13
1926–27	26	20	3	3	43	360	145	1 from 14
1927–28	24	19	0	5	38	365	122	2 from 13
1928–29	24	14	1	9	29	311	218	5 from 13
1929–30	24	12	2	10	26	210	242	6 from 13
1930–31	26	12	2	12	26	251	169	8 from 14
1931–32	26	12	1	13	25	320	355	8 from 14
1932–33	26	9	3	14	21	252	266	10 from 14
1933–34	26	9	1	16	19	276	325	12 from 14
1934–35	26	13	1	12	27	267	257	6 from 14
1935–36	28	8	1	19	17	182	326	13 from 15
1936–37	28	13	2	13	28	226	260	8 from 15
1937–38	26	10	1	15	21	215	348	10 from 14
1938–39	26	5	0	21	10	149	325	12 from 14
	498	**244**	**27**	**227**	**515**	**5,188**	**4,515**	

Challenge Cup

1896–97

R1	Bye			
R2	Rochdale Hornets	8	St Helens Recs	0 (Recs amateurs)

1897–98

R1	Halifax	17	St Helens Recs	0

1919–20				
R1	Hunslet	0	St Helens Recs	9
R2	St Helens Recs	9	Barrow	2
R3	Huddersfield	2	St Helens Recs	2
Rep	St Helens Recs	6	Huddersfield	8
1920–21				
R1	St Helens Recs	9	Wigan	6
R2	St Helens Recs	0	Widnes	7
1921–22				
R1	St Helens Recs	5	Leeds	20
1922–23				
R1	Barrow	8	St Helens Recs	0
1923–24				
R1	St Helens Recs	0	Wakefield Trinity	2
1924–25				
R1	St Helens Recs	15	Hull	5
R2	St Helens Recs	74	Dalton (amateurs)	5
R3	Rochdale Hornets	9	St Helens Recs	5
1925–26				
R1	Castleford (amateurs)	12	St Helens Recs	18
R2	Warrington	17	St Helens Recs	12
1926–27				
R1	Hull	6	St Helens Recs	5
1927–28				
R1	St Helens Recs	12	Wakefield Trinity	0
R2	Leeds	13	St Helens Recs	12
1928–29				
R1	Broughton Rangers	2	St Helens Recs	13
R2	Featherstone Rovers	0	St Helens Recs	13
R3	St Helens Recs	21	Halifax	0
SF	Wigan	7	St Helens Recs	7
Rep	Wigan	13	St Helens Recs	12
1929–30				
R1	St Helens	9	St Helens Recs	7
1930–31				
R1	St Helens Recs	19	Barrow	11
R2	Warrington	9	St Helens Recs	0
1931–32				
R1	St Helens Recs	10	Salford	6
R2	St Helens Recs	8	Castleford	11
1932–33				
R1	St Helens Recs	5	Hunslet	19
1933–34				
R1	St Helens Recs	32	Pendlebury Jnrs (amateurs)	3
R2	St Helens Recs	7	Oldham	7
Rep	Oldham	18	St Helens Recs	5
1934–35				
R1	Wakefield Trinity	23	St Helens Recs	8
1935–36				
R1	Salford	20	St Helens Recs	3
1936–37				
R1	Hull KR	13	St Helens Recs	5
1937–38				
R1	St Helens Recs	11	Dewsbury	10
R2	St Helens Recs	18	Rochdale Hornets	10
R3	Salford	19	St Helens Recs	0
1938–39				
R1	Liverpool Stanley	2	St Helens Recs	2
Rep	St Helens Recs	12	Liverpool Stanley	3
R2	St Helens Recs	3	Wigan	8

Lancashire Cup

1919–20				
R1	Bye			
R2	Widnes	7	Barrow	2
1920–21				
R1	St Helens Recs	16	Barrow	0
R2	Warrington	5	St Helens Recs	9
R3	Leigh	9	St Helens Recs	3
1921–22				
R1	St Helens Recs	0	Swinton	0
Rep	Swinton	2	St Helens Recs	8
R2	Warrington	5	St Helens Recs	3
1922–23				
R1	Bye			
R2	Wigan	14	St Helens Recs	3
1923–24				
R1	Bye			
R2	St Helens Recs	21	Rochdale Hornets	0
SF	St Helens Recs	13	Oldham	11
Final	St Helens Recs	17	Swinton	0
1924–25				
R1	St Helens Recs	17	Wigan	2
R2	St Helens Recs	36	Salford	5
SF	Barrow	5	St Helens Recs	7
Final	Oldham	10	St Helens Recs	0
1925–26				
R1	Bye			
R2	St Helens Recs	7	Swinton	8
1926–27				
R1	St Helens Recs	21	Leigh	3
R2	St Helens Recs	26	Rochdale Hornets	2
SF	St Helens Recs	8	Salford	8
Rep	Salford	0	St Helens Recs	14
Final	St Helens Recs	2	St Helens	10
1927–28				
R1	St Helens Recs	41	Broughton Rangers	5
R2	St Helens Recs	7	Wigan	10
1928–29				
R1	St Helens Recs	7	Warrington	7
Rep	Warrington	10	St Helens Recs	2
1929–30				
R1	Bye			
R2	Oldham	8	St Helens Recs	2
1930–31				
R1	Bye			
R2	St Helens Recs	24	Leigh	7
SF	St Helens Recs	6	Oldham	4
Final	St Helens Recs	18	Wigan	3
1931–32				
R1	Warrington	11	St Helens Recs	2
1932–33				
R1	St Helens Recs	5	Oldham	5
Rep	Oldham	4	St Helens Recs*	0
Rep2	Oldham	7	St Helens Recs	7
Rep3	St Helens Recs	9	Oldham**	6
R2	Warrington	11	St Helens Recs	8
1933–34				
R1	St Helens Recs	5	Warrington	0
R2	St Helens Recs	19	Swinton	5

SF	St Helens Recs	9	St Helens	2
Final	Oldham	12	St Helens Recs	0
1934–35				
R1	St Helens Recs	8	Wigan	20
1935–36				
R1	St Helens Recs	17	Barrow	5
R2	St Helens	2	St Helens Recs	2
Rep	St Helens Recs	8	St Helens	21
1936–37				
R1	St Helens Recs	7	Leigh	7
Rep	Leigh	4	St Helens Recs	8
R2	St Helens Recs	10	St Helens	4
SF	Wigan	15	St Helens Recs	2
1937–38				
R1	Barrow	11	St Helens Recs	2
1938–39				
R1	St Helens Recs	12	Barrow	7
R2	St Helens Recs	8	Liverpool Stanley	10

* Game abandoned after 40 minutes (result stood) ** Match played at Salford (The Willows)

Team and Individual Records

Honours

Lancashire League Winners 1926–27
Lancashire Cup Winners 1923–24; 1930-31. Runners-up 1924–25; 1926–27; 1933–34
Championship Finalists 1926–27
Challenge Cup semi-finalists 1928–29

Team records
First match: Swinton (H) 23 August 1919
Last match: Hull KR (A) 29 April 1939
Record victory: 74–5 v Dalton (H) (Challenge Cup) 28 February 1925
Record defeat: 0–46 v Salford 8 April 1933
Record away win: 40–13 versus Bramley 8 October 1921
Record league win: 64–14 versus Bradford Northern 5 September 1931
Record home defeat: 17–45 versus York 4 November 1933
Most League points in a season: 61 (1926–27)
Least League points in a season: 22 (1938–39)

Individual career records

Most appearances:	469	Tommy Smith
Most tries:	166	Albert Bailey
Most goals:	509	Tommy Dingsdale
Most points:	1,096	Tommy Dingsdale

Match records

Tries:	6	Joe McComas versus Dalton (Challenge Cup) 28/02/25
Goals:	12	Tommy Dingsdale versus York 16/10/26
Points:	24	Tommy Dingsdale versus York 16/10/26

Seasonal records

Appearances:	46	Jack Wilson 1926–27
Tries:	37	Jack Wilson 1928–29
Goals:	101	Tommy Dingsdale 1926–27
Points:	208	Tommy Dingsdale 1926–27

The Championship of St Helens: Recs versus Saints 1919 to 1939

Date	Venue	Comp.	Score R	S	Recs Scorers Tries	Goals
25/12/1919	City Road	Lge	21	6	G. Ashall (2), McComas, Bates, J. Greenall	Pyke (3)
01/01/1920	Knowsley Road	Lge	8	9	W. Ashall, Owen	McNulty
25/12/1920	Knowsley Road	Lge	5	0	Bowen	McComas
01/01/1921	City Road	Lge	39	0	W. Ashall (2), F. Bowen (2), McComas (2), Pierce, H. Grundy, Leyland	McComas (4), Mulvanney, Dolan
24/12/1921	City Road	Lge	6	0	Smith (2)	
01/01/1922	Knowsley Road	Lge	6	7	W. Ashall, McComas	
25/12/1922	Knowsley Road	Lge	14	2	Owen, J. Greenall J. Greenall (DG)	McComas (3)
01/01/1923	City Road	Lge	8	13	Gormley, Hughes	Owen
25/12/1923	City Road	Lge	21	2	Dingsdale, Bates, Innes, Hughes, H. Grundy	Dingsdale (3)
01/01/1924	Knowsley Road	Lge	0	4		
25/12/1924	Knowsley Road	Lge	5	7	H. Grundy	McComas
01/01/1925	City Road	Lge	5	5	Smith	Wallace
25/12/1925	City Road	Lge	3	3	Wallace	
01/01/1926	Knowsley Road	Lge	2	4		Ashcroft
20/11/1926	Warrington	LCF	2	10		Pyke
25/12/1926	Knowsley Road	Lge	6	6		Dingsdale (3)
01/01/1927	City Road	Lge	17	8	McComas, Fildes, Wallace	Dingsdale (3 and DG)
23/04/1927	City Road	CPO	33	0	Wilson (2), Smith (2), Wallace, J. Greenall, Innes J. Greenall (DG)	Dingsdale (5)
24/12/1927	City Road	Lge	5	2	Smith	Dingsdale
29/12/1927	Knowsley Road	Lge	22	5	Smith (2), Halton, McComas	Dingsdale (5)
25/12/1928	Knowsley Road	Lge	5	0	Wilson	Dingsdale
01/01/1929	City Road	Lge	8	2	Smith, Bailey	Dingsdale
25/12/1929	Knowsley Road	Lge	3	8	Mulvanney	
01/01/1930	City Road	Lge	3	0	Mulvanney	
08/02/1930	Knowsley Road	CC	7	9	Fildes	Dingsdale (2)
25/12/1930	Knowsley Road	Lge	6	7	Wilson, Highcock	
01/01/1931	City Road	Lge	5	3	Frodsham	Dingsdale
25/12/1931	City Road	Lge	13	2	Bailey, Frodsham, W. Bowen	Dingsdale (2)
01/01/1932	Knowsley Road	Lge	7	7	Highcock	Dingsdale (2)
25/12/1932	Knowsley Road	Lge	3	8	Laithwaite	
02/01/1933	City Road	Lge	5	10	Smith	Frodsham
02/11/1933	City Road	LCSF	9	2	W. Greenall	Heaton (3)
25/12/1933	City Road	Lge	11	9	R. Grundy	Heaton (3), Prescott (DG)
01/01/1934	Knowsley Road	Lge	2	10		Barnes
25/12/1934	Knowsley Road	Lge	2	6		Liptrot
01/01/1935	City Road	Lge	2	2		Barnes
25/09/1935	Knowsley Road	LC2	2	2		Liptrot
30/09/1935	City Road	LC (R)	8	21	Bailey, W. Greenall	Liptrot
25/12/1935	City Road	Lge	0	3		
01/01/1936	Knowsley Road	Lge	3	5	Blakeley	
23/09/1936	City Road	LC2	10	4	Pimblett, J. Howard	Liptrot (2)
25/12/1936	Knowsley Road	Lge	0	4		
01/01/1937	City Road	Lge	10	3	Pimblett (2)	E. Dixon (2)
25/12/1937	City Road	Lge	2	10		Winstanley
01/01/1938	Knowsley Road	Lge	3	8	H. Dixon	
26/12/1938	Knowsley Road	Lge	5	4	H. Dixon	Winstanley
02/01/1939	City Road	Lge	3	5	Tracey	

Championship of St Helens summary

					Recs			Saints		
	P	W	D	L	T	G	Pts	T	G	Pts
League	40	17	5	18	62	54	294	39	41	199
Championship Play Off	1	1	0	0	7	6	33	0	0	0
Lancashire Cup	5	2	1	2	5	8	31	7	9	39
Challenge Cup	1	0	0	1	1	2	7	1	3	9
Overall	**47**	**20**	**6**	**21**	**75**	**70**	**365**	**47**	**53**	**247**
League at City Road	20	12	3	5	41	32	187	18	17	88
League at Knowsley Road	20	5	2	13	21	22	107	21	24	111

Recs' top try scorer versus Saints: Tommy Smith 10
Recs' top goal scorer versus Saints: Tommy Dingsdale 30

Representative honours (by surname)

Forename	Surname	Status	Team	Pos	Date	Opponents	F	A	Venue	Pts
Jack	Atherton	CC	Lancashire	SR	18/09/1937	Cumberland	23	17	Workington	0
Albert	Bailey	CC	Lancashire	LW	26/10/1929	Cumberland	15	7	Whitehaven	0
Albert	Bailey	Int	England	LC	15/04/1934	France	32	21	Paris	1T
Albert	Bailey	Rep	RLXIII	LW	28/04/1935	French XIII	32	12	Paris	0
Albert	Bailey	CC	Lancashire	LC	21/09/1935	Cumberland	7	4	Whitehaven	0
Albert	Bailey	CC	Lancashire	RW	12/10/1935	Yorkshire	16	5	Widnes	1T
Frank	Bowen	Rep	Lancs Lge	SR	30/11/1921	Australia	6	29	Goodison Park	0
Frank	Bowen	Test	Great Britain	SR	04/08/1928	New Zealand	13	17	Auckland	0
Frank	Bowen	Test	Great Britain	SR	18/08/1928	New Zealand	13	5	Dunedin	1T
Frank	Bowen	Test	Great Britain	SR	25/08/1928	New Zealand	6	5	Christchurch	0
Frank	Bowen	CC	Lancashire	SR	03/11/1928	Yorkshire	33	10	Halifax	0
Frank	Bowen	CC	Lancashire	SR	17/11/1928	Cumberland	10	5	Swinton	0
Frank	Bowen	Rep	Lancashire	SR	26/09/1929	Australia	14	29	Warrington	0
William	Bowen	CC	Lancashire	SH	29/10/1932	Yorkshire	3	30	Wakefield	0
Tommy	Dingsdale	CC	Lancashire	FB	29/10/1924	Cumberland	8	0	Warrington	0
Tommy	Dingsdale	CC	Lancashire	FB	29/11/1924	Yorkshire	28	9	Halifax	3G
Tommy	Dingsdale	CC	Lancashire	FB	26/09/1925	Cumberland	6	5	Whitehaven	0
Tommy	Dingsdale	CC	Lancashire	FB	12/12/1925	Yorkshire	26	10	City Road	2G
Tommy	Dingsdale	CC	Lancashire	FB	30/10/1926	Yorkshire	18	13	Wakefield	1G
Tommy	Dingsdale	Int	England	FB	11/01/1928	Wales	20	12	Wigan	1G
Tommy	Dingsdale	CC	Lancashire	FB	26/10/1929	Cumberland	15	7	Whitehaven	1G
Tommy	Dingsdale	CC	Lancashire	FB	04/10/1930	Cumberland	24	17	Warrington	3G
Tommy	Dingsdale	CC	Lancashire	FB	18/10/1930	Yorkshire	15	25	Wakefield	3G
Tommy	Dingsdale	CC	Lancashire	FB	22/11/1930	Glam & Mon	10	14	Salford	2G
Tommy	Dingsdale	CC	Lancashire	FB	03/10/1931	Cumberland	17	11	Whitehaven	4G
Tommy	Dingsdale	CC	Lancashire	FB	17/10/1931	Yorkshire	11	8	Warrington	1G
Oliver	Dolan	CC	Lancashire	H	15/10/1932	Cumberland	3	9	Barrow	0
Oliver	Dolan	CC	Lancashire	H	29/10/1932	Yorkshire	3	30	Wakefield	0
Oliver	Dolan	Int	England	H	30/11/1932	Wales	14	13	Leeds	0
Albert	Fildes	CC	Lancashire	LF	30/10/1926	Yorkshire	18	13	Wakefield	0
Albert	Fildes	Int	England	SR	06/04/1927	Wales	11	8	Broughton	0
Albert	Fildes	CC	Lancashire	SR	29/10/1927	Yorkshire	35	19	Warrington	0
Albert	Fildes	CC	Lancashire	SR	12/11/1927	Glam & Mon	7	12	Pontypridd	0
Albert	Fildes	Test	Great Britain	SR	23/06/1928	Australia	15	12	Brisbane	0
Albert	Fildes	Test	Great Britain	SR	14/07/1928	Australia	8	0	Sydney	0
Albert	Fildes	Test	Great Britain	SR	21/07/1928	Australia	14	21	Sydney	0
Albert	Fildes	Test	Great Britain	SR	04/08/1928	New Zealand	13	17	Auckland	0
Albert	Fildes	Test	Great Britain	SR	18/08/1928	New Zealand	13	5	Dunedin	0
Albert	Fildes	Test	Great Britain	SR	25/08/1928	New Zealand	6	5	Christchurch	0
Albert	Fildes	CC	Lancashire	SR	03/11/1928	Yorkshire	33	10	Halifax	0

Albert	Fildes	CC	Lancashire	SR	17/11/1928	Cumberland	10	5	Swinton	0
Albert	Fildes	CC	Lancashire	SR	08/12/1928	Glam & Mon	25	10	Leigh	1T
Albert	Fildes	Int	England	SR	20/03/1929	Other Nat	27	20	Leeds	0
Albert	Fildes	Rep	Lancashire	SR	26/09/1929	Australia	14	29	Warrington	0
Albert	Fildes	CC	Lancashire	SR	26/10/1929	Cumberland	15	7	Whitehaven	0
Albert	Fildes	Test	Great Britain	SR	09/11/1929	Australia	9	3	Leeds	0
Albert	Fildes	Rep	NL XIII	SR	04/12/1929	Australia	18	5	Wigan	0
Albert	Fildes	Test	Great Britain	SR	04/01/1930	Australia	0	0	Swinton	0
Albert	Fildes	Test	Great Britain	SR	15/01/1930	Australia	3	0	Rochdale	0
Albert	Fildes	CC	Lancashire	SR	22/03/1930	Yorkshire	18	3	Rochdale	0
John	Greenall	CC	Lancashire	SH	06/10/1920	Cumberland	16	12	St Helens	1T
John	Greenall	Rep	Lancs Lge	SH	30/11/1921	Australia	6	29	Goodison	0
John	Greenall	Rep	Lancashire	SH	14/12/1921	Australia	8	6	Warrington	0
John	Greenall	Test	Northern Un	SH	14/01/1922	Australia	6	0	Salford	0
John	Greenall	CC	Lancashire	SH	21/01/1922	Cumberland	18	7	Ellenborough	0
John	Greenall	CC	Lancashire	SH	15/11/1922	Cumberland	46	9	Swinton	0
John	Greenall	CC	Lancashire	SH	07/12/1922	Yorkshire	11	11	Hull KR	0
John	Greenall	Int	England	SH	07/02/1923	Wales	2	13	Wigan	0
John	Greenall	CC	Lancashire	SH	29/09/1923	Cumberland	24	5	Whitehaven	0
John	Greenall	Int	England	SH	01/10/1923	Wales	18	11	Huddersfield	0
John	Greenall	CC	Lancashire	SH	08/12/1923	Yorkshire	6	5	Oldham	0
John	Greenall	CC	Lancashire	SH	30/10/1926	Yorkshire	18	13	Wakefield	0
Billy	Greenall	Rep	Lancashire	SH	20/09/1933	Australia	7	33	Warrington	0
Billy	Greenall	CC	Lancashire	SH	25/09/1933	Yorkshire	12	15	Oldham	1T
George	Highcock	CC	Lancashire	FR	22/11/1930	Glam & Mon	10	14	Salford	0
George	Highcock	CC	Lancashire	FR	17/10/1931	Yorkshire	11	8	Warrington	0
William	Liptrot	CC	Lancashire	FR	15/10/1932	Cumberland	3	9	Barrow	0
William	Liptrot	CC	Lancashire	FR	09/01/1934	Yorkshire	5	5	Leeds	1G
William	Liptrot	CC	Lancashire	FR	21/09/1935	Cumberland	7	4	Whitehaven	2G
William	Liptrot	CC	Lancashire	FR	12/10/1935	Yorkshire	16	5	Widnes	0
Pat	Martin	CC	Lancashire	LC	29/10/1932	Yorkshire	3	30	Wakefield	1T
Joe	McComas	CC	Lancashire	LW	06/10/1920	Cumberland	16	12	St Helens	1T
Joe	McComas	CC	Lancashire	LW	21/10/1920	Yorkshire	3	18	Hull FC	0
Joe	McComas	Rep	Lancashire	LW	14/12/1921	Australia	8	6	Warrington	1G
William	Mulvanney	CC	Lancashire	SR	24/09/1919	Yorkshire	15	5	Broughton	1T
William	Mulvanney	CC	Lancashire	SR	06/10/1920	Cumberland	16	12	St Helens	0
Jimmy	Owen	Int	England	LW	19/01/1921	Wales	35	9	Leeds	1T
Jimmy	Owen	Int	England	LW	05/02/1921	Other Nat	33	16	Workington	1T
Jimmy	Owen	CC	Lancashire	LW	04/10/1921	Yorkshire	2	5	Rochdale	0
Jimmy	Owen	Int	England	LW	10/10/1921	Australia	5	4	Highbury Lnd	0
Jimmy	Owen	Rep	Lancashire	RW	14/12/1921	Australia	8	6	Warrington	0
Jimmy	Owen	Test	Northern Un	LW	14/01/1922	Australia	6	0	Salford	0
Jimmy	Owen	CC	Lancashire	RW	15/11/1922	Cumberland	46	9	Swinton	1T
Jimmy	Owen	CC	Lancashire	RW	07/12/1922	Yorkshire	11	11	Hull KR	1T
Jimmy	Owen	Int	England	RW	07/02/1923	Wales	2	13	Wigan	0
Jimmy	Owen	CC	Lancashire	RW	29/09/1923	Cumberland	24	5	Whitehaven	2T
Jimmy	Owen	Int	England	LW	01/10/1923	Wales	18	11	Huddersfield	2T
Jimmy	Owen	CC	Lancashire	LW	08/12/1923	Yorkshire	6	5	Oldham	0
Albert	Pimblett	CC	Lancashire	RW	18/09/1937	Cumberland	23	17	Workington	1T
Albert	Pimblett	Rep	Lancashire	RW	29/09/1937	Australia	7	5	Warrington	0
Albert	Pimblett	CC	Lancashire	RW	14/09/1938	Cumberland	8	7	Wigan	0
Albert	Pimblett	CC	Lancashire	RW	26/10/1938	Yorkshire	10	10	Leeds	0
Jim	Pyke	CC	Lancashire	LC	06/10/1920	Cumberland	16	12	St Helens	1T
Jim	Pyke	CC	Lancashire	LC	21/10/1920	Yorkshire	3	18	Hull FC	0
Tommy	Smith	CC	Lancashire	SR	29/10/1924	Cumberland	8	0	Warrington	0
Tommy	Smith	CC	Lancashire	SR	26/09/1925	Cumberland	6	5	Whitehaven	0
John	Wallace	Int	England	LW	30/09/1925	Wales	18	14	Wigan	0
John	Wallace	CC	Lancashire	RW	12/12/1925	Yorkshire	26	10	City Road	0
John	Wallace	Int	England	LW	04/02/1926	Other Nat	37	11	Whitehaven	0
John	Wallace	CC	Lancashire	LW	30/10/1926	Yorkshire	18	13	Wakefield	0

Pilkington Recs amateur honours 1949 to 2008

Open Age

(N.B. Some records not confirmed)

Season	Honour
1951–52	St Helens and District League Leaders
1953–54	St Helens and District League Leaders
1953–54	St Helens Cup Winners
1953–54	West Lancashire League Cup Winners
1953–54	Bootle Charity Cup
1956–57	St Helens and District League Leaders
1956–57	West Lancashire League Cup Winners
1956–57	West Lancashire League Leaders
1956–57	Lancashire Cup Winners
1957–58	St Helens and District League Champions
1958–59	St Helens and District League Champions
1959–60	St Helens and District League Champions
1960–61	St Helens and District League Champions
1960–61	St Helens Cup Winners
1961–62	St Helens and District League Champions
1962–63	St Helens and District League Champions
1963–64	St Helens and District League Champions
1963–64	St Helens Cup Winners
1968–69	Warrington League Leaders
1969–70	Lancashire Cup Runners–up
1973–74	**National Cup Winners**
1973–74	Lancashire Cup Winners
1973–74	Warrington and Dist League Champions
1973–74	Greenall Whitley Cup Winners
1974–75	Eric Bromilow Cup Winners
1975–76	Division One Champions
1975–76	Division Three Runners–up ('A' team)
1975–76	Eric Bromilow Cup Winners
1975–76	Greenall Whitley Cup Winners
1976–77	Lancashire Cup Winners
1977–78	Premier Division Champions
1977–78	Division One Champions ('A' team)
1977–78	Lancashire Cup Winners
1977–78	Eric Bromilow Cup Winners
1977–78	National Sevens Runners–up
1978–79	**National Cup Winners**
1978–79	National Youth Sevens Runners–up
1979–80	**National Cup Winners**
1979–80	Premier Division Champions
1979–80	Eric Bromilow Cup Winners
1979–80	S. Garner: Youth Player of the Year
1980–81	Lancashire Cup Winners
1980–81	Premier Division Runners-up
1980–81	Lancashire Youth Cup Runners-up
1980–81	Eric Bromilow Cup Winners
1981–82	**National Cup Winners**
1981–82	Premier Division Runners-up
1981–82	Eric Bromilow Cup Winners
1981–82	John Player Amateur Sevens Winners
1982–83	Premier Division Runners-up
1982–83	Eric Bromilow Cup Runners-up
1985–86	St Helens Cup Winners
1985–86	Division One Champions
1986–87	Lancashire Cup Runners-up
1986–87	Niel Wood National Lge Player of the Year
1991–92	Division One Champions
1992–93	Alliance Division One Runners-up
1994–95	St Helens Cup Runners-up
1996–97	Division One Runners-up
1996–97	Lancashire Youth Cup Runners-up
1997–98	Alliance Division One Runners-up
1999–00	Division One Runners-up
1999–00	Division Six Champions ('A' team)
2004–05	Division One Champions
2004–05	St Helens Cup Runners-up
2005–06	NWC Fair Play Award
2007–08	NWC Premier League Runners-up
2007–08	NWC Premiership Trophy Winners

Under–18

1995–96 Premier Division Winners
1996–97 Premier Division Runners–up
1996–97 Lancashire Cup Runners–up
2002–03 Division One Winners
2003–04 Division One Winners
2005–06 Premier Division Winners
2007–08 National Cup Winners
2007–08 Premier Division Runners–up
2007–08 North West Counties Cup Winners

Under–17

2007-08 Lancashire Cup Runners-up

Under–16

2001–02 Lancashire Cup Runners-up
2006–07 NW Counties Division 2 Runners-up

Under–15

2000–01 NW Counties Division 1 Winners
2004–05 NW Counties Cup Winners
2006–07 NW Counties Play-off Winners

Under– 14

2005-06 NW Counties Cup Winners

Under–12

2006-07	Lancashire Cup Winners	2007-08	Lancashire Cup Winners 2007-08
2006-07	NW Counties Cup Runners-up	2007-08	NW Counties Cup Winners
2006-07	NW Counties Plate Winners		

Individual honours: county and country

Open age internationals

BARLA Under 21s / 23s
Mark Ashton

Full Internationals
Bob Bolan
Kevin Casey
Andy Casey
Ken Cross
Kenny Gill
Peter Glover (1978 T)
Jeff Gormley
Paul Hankinson (1991 T)
Joey Hull (1978 T)
Bernard Jeffries
Ronald Leyland
John McCabe (1978 T)
Ray Shuker
Billy Simmons
Kevin Whittle
Bob Williams
Niel Wood
(T) BARLA Tourist (Australasia)

Youth (18s/19s) Internationals
Danny Davies
Nicholas Cammann
Geoff Fletcher
Gareth Frodsham
Steve Garner
Mark Gleave
John McCabe
Gareth Roberts
Derrick Seabrook
John Tabern

England Students Under 19s
Ben Gravener
Ian Marren

England Schoolboys
Gareth Frodsham

Open Age County
Mark Ashton
Bob Bolan
Kevin Casey
Andy Casey
Alan Corrigan
Graham Cranny
Ken Cross
John Forster
Eric Frodsham (Sen)
Kenny Gill
Peter Glover
Jeff Gormley
Paul Hankinson
William Hill
David Hull
Joey Hull
Bernard Jeffries
Ronald Leyland
Andy Lyons
John McCabe
Peter Metcalfe
Geoff Phillips
John Rees
Ray Shuker
Billy Simmons
Andy Traverse
Jimmy Walker
Kevin Whittle
Bob Williams
Niel Wood
Sid Wright

Youth (18s/19s) County
Bernard Bibby
Mark Briody
Nicholas Cammann
Tom Connick
Danny Filson
Geoff Fletcher
Tommy Frodsham
Ian Frodsham
Eric Frodsham
Steve Garner
Jamie Hill
Danny Lynch
Anthony Marsh
John McCabe
Jonathon Peers
John Rees
Gareth Roberts
Derrick Seabrook
Alan Shea
Greg Smith
John Tabern

NW Counties ARFL Australasian Tour 1997 (Under 18s)
Nicholas Cammann

NW Counties ARFL Australasian Tour 2001 (Under 16s)
James Lacey
(club's youngest-ever tourist)

Club officials

Chairmen	Era
Stan Brittle	1960s
Roy Britch	1970s
Jim Burkhill	1950s
Bill Chester	1970s
Jim Clitheroe	1960s
David Corless	1990s
Billy Dillon	1990s
Albert Garner	1990s
James Glen	1930s
Jeff Gormley	1980s
Billy James	1950s
Tom Metcalfe	1950s
George Parsons	1960s
Ralph Rawsthorne	2000s
Joseph Rigby	1920s
Joe Robinson	1950s
Ray Ryan	1990s
James Stewart	1930s
Brian Woodward	1970s

Secretaries	Era
Thomas Ashcroft	1920s
Roy Britch	1970s
Jim Clitheroe	1960s
Derek Cross	1980s
Eric Cunliffe	1960s
Billy Dillon	2000s
Wilfred Ellison	1890s
Eric Frodsham	1980s
Albert Garner	1990s
Darren Haigh	1990s
Billy James	1950s
Jimmy Parr	1950s
Ralph Rawsthorne	1990s
Billy Simmons	1970s
Ken Vines	1950s
Bill Webster	1960s
Kevin Whittle	1980s
Joseph Wood	1920s
Brian Woodward	1970s

Coaches	Era
Shaun Allen	1990s
Chris Arkwright	2000s
Billy Benyon	1980s
Dave Chisnall	1990s
John Dickinson	1960s
Eric Frodsham	2000s
Austin Gillin	1960s
Jeff Gormley	1980s
John Ledger	2000s
Dave Manning	1990s
John Mantle	1980s
Ged Marsh	1980s
Vinty Matthews	1950s
Peter Metcalfe	1960s
Ron Prescott	1950s
Austin Rhodes	1970s
Billy Sheils	1960s
Billy Simmons	1980s
Johnny Smith	1990s
Kevin Thompson	2000s
Colin Whittaker	1980s
Kevin Whittle	1970s
Frank Wilson	1980s

Players who turned professional from Pilkington Recs

	Professional club	Era
Danny Allender	St Helens	1950s
Alan Baldwin	Leigh	1960s
Ronnie Barton	Liverpool City	1950s
Bernard Bibby	Barrow	1980s
Bob Bolan	Widnes	1970s
Liam Bostock	St Helens	2000s
Mike Bowes	St Helens	1980s
Frank Briers	Liverpool City	1950s
Jeff Brown	Swinton	1980s
Bill Burrows	Huyton	1970s
Nicholas Cammann	St Helens	1990s
Mike Carr	Runcorn	1980s
Mike Carr	Highfield	1990s
Bobby Chisnall	Wigan	1950s
Eric Chisnall	St Helens	1960s
Les Chisnall	Huyton	1960s
Peter Cook	St Helens	2000s
Andy Crehan	Swinton	1980s
Andy Crehan	Prescot Panthers	1990s
Gordon Crosby	Liverpool City	1950s
Eddie Cunningham	Wigan	1960s
Mike Denning	Highfield	1990s
Brian Dunn	Wigan	1980s
Gordon Edgerton	St Helens	1960s
John Evans	Huyton	1970s
Steve Fenney	St Helens	1980s
Bill Finnan	St Helens	1950s
Geoff Fletcher	Leigh	1960s
Ernie Forber	Liverpool City	1960s
Gareth Frodsham	St Helens	2007
Peter Frodsham	Blackpool Borough	1980s
Tommy Frodsham	Swinton	1980s
Steve Garner	Swinton	1980s
Brian Garrity	Highfield	1990s
Ken Gill	Salford	1970s
Mark Gleave	Warrington	1980s
Brian Glover	Warrington	1950s
Peter Glover	Huyton	1980s
Bert Grice	Leigh	1950s
Roy Haggerty	St Helens	1970s
Gary Haggerty	Wakefield	1980s
Kurt Haggerty	St Helens	2000s
Andy Hardman	St Helens	1950s
Derek Harrison	Huyton	1970s
William Hill	Swinton	1970s
Gary Holden	Prescot Panthers	1990s
Neil Holding	St Helens	1970s
Steve Houghton	St Helens	1970s
Frank Hudson	Warrington	1950s
David Hull	St Helens	1970s
Phil Hurst	Salford	1970s
Geoff Irwin	Liverpool City	1960s
Mark Jackson	Highfield	1990s
Bernard Jeffries	Liverpool City	1950s
Ian Jones	Leigh	1960s
Hughie Leyland	Wigan	1950s
Denis Litherland	St Helens	1970s
Roy Litherland	Halifax	1980s
Roy Litherland	Highfield	1990s
Ged Marsh	Blackpool Borough	1970s
John McCabe	Huyton	1980s
Dave McConnell	St Helens	1990s

Neil Meadowcroft	Swinton	1990s
Peter Metcalfe	St Helens	1950s
Paul Parnell	Highfield	1990s
Ken Parr	Rochdale H Warrington	1950s
Jimmy Rigby	Leigh	1950s
Wilf Roach	St Helens	1950s
Jake Round	Liverpool City	1950s
Derrick Seabrook	St Helens	1980s
Jamie Smith	Leigh	2000s
Malcolm Smith	St Helens	1970s
Jack Topping	Leigh	1950s
Andy Traverse	Prescot Panthers	1990s
Steve Traverse	Prescot Panthers	1990s
Norman Unsworth	Rochdale H	1950s
Austin Vallet	Leigh	1950s
Tommy Vose	Wigan	1960s
Albert Walsh	Liverpool City	1950s
Kevin Wellens	St Helens	1980s
Les Westhead	Huyton	1970s
Kevin Whittle	Swinton	1970s
Chris Willett	Wigan	1960s
John Wills	St Helens	1960s

Players joining Pilkington Recs from professional clubs

	Professional club	**Era**
Shaun Allen	St Helens	1990s
Chris Arkwright	St Helens	1990s
Dennis Brown	Liverpool City	1960s
Les Chisnall	Leigh, Huyton	1970s
Dennis Colbon	St Helens	1960s
Terry Cooke	Wigan	1960s
Bob Dagnall	Rochdale H St Helens	1970s
Brian Highcock	Leigh	1970s
William Hill	Swinton	1970s
Bob Jones	Leigh	1960s
Ian Jones	St Helens	1960s
Barrie Ledger	Runcorn Highfield	1990s
Denis Litherland	St Helens	1990s
Michael Loughlin	St Helens	2000s
Ged Marsh	Blackpool B Widnes	1980s
Jimmy Mustard	St Helens Liverpool City	1970s
Terry O'Loughlin	Wigan	1960s
Geoff Phillips	Wigan	1960s
John Phillips	Blackpool	1960s
Tim Pickup	Blackpool	1970s
Jackie Pimblett	St Helens	1970s
Phil Price	St Helens	1980s
Richard Rafferty	Blackpool Panthers	2000s
Ray Shuker	Salford	1970s
Johnny Smith	St Helens	1980s
John Stephens	St Helens, Widnes	1970s
Peter Twist	Liverpool City	1960s
Kevin Whittle	Swinton	1980s

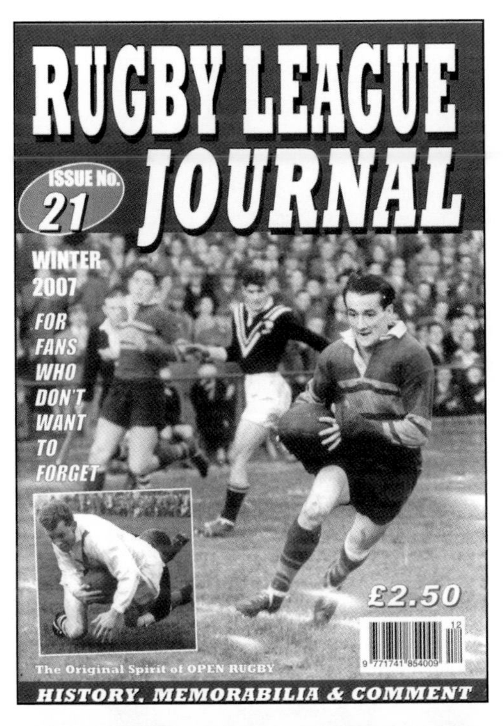

Published quarterly

History, Memorabilia and Comment with every issue packed with wonderful old black and white photographs.

www.rugbyleaguejournal.net

For more details: e-mail:
rugbyleague.journal@virgin.net

Or write to: "Rugby League Journal," PO Box 22, Egremont, Cumbria, CA23 3WA.

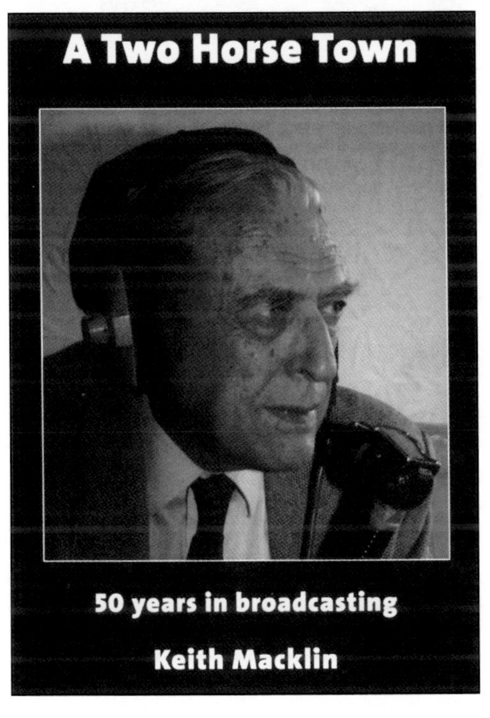

The fascinating autobiography of one of the north's leading broadcasters in the post war period. Published in 2007, available post free at a special offer for £8.00 (hardback) from London League Publications Ltd, PO Box 10441 London E14 8WR. Credit card orders via www.llpshop.co.uk

The book can be ordered from any bookshop at £14.95.

Rugby league in Liverpool has a long history. Older fans have memories of visits to watch Liverpool Stanley before the war and Liverpool City in the 1950s and 1960s. This history of rugby league in Liverpool covers from the 1850s to the present day. It includes the first Liverpool City RLFC, Wigan Highfield and London Highfield, the forerunners to Liverpool Stanley RLFC, and the club after it moved to Huyton in 1969 until it was wound up in 1997. Based on extensive research and interviews, this fascinating story will be of interest to all rugby league fans and people interested in Liverpool's sporting history. Mike Brocken was born in Liverpool and supported Liverpool City. He is a senior lecturer at Liverpool Hope University and has a lifetime's involvement in sport and popular culture in the city.

Published in October 2008 at £14.95. Order from London League Publications for £14.00 post free.

Rugby League Review No.2 – articles on current issues, history, international development, obituaries and book reviews. Published in September 2008 at £12.95. Order for just £12.00 post free.

Rugby League books from London League Publications Ltd:

Peter Fox – The Players' Coach
by Graham Williams and Peter Lush.
Authorised biography of former Great Britain coach.
Published in June 2008 at £14.95,
order for just £14.00 post free.

***The Patience of a Saint* by Mike Critchley**.
St Helens RLFC from 1978 to 1996 combined with reflections on growing up in St Helens.
Special offer – order direct from us for just £5.00.

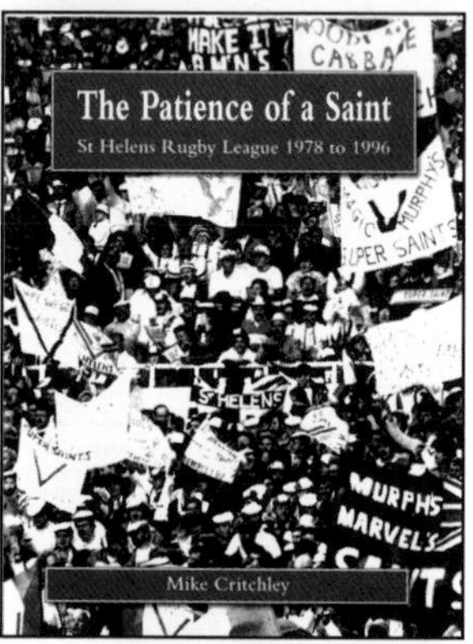

Newlove – At the Centre of Rugby League
by Paul Newlove with Andrew Quirke.
Autobiography of former St Helens and Great Britain player. Special offer – order direct from us for just £5.00.

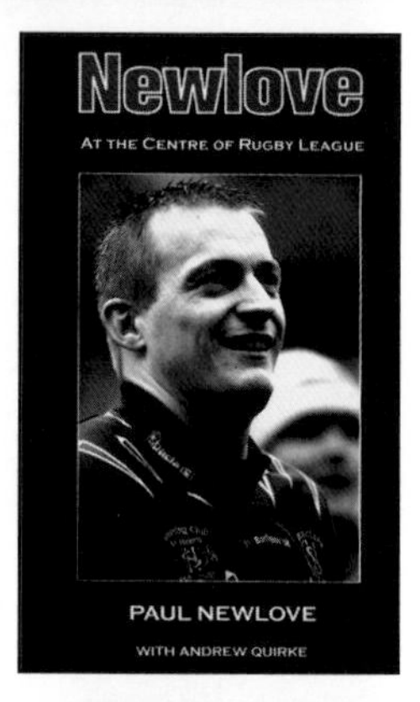

A Dream Come True by Doug Laughton with Andrew Quirke. Autobiography of former Leeds and Widnes coach who played for St Helens, Wigan and Widnes.
Special offer – order direct from us for just £5.00.

Orders by cheque (payable to London League Publications Ltd) to London League Publications Ltd, PO Box 10441 London E14 8WR. Credit card orders via www.llpshop.co.uk
To see all our books in print, visit www.llpshop.co.uk